NEW ORLEANS

Elegance

— *and* —

Decadence

THE PHOTOGRAPHS OF
RICHARD SEXTON

NARRATIVE BY
RANDOLPH DELEHANTY

CHRONICLE BOOKS

SAN FRANCISCO

For permission to use a quotation from THE MOVIEGOER by Walker Percy © 1960, 1961, we would like to thank
Alfred A. Knopf, Inc.

Library of Congress Cataloging-in-Publication Data:
Sexton, Richard
      New Orleans: elegance and decadence / the photography of Richard Sexton; narrative by Randolph Delehanty.
      p. cm.
      Includes index
      ISBN: 0-8118-4131-6
      1. Architecture—Louisiana—New Orleans—Pictorial works. 2. New Orleans (La.)—Buildings, structures, etc.—Pictorial works.
3. New Orleans (La.)—Social life and customs—Pictorial works.
I. Sexton, Richard. II. Title.
NA735.N4D46 1993
720'.9763'35—DC20   92—46174
                          CIP

Manufactured in Hong Kong

Book and cover design: Chuck Routhier
Editing: Suzanne Kotz
Maps: Françoise St. Clair
Typesetting: On Line Typography
Typeset in Sabon and Century Old Style

Distributed in Canada by Raincoast Books
9050 Shaughnessy Street
Vancouver, BC V6P 6E5

10 9 8 7 6 5 4 3 2 1

Chronicle Books LLC
85 Second Street,
San Francisco, CA 94105

www.chroniclebooks.com

DEDICATION

We dedicate this book to the New Orleanians—past, present, and future—who have created and who will sustain this most distinctive city. We like what Hélène D'Aquin Allain wrote:

Chère Nouvelle Orléans, patrie de ma jeunesse, berceau de quelques-uns de mes ancestres, tombeau d'un grand nombre de ceux que j'ai aimés. Je demande à Dieu de te protéger, de te garder, de te bénir. Par une Créole.

Dear New Orleans, home of my youth, cradle of many ancestors, tomb of many I have loved, I ask of God to protect, to preserve, and to bless thee. From a Creole.

—Hélène D'Aquin Allain
Souvenirs d'Amerique et de France par une Créole, 1868

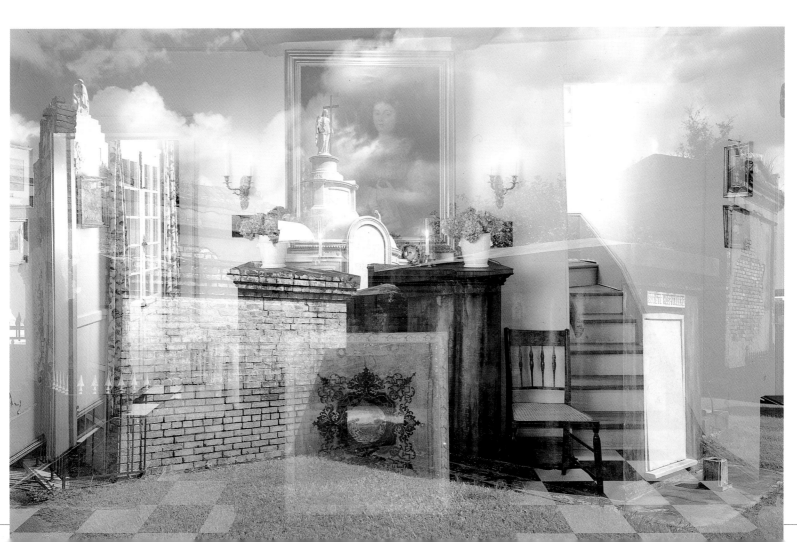

TABLE OF CONTENTS

PREFACE

As a child growing up in the Deep South only a short car drive from the sawgrass, palmettos, and sandy scrub of the Gulf Coast, I saw New Orleans as an exotic and far-away place. Adults talked of it in grandiose terms, but despite all the talk, I knew only superficial things about it. I knew it was old, located on the Mississippi, and had been settled by the French. Before I ever visited, though, I could sense that it was a city somehow *different* from other southern cities, different in that overstated way that some would infer as superior.

I can't say that New Orleans was entirely what I expected, when, as a visitor, I first experienced it. After an unsuccessful attempt to book a room at a boarding house on Decatur Street (it was too hot for the old guy clad only in his underwear to get far enough from his bottle of Bourbon, or window fan, to see if anyone had checked out recently), an unsuspecting encounter with a transvestite near the Old Mint, and an evening stroll down decadent Bourbon Street, I concluded that this was a place not lacking in ambience, interesting residents, or pleasure-seeking pursuits.

The next time I came to New Orleans, it was not as a visitor but to become a resident. True to her character, New Orleans had gone out of her way to make a mediocre first impression, setting the stage for a dramatic come-on at a more appropriate time. It's difficult to account for differing impressions of the same place over time, but I don't think New Orleans had changed nearly as much as I had in the intervening fifteen years, living in San Francisco. Relocating to New Orleans was a move to a new and exotic city and a return to the familiar climate and terrain of the Gulf South. This created a truly rare opportunity to experience the exotic and the familiar all in one complex bundle. In a beguiling way, New Orleans impresses me as being the most intensely southern place imaginable, while at the same time not being southern at all. It is southern in all the typical ways that any Southerner would recognize, but it has an exotic underlayment that reflects its Creole origins, a foreign culture buried in the heart of the Deep South.

Many things make New Orleans a compelling place of national and international interest. The Vieux Carré is one of the most pristine examples of an eighteenth-century town plan in America. The city is rich in French and Spanish Colonial, Greek Revival, Victorian, Richardsonian Romanesque, Neoclassical, and Craftsman architecture. The musical traditions of New Orleans—the pervasive genres of jazz, blues, rhythm and blues, rock and roll—made some of the most significant and innovative contributions to twentieth-century American popular music. The same dynamic influences that make New Orleans architecture and music so unmistakably unique are characteristic of its culinary tradition, as well. Great architecture and a culturally vibrant city provide the setting, food and music add the sensory pleasure for a style—a lifestyle—that is distinctly New Orleanian. It is this lifestyle, as manifested in the city streetscapes, individual houses and shops, gardens, and the flavorful celebration of local culture, that our book explores. Not a history, this book is about the city of New Orleans today and the manner in which its residents live.

Just what is the "style" of New Orleans and why do the seemingly contradictory terms elegance and decadence describe it? These words best describe the elements of contemporary New Orleans that we find most compelling: the patina of an eighteenth-century Louisiana armoire; the unabashed display of ruined finery; the stained and weathered empire-yellow wash of a crumbling plaster wall; the moss on the brick floor of a Vieux Carré courtyard; the flicker of candlelight casting a warm glow on dusty mantel mementos; the textural delicacy of peeling paint. The city's elegant architecture, furniture, decoration, and objects worth keeping and treasuring forever exhibit the traits of midlife, somewhere between creation and eternity. They have the battle scars of enduring things, that property which antiques have and modern objects lack, the sense of the millennium that envelops Venice, Italy but not hip and happening Venice, California.

The residences included here are in an objective sense typical, not landmark, houses. In a subjective sense, they are quite extraordinary, not necessarily because of their original resplendence, but because of the way they are lived in today. Many whose homes are included are artists. Others are antique dealers, architects, and the like. Regardless of profession, they all pursue a lifestyle that is, in itself, an art form. Therefore, they are all artists, and living is their medium; this book is their document. My photographs are not highly choreographed; the furniture, arrangements, art, collectibles, flowers, tableaux, and table settings are those of the occupants. In many cases the work of artisans such as *faux* finishers, cabinet makers, and tile setters is apparent, but in no case do the interior elements reflect the design sensibilities of anyone other than those who live there. Another distinguishing element of this work is that we attempt to encompass those factors—climatological, cultural, architectural, musical, and culinary—that make the New Orleans lifestyle what it is. My hope is that the viewer will not only experience how New Orleans is different from other places, but why.

Those whose homes and shops fill these pages are content to live in architectural relics of the eighteenth and nineteenth centuries. Old houses are indeed expected to look old. New Orleanians will tell you that this is not a design trend or a political statement, but merely an existing condition. It is an attitude that pervades the old sections of the city. In the 1990s many of us everywhere are attracted to rusticity, funk, and patina as a counterpoint to a hard-edged, high-tech work environment and as solace from the alienation of strip developments, asphalt paving, and other trappings of the contemporary age. And, in practical terms, accepting old houses as they are is far cheaper than total renovation and modernization. An old house can be treated like antique furniture. Much of its allure is in its patina, and if that is taken away, it becomes indistinguishable from a reproduction.

The grand opulence of high ceilings, ornately carved crown mouldings, Georgian sash windows, and operable cypress shutters offer a rare kind of satisfaction. And when the plaster of those high ceilings has a few cracks, the crown mouldings develop a crazed finish, the sash rattles wildly in the wind, and the shutters lose some of their louvers, we feel the inevitable effects of age and are enraptured by the gravity of human experience that all those telltale signs evoke. Nowhere more than New Orleans is this experiential lesson taught. One develops a rapport with and discrimination about old things: whereas the termite infestation may need to be dealt with at any expense, perhaps the peeling paint can be integrated into the motif.

New Orleans exudes age, and New Orleanians work with it rather than lament it. The city has long inspired and thrived on decadence. New Orleans photographer Clarence John Laughlin chose to photograph not the restored plantations of the lower Mississippi River valley, but derelict ones rich in symbolism. His book of these photographs, *Ghosts Along the Mississippi,* has become a classic. The most famous photographic portraits of New Orleanians are E. J. Bellocq's haunting portraits of the prostitutes of Storyville. Jazz was considered by contemporary musical arbiters of its formative days to be degenerative, uncontrolled, a fleeting aberration outside of the mainstream. New Orleans' literary inspirations—Tennessee Williams's Stanley Kowalski and Blanche du Bois in "A Streetcar Named Desire," Walker Percy's Binx Bolling in *The Moviegoer,* John Kennedy Toole's Ignatius Reilly in *A Confederacy of Dunces,* all are an enigmatic and decadent lot.

Modernization and efficiency frequently prove incompatible with a city known for old world charm, a friendly, relaxed attitude, and an appreciation for handmade craftsmanship. It is very satisfying to live within this embrace, for it gives a warm feeling of security—that jazz will always be heard wafting through the streets, the Tuesday before Ash Wednesday will always be the most important day of the year, coffee with chicory and *beignets* will be served every morning at Café du Monde, and New Orleans will continue to remain elegant and decadent forever.

Richard Sexton
New Orleans

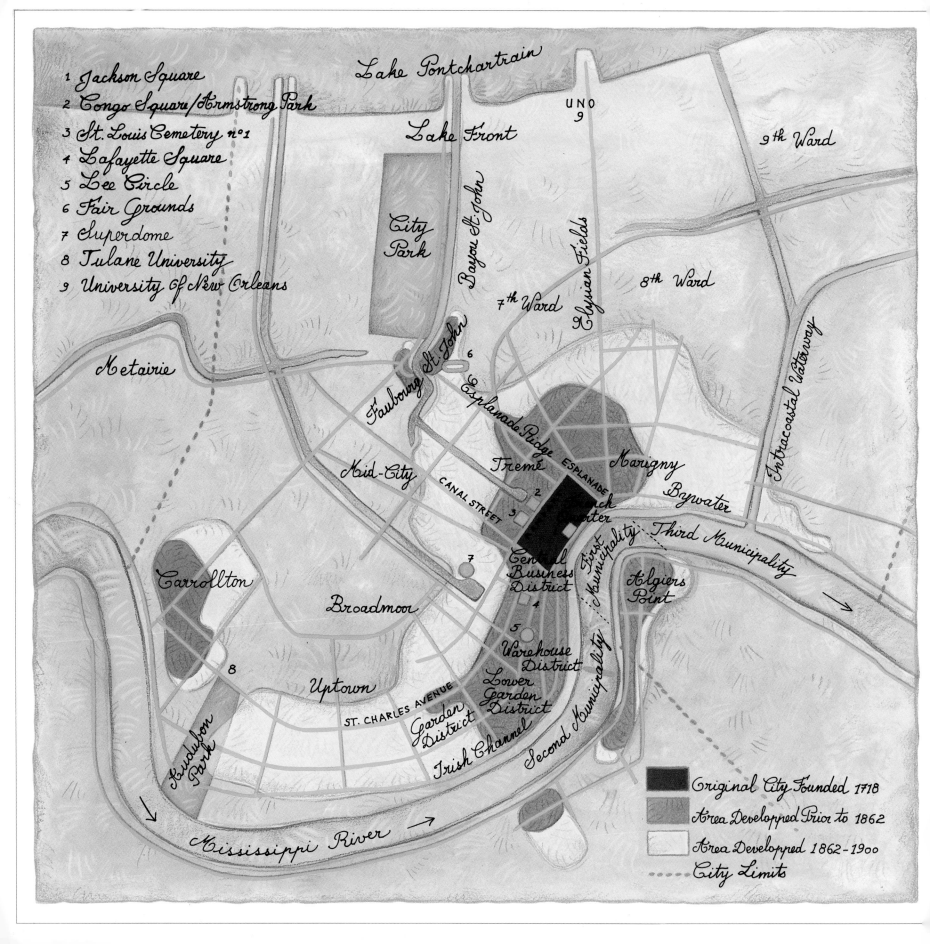

1 Jackson Square
2 Congo Square/Armstrong Park
3 St. Louis Cemetery n°1
4 Lafayette Square
5 Lee Circle
6 Fair Grounds
7 Superdome
8 Tulane University
9 University of New Orleans

Lake Pontchartrain

Lake Front

UNO
9

9th Ward

City Park

Bayou St. John

Elysian Fields

8th Ward

Metairie

Faubourg St. John

7th Ward

Esplanade Ridge

Intracoastal Waterway

Mid-City

CANAL STREET

Tremé

ESPLANADE

Marigny

Bywater

2
3
French Quarter

Central Business District

First Municipality

Third Municipality

Carrollton

7

Algiers Point

Broadmoor

4

Uptown

ST. CHARLES AVENUE

Warehouse District

5

Lower Garden District

Second Municipality

8

Audubon Park

Garden District

Irish Channel

Mississippi River

Original City Founded 1718

Area Developped Prior to 1862

Area Developped 1862-1900

- - - - City Limits

INTRODUCTION

NEW ORLEANS: THE VENICE OF NORTH AMERICA

"New Orleans is North America's Venice; both cities are living on borrowed time. Here we are fighting the mud, the heat, the rain, and the insects, trying—if you squint your eyes a bit—to create a Paris in the swamps. Our architecture, and the way we live, are here because of a particular attitude, an attitude about time that is different from that of the rest of the United States. New Orleans won't change—this is the source of its decline—and yet it does change: but somehow, layer after layer, it stays the same. New Orleans doesn't want to be practical, or to follow the trends in the rest of the country, yet it still works as a place to live; I don't know how. And it sure is fun living here!"

Joel Lockhart Dyer—artist and New Orleanian

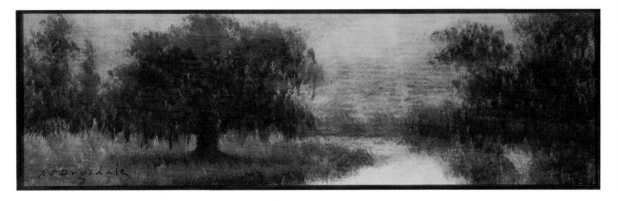

ALEXANDER JOHN DRYSDALE, *Sunset on Bayou Saint John*, circa 1920
The southern Louisiana landscape is a moody world of water, swamps, cypress, and Spanish moss–draped live oaks. Bayou Saint John was the Native-American portage that fixed the location of the French city of La Nouvelle Orléans. (Roger Houston Ogden Collection, New Orleans)

THIS BOOK: A PARTIAL VIEW IN BOTH SENSES

These photographs share a personal, impressionistic vision of New Orleans, a paradoxical vision that sees beauty in decay, in peeling paint, in faded walls, in timeworn facades, and in lived-with furnishings. This is a partial view of the Cresent City in both senses: it selects one particular aspect of the city for its focus, and it looks with favor on what others might overlook. We want this to be a loving view, just the way one looks at the face of one's favorite grandparent with love for every wrinkle and white wisp of hair because, to our eyes, there's more beauty in that face than in smooth youth.

The suites of photographs in this book explore and record four dimensions of this unusual and venerable city. They look sequentially at: (1) the threads in the city's distinctive urban fabric; (2) the hospitable, private worlds of some of New Orleans' most evocative rooms; (3) the lush *jardins sauvage* of her increasingly tropical gardens and courtyards, and lastly; (4) at the city's long, vibrant tradition of cultural revelry — gaudy, boisterous fun — whereby life and art fuse here to produce a community with a joyous soul like no other.

FIVE FEET OF RAIN A YEAR

So much about New Orleans is peculiar, dramatic, and memorably sensuous, not the least being her semitropical climate. In this city, surrounded by swamps, a great river and large lakes, water is as important as the earth itself. Moisture and heat saturate the atmosphere. The mean annual rainfall in New Orleans is a remarkable 59.45 inches (almost five feet!), and the average annual temperature is a warm 69.5 degrees Fahrenheit. More Caribbean than North American, the climate has had a marked impact on the architecture, gardens, clothing, and lifestyle of New Orleanians. The louvered shutters, cast-iron galleries (porches), and the steep pitch of house roofs; the banana trees and shell ginger in gardens; the light, baggy Haspel suits of local businessmen and the bold flower prints favored by local women; the cultivation of drinks and talk — all are local responses to the south Louisiana climate. The languid atmosphere here slows things down and gives New Orleanians time to elaborate their hospitable instincts.

Mild winters and soft springs compensate for the steamy summers. The climate nurtures a lush, profligate evergreen flora that enfolds the old city in ancient-seeming live oaks and drapes it in junglelike vines. It's hard *not* to garden in New Orleans. Mixed in with the prolific native vegetation are imported bananas, bougainvillea, palms, citrus, and bright pink crepe myrtle, among many other showy, exotic plants. Nature here sends seeds to sprout in the most unlikely places. Unattended rain gutters become miniature forests; trees take root on roofs; brick walls are patinated with soft mosses and microscopic plants; resurrection ferns sprout from trees and tombs. Everything seems alive.

The rich, black alluvial soils carried down the Mississippi River, the abundant rain, and the strong sun produce bountiful crops in the Delta of sugar cane, rice, cotton, vegetables, tobacco, oranges, and in the past, indigo and lemons. It was this great agricultural abundance that built the city and gave its port riches to export in exchange for all of the world's luxuries.

Flourishing in this abundant flora is a rainbow world of iridescent dragonflies, jewellike insects, and bright green gekkos (lizards) that mimic leaf and flower shapes as they press against walls and windows. Every twilight, purple martins swarm and swoop over the old French Quarter, twittering as they feed on airborne insects. So beautiful and compelling is this insect world that the theme of one recent Mardi Gras parade was the entomological empire. It's hard to think of another North American city celebrating its insect life.

The climate has another compensation — the dramatic thunderstorms that create baroque skies and the startling lighting effects that painters dream of. After a hot, humid summer morning come brief, furious, and cooling afternoon rainstorms. The skies suddenly turn gray, black, and saffron. Great lightning bolts flash and sharp thunder cracks so loudly that it shakes the earth and rattles the windows. Torrents of rain flail the trees and drench the tropical foliage. Gutters become rivulets and the streets become temporary shallow streams as the water rushes toward the city drains. You quickly note that the house lots, sidewalks, and streets that looked so flat are actually pitched to quickly shed the rain and send it toward the storm sewers. These afternoon rains clear the air, wash the city's buildings, refresh her plants, cool the populace, and then quickly disappear. The sun comes out and soon everything is bright again.

In the old days Louisiana's climate had an even more marked effect on the city's life. Wealthy New Orleanian families summered in Newport, Rhode Island, New York City, Paris, or resorts along the Gulf Coast to escape not so much the heat as the diseases that came with the warm weather. On the other side of this climatic coin, in winter, after the sugar and cotton harvests were in, planters from the country came down to New Orleans for the social season: a round of dinners, balls, theater, opera—and business deals and matrimonial alliances—that made the city a regional capital and the only true metropolis in the South. The well-to-do of distant parishes (counties) came here to display and enjoy themselves, and to stimulate the commerce of the South's great entrepôt. The very wealthy built fine city houses to which they repaired in winter; the rest of the year they resided on their remote and vast plantations. Planters came to New Orleans to do business with brokers and bankers; women came to shop and absorb culture; the children of the wealthy came to be educated and to socialize. With the predictable rhythm of the natural seasons, the winter social season annually enlivened the city's cultural life.

THE NEAR SEA-LEVEL CRESCENT CITY

The topography of New Orleans is as distinctive as its climate, and the two together have produced this city's special challenge: drainage. Southern Louisiana is a creation of the great Mississippi River. Over eons this tawny river, draining about a third of North America, has carried silt and organic matter south toward the Gulf of Mexico. In times past this mighty river overflowed its banks during annual spring floods. Like the Nile in Egypt, the Mississippi created fertile lands and waterlogged swamps. Slowly twisting back and forth in its serpentine bed, the restless river alternately cut down one bank and built up the opposite side. On one of these built-up bends, or crescents, New Orleans was founded. Hence the city's historic nickname: the Crescent City.

Each time the Mississippi flooded, it would gradually shrink back into its shifting bed. As it did so, clay and silt were left behind, causing natural levees (high grounds) to form along both banks. Behind these low ridges stretched vast cypress swamps and marshes. The French sited New Orleans on the widest part of this natural levee, on a curving ridge of land just above sea level. Here the soil was firmer and settlers felt more secure. But they soon discovered that even the "high" ground could be inundated, and within a few years of settlement the French began construction of man-made levees to protect the city from flooding. The process of levee improvement, which lasted almost two hundred years, effectively walled off the city from the river.

Looking down New Orleanian streets today one often sees large ships floating above the level of the low-lying city, a disconcerting sight.

The levees prevent heavy rains from draining away naturally into either the river or Lake Pontchartrain. New Orleans is often likened to a shallow saucer designed to catch rain. The early French settlers dug drainage ditches around French Quarter blocks, which became known as "islets." Alongside these ditches they used cypress planks for sidewalks, known as "banquettes" (literally, little benches, pronounced "ban-kets"), the term by which New Orleanians still describe their sidewalks. Some early houses, called "raised cottages," were lifted off the ground on wood or brick piers so that when a "crevasse" broke the levee, the house and its furnishings could ride out the flood undamaged. The waterlogged state of the early city and its swampy surroundings bred mosquitoes that carried malaria and yellow fever (which became so familiar it was called "bronze John") and spread waterborne typhoid and cholera. Early missionaries assigned to Louisiana branded it "the wet grave."

The drainage problem confined the early settlement to the natural levee, giving the eighteenth- and nineteenth-century city a sickle shape that followed approximately along the line of what is now St. Charles Avenue. It was not until 1896 and the establishment of the New Orleans Drainage Commission, and then the organization of the Sewerage and Water Board in 1903 with its own taxing powers, that flooding inside the city was brought under control. Great canals, set like the ribs of a fan, were excavated and pointed toward Lake Pontchartrain, north of the city. At the head of the canals, powerful screw pumps lift water from the channels and dump it into the lake. Engineer James S. Janssen has calculated that, by 1984, this remarkable system consisted of eighteen large and two small pumping stations with a total of fifty-four huge electric pumps, 83 miles of covered canals, 87 miles of open canals, 57 miles of large diameter pipelines, 1,258 miles of subsurface drains, and forty thousand curbside catch basins. The system can pump up to twenty-four billion gallons of rainwater a day from the city into the lake. This twentieth-century engineering marvel, which makes rainwater disappear so quickly, finally broke the deadly cycle of summer epidemics.

The covered canals have become an aesthetic boon to the city. Located under the medians of the city's many wide boulevards (the so-called neutral grounds), these concrete rectangular boxes range in size from six feet wide and eight feet high to a colossal twenty-eight feet wide and fourteen feet high. The canals are covered over to reduce the growth of unwanted vegetation, to prevent the dumping of trash, to increase safety for vehicles and children, and to improve the city's appearance. Lined with trees, often live oaks, and with planted medians, the great boulevards of New Orleans are the handsomest feature of many neighborhoods. A city noted for its romantic self-image in fact relies on an efficient technology and powerful pumps that never stop working. In the struggle to protect, then drain, this site some of the most beautiful tree-lined boulevards in America have been created.

UPTOWN, DOWNTOWN, RIVERSIDE, LAKESIDE:
A UNIQUE SENSE OF DIRECTION

Because the Crescent City is set on a bend in the river, many of its principal streets are curved, and a compass is almost useless. North, south, east, and west mean little here and are rarely referred to. Instead (and how New Orleanian it is!), this city has created its own unique sense of direction. Rather than referring to the southeast corner of Canal and Carondelet streets, a New Orleanian will speak of the "uptown-riverside" corner of this important intersection. (It's where residents and tourists board the St. Charles Avenue streetcar to head uptown to the fashionable residential districts.) The matrix for directions in New Orleans is this:

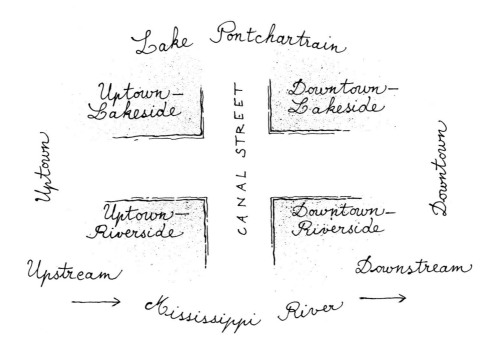

What counts are the unseen river and the unseen lake, and being upstream or downstream from Canal Street, the historical divide between the original French city downtown (today the French Quarter) and the eventually dominant American city uptown.

The sun rises across the Mississippi River from Saint Louis Cathedral in the French Quarter, which faces toward the southeast, even though it is on the east bank of the Mississippi River. (It's disorienting, I know. That's the whole point.) "Downtown" does not mean in New Orleans what it does in other American cities. Here CBD (Central Business District) is used to refer to the office and retail core. "Downtown" means downriver from Canal Street, essentially from the French Quarter downstream to the working-class side of the city.

Uptown New Orleans, today generally understood to be upstream from Lee Circle on the edge of the CBD, became the fashionable residential district as the American city expanded. Uptown's principal axis is curving St. Charles Avenue, which follows the natural levee. Uptown's most famous neighborhood is the Garden District, distinguished, as its name states, by fine houses standing in lush gardens. This tony district, one of the nation's first "garden suburbs," is now deep within the contemporary city limits. Some claim that Uptown is not just a place but a state of mind, an attitude both superior and unassailable. There is even an Uptown manner of speech with its own distinctive pronunciation of New Orleans with four clipped syllables, the third one extra: Noo OR-li-unz.

It is comforting to know, as you drive "west" on the Greater New Orleans Bridge with the sun setting behind you, that you are re-entering the world of the compass as most mortals know it. But then you are, unfortunately, leaving New Orleans.

PORTAGE AND PORT:
THE REASON FOR THIS UNLIKELY LOCATION

Given all these geographic difficulties, why is there a city here at all? Why has this unforgettable place developed some 125 miles upstream from the mouth of the Mississippi River? The historical explanation is that French settlers approached the Mississippi from the east, from their first capital at Mobile, Alabama. Sailing west along the Gulf Coast, they sought a shortcut to the great river to avoid navigating its treacherous and bewildering delta. In 1699 Choctaw guides showed the French how to reach the river from the Mississippi Sound and Lake Borgne, through the passes called the Rigolets, and into Lake Pontchartrain. On the south shore of that lake was a small stream, later named Bayou Saint John, which penetrated about four miles south toward the Mississippi River. From the Bayou Saint John headwater it was but a two-mile portage to the river itself, the highway into the North American interior. And up that great river were more rivers and the Great Lakes, links in a watery chain that connected French Louisiana with long-established French Canada. So the French decided to move their colonial capital from Mobile Bay to where the French Quarter now stands. Today the eccentric angle of Bayou Road across the later grid of city streets preserves the route of that ancient Choctaw portage. (Bayou Road becomes Governor Nicholls Street when it crosses Rampart Street and enters the Cartesian grid of the French Quarter.)

The French protected their new town with a three-foot-high man-made levee. All around it were cypress swamps, alligators, and thickets of rozo cane. The area between the Gulf of Mexico, the Mississippi River, and the narrow Amite River came to be called the Isle of Orleans, a wilderness of water and dense vegetation with a small, rectilinear settlement precariously placed within it, like an island within an island.

The Bayou Saint John portage soon lost its importance as New Orleans found its place on the river that was both its blessing and its constant menace. The riverfront *place d'armes* (parade grounds), today's Jackson Square, became the meeting point between sailing ships that came up the river from the Gulf of Mexico and flatboats and other small vessels that coursed down the river from the interior. New Orleans was where the sea met the rivers and where the southern and midwestern United States met the world.

The first natural resource exploited by the French were furs and pelts obtained from Native Americans in the upper Mississippi valley. When settlers came, profitable crops that would command high prices on world markets were cultivated. They were, in turn, indigo (used as a blue dye), tobacco, cypress lumber, rice, sugar extracted from cane, cotton, grain from the upper Midwest, and today, petrochemicals. Into the port came manufactured goods, slaves from West Africa to work the land (New Orleans became the largest slave trading center in the South), and luxuries, such as wine from Bordeaux and silks from Lyons, to satisfy the desires of a cosmopolitan city. Later came sisal for bags, bananas and tropical fruit, sugar from Cuba and the Caribbean, tropical woods such as mahogany from Honduras, and coffee from Central America and Brazil. New Orleans became the greatest cotton port in the world, feeding the "dark, satanic mills" in England and New England and creating great fortunes for her cotton brokers and many merchants.

PAUL POINCY, *Portrait of J. P. Marchand*, 1873
This portrait of a Creole gentleman epitomizes the elegant French-speaking elite of New Orleans. (Roger Houston Ogden Collection, New Orleans)

EXPLORERS, FOUNDERS, AND COLONISTS

The first Europeans to explore the lower Mississippi River valley were Spaniards fanning out from Mexico in search of precious metals. But it remained for the French to claim the vast valley, and they approached it first not from the Gulf of Mexico but down the Mississippi River from French Canada and Quebec, which they had founded in 1608. Reaching out from their settlements along the Saint Lawrence River in Canada, French fur trappers penetrated the Great Lakes, the upper Mississippi valley, and the Ohio valley, bartering with native peoples for furs along the way. Both Jesuit missionaries and French *coureurs des bois* (trappers) explored the heart of North America. Native Americans told the French of a great river to the west, and in 1673 the Jesuit Père Marquette and the fur trader Louis Joliet traveled by canoe from Lake Michigan down the Mississippi as far as the mouth of the Arkansas River. The French and English became fierce rivals over the Mississippi valley fur trade and formed shifting alliances with various tribes.

A wealthy French Canadian in the Illinois fur trade, René-Robert Cavelier, sieur de la Salle, determined to build a fort at the mouth of the Mississippi. He wished to find a way to ship heavy, bulky skins down the Mississippi rather than by over the many portages to Montreal. In 1682 La Salle led an expedition of fifty-six people, including ten native women, down the sinuous river to its mouth. On March 31, the party stopped at Maheoula, a Tangipahoa village near the Bayou Saint John portage and the present site of New Orleans. On April 9, La Salle erected a monument in the mud near the river's mouth and claimed the enormous valley for his king, Louis XIV, naming it Louisiane in his honor. ("Louisiana" is a local amalgamation of the French Louisiane and the Spanish Luisiana.)

The French had strategic as well as economic reasons for wanting to control the Mississippi. France's richest colonies were the sugar islands of Saint Domingue (Haiti) and Guadaloupe in the Caribbean. Far to the north was French Canada with its string of farms and settlements. Between the two were the remote French fur trading outposts of the upper Mississippi valley. And along the eastern Atlantic seaboard were the vigorous English colonies, already propelling frontiersmen across the Appalachian Mountains into the disputed Ohio River valley. A colony on the Gulf would be not only a bridge between French New World holdings but a barrier to westward English expansion. In 1699 the French established a settlement at Biloxi Bay (Mississippi). In 1702 the capital of Louisiana was established at Fort Saint Louis de la Mobile (Alabama). In 1715 the first permanent French settlement in what is now Louisiana was founded at Natchitoches on the Cane River near the center of the present-day state.

Finally, in the spring of 1718, Jean-Baptiste Lemoyne, sieur de Bienville, with Adrien de Pauger and Pierre Blond de la Tour, made a clearing in the dense cane break on the natural levee of the Mississippi near the Bayou Saint John portage—"on one of the most beautiful crescents of the river"—and there founded the Ville de la Nouvelle Orléans. The town was named for the duc d'Orléans, regent of France during the minority of Louis XV and a notorious debauchee. In 1721 de Pauger, a military engineer, made an orderly plan for the site, and its streets and blocks were surveyed. The focal point of the plan was the *place d'armes* (parade grounds), today's Jackson Square, which fronted the quay. On the land side of the square a site was reserved for the principal church, today Saint Louis Cathedral. Eventually the church was flanked by the seat of government, the Cabildo, and a residence never used by the church's priests, the Presbytère. This trio, plus the later Pontalba Buildings that flank it, composes one of the great colonial architectural ensembles in the United States.

De Pauger laid out four blocks above and below the central square and platted out a town six blocks deep. Behind the central church he surveyed a wider axial street, the Rue d'Orléans. Most of the streets were roughly thirty-eight feet wide, which gives the French Quarter its intimate scale. The streets were named after the saint names of figures associated with the French crown. Later, additional blocks were added to the plan, creating a rectangular grid eleven blocks long and six blocks deep. Each block was subdivided into twelve rectangular lots, and drainage ditches were dug around each block. Space was left around the town for fortifications, but they were not begun until 1760 and the fall of Quebec to the English. De Pauger's plan for palisades and five forts was never fully executed. Rampart Street behind the French Quarter preserves in its name its intended function.

THE NEW WORLD CREATES NEW PEOPLES:
THE MAKING OF THE CREOLES

Laying out a town was one thing, populating it was another. Louisiana became a private enterprise when the Scottish-born gambler and financier John Law persuaded the cash-hungry French crown to grant the infant colony to his Company of the West (later the Company of the Indies). Law had the modern idea of creating a state bank that would issue notes secured by anticipated crown revenues, including those from a productive Louisiana. A great wave of speculation in the company's stock swept Paris and the French court. But the notorious "Mississippi Bubble" burst in 1720, and Law fled France.

Before its spectacular collapse, however, the Company of the Indies sent several thousand colonists to its semitropical New World property. Some of these early colonists were adventurers; others were vagrants, petty criminals, and prostitutes deported from Paris and the provinces. Early efforts by the company to enslave the native peoples failed as the aborigines fled inland. Between 1717 and 1721, the Company of the Indies sent 7,020 colonists to Louisiana. Of these, 199 held land concessions, 2,462 were indentured servants, and 1,278 were convicted salt smugglers. Only 1,215 were women, and 502, children. It was not a promising beginning. One French official lamented in 1720, "What can one expect from a bunch of vagabonds and wrong-doers in a country where it is harder to repress licentiousness than in Europe?"

When it became clear that urban deportees would not create a prosperous agricultural colony, the company determined to grant land to colonists who would bring it under cultivation with slave labor and provide the company with valuable staples for export. The company began to recruit German peasants from the Rhineland and the German cantons of Switzerland. It settled these farmers upriver from New Orleans in an area that became known as the German Coast. They quickly became gallicized and even translated their German surnames into French; Zweig, for example, became La Branche. To this mixture were added West African slaves from the region between the Senegal and Gambia rivers. (The Company of the Indies also held the French monopoly on slave trading.)

Naval stores, tobacco, and indigo were the first important crops. The African slave ships also brought rice seed and slaves who knew how to grow it in swampy lands. Rice became the most reliable food crop in Louisiana and an important ingredient in Creole cuisine. But in 1731 the Company of the Indies relinquished Louisiana to the French crown after having sunk twenty million livres into the enterprise. By about 1750 the royal colony in Louisiana was costing the crown some eight hundred thousand livres a year. The colony was poor, unhealthy, and disorderly. Drout de Valdeterre reported in 1726 that Louisiana was a place "without religion, without justice, without discipline, without order, and without police."

A unique society emerged from these difficult conditions. The lack of French women resulted in some colonists ignoring the prohibitions of the 1724 Code Noir against interracial relationships. Some French men cohabited with native women or with their West African slaves, producing children of mixed race. "The greatest strength of the Canadian and French settlers of Louisiana," historian Gwendolyn Midlo Hall has recently written, "was their openness to peoples of other races and cultures. Surely, it was the main reason for their survival in this dangerous and inhospitable land." There were whites, mulattoes, quadroons, octaroons, griffes, and "half-breeds." The mulattoes were children of whites and Africans; quadroons were the children of whites and mulattoes; octaroons were the children of whites and quadroons; griffes were the children of mulattoes and Africans; and "half-breeds" were the children of whites and Native Americans. Many of these people of mixed race were free and not slaves. (The first record of the legal existence of a free man of color in Louisiana dates from 1722.)

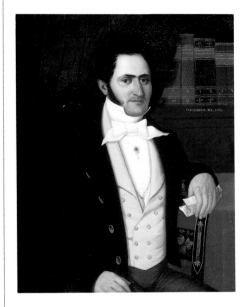

FRANCOIS FLEISCHBEIN, *Judge Benjamin Christopher Elliot,* 1834 The English-speaking Anglo-Americans became dominant in New Orleans by the 1850s. (Roger Houston Ogden Collection, New Orleans)

The scarcity of women led the French crown to recruit wives for the colonists. Beginning in December 1728, the first group of *filles à la cassette,* young women with state-provided trousseaus, arrived to help populate the distant colony. Very quickly the New World created a new people: the Creoles, both white and of color. The blending of peoples had remarkable effects. The architect Benjamin Latrobe commented in 1818 that "there are collected at New Orleans at a ball, many women, below the age of twenty-four or twenty-five, of more correct and beautiful features, and with faces and figures more fit for the sculptor, than I ever recollect to have seen together elsewhere in the same number." New Orleans still has her beauties.

The word "Creole" has a complex history. Its root is the Portuguese *crioulo,* meaning a slave of African descent born in the New World. The word was later extended to include white Europeans born in the Americas. "White" Louisianans in the nineteenth century later rejected the racial openness of early Louisiana and redefined Creole to mean exclusively white. (In the 1930s Huey Long claimed that you could feed all the "pure" white people in New Orleans with half a cup of beans and half a cup of rice, and still have food left over!) The phrase "Creoles of color" then emerged to indicate the many people of mixed racial descent in Louisiana. Creole also refers to the dialect and folk culture that developed in south Louisiana where French, African, and, later, Spanish influences blended.

After the revolution in Saint Domingue (Haiti) in 1791, a substantial number of Haitian Creole planters and their slaves, and also Haitian free people of color of mixed race, migrated to New Orleans and Louisiana in general. These later émigrés had a great impact on French-speaking Creole culture and brought French journals, theater, and higher Francophone culture to New Orleans. When Anglo-Americans began to filter into Louisiana in the early 1800s, Creole came to mean culturally and linguistically French as opposed to English speaking.

The French brought building traditions from both Quebec and the French West Indies to their new colony. From French Canada came house forms with their roots in Normandy and post-medieval French farmhouses. These houses had steeply pitched hip roofs, few windows, and no porches. Early New Orleans dwellings, *poteaux-en-terre* (post-in-the-ground) houses, were built of cypress timbers placed directly on the swampy soil. They quickly rotted in the wet climate. These dwellings had few doors and windows and were unbearably hot in the summer.

When French West Indian Creoles came to Louisiana, they brought with them a more environmentally suitable way of building. Following the Spanish Caribbean style, raised cottages completely surrounded by galleries were erected. This lifted the buildings off the soggy, flood-prone soil, while the gallery roofs shielded the walls from the baking sun and torrential rains. Raising the building also caught the cooling breeze. The ground floor under the principal floor, called the *rez-de-chaussée,* was used as a storage area or cool work space. The sheltered galleries supported by light wooden colonnettes provided shady places to live and work, and even to sleep at night behind temporary curtains. Double-leaf "French" doors supplanted the earlier small doors and windows and allowed much better ventilation. Eventually Creole carpenters introduced a French door in every other bay of the house facade, making windows and doors one. In the country, where there was space, the Creole plantation house became a raised building under a double-pitched roof like a great sun-and-rain-shedding parasol. Pronounced dormers in the roof ventilated the house by letting hot air rise up through the building. There is great beauty and utility in these early Louisiana vernacular buildings.

In New Orleans, where space was precious and town lots were long and narrow, an urban Creole cottage evolved. These houses were built right out to the sidewalk and raised one or two steps above it, creating well-defined, corridor-like streets. Behind the houses were sheltered gardens and work areas. The steeply pitched gable roof was frequently extended beyond the walls to create *abat-vents* (wind breakers) that projected two or three feet over the sidewalk. Along the front of the house, every other bay was occupied by double-leaf French doors with windows in their upper sections. Spanish-inspired louvered jalousies (shutters) covering the doors allowed privacy, security, and ventilation. Fire- and rot-resistant brick with a stucco finish replaced timber construction. Many of these Creole cottages survive in the French Quarter and the Faubourg Marigny.

The distinctive floor plan of the Creole cottage usually consisted of four rooms symmetrically arranged, each from twelve to fourteen feet square. There were no hallways, just French doors connecting the two front rooms to each other, and to the two back rooms. Two chimneys, each with two fireplaces, were placed in the shared interior wall between front and back rooms, with a fireplace facing each room. Two additional small rooms, called *cabinets,* were placed in the two rear corners of the cottage. One *cabinet* housed a spiral stair to the attic (used as sleeping quarters for children); the other was a storeroom. Cooking was often done in a separate building in the back garden. Creole families did not assign set functions to their four principal rooms; any might be used for sleeping, dining, or receiving guests (although visitors were often received in one of the front rooms). The Creoles furnished their rooms sparingly with portable chairs and tables. Clothes and linens were kept in tall armoires. These cottages (and the larger Creole townhouses that followed them) differ sharply from the homes with hallways and rooms dedicated to specific uses that English-speaking Americans introduced to New Orleans after 1803. The differences between the promiscuous Latin culture and the privacy-oriented Anglo culture can be read in the city's old house plans.

French Creole culture was Roman Catholic in its religion but tended to be more ritualistic than moralistic. Notre Dame de Prompt Secours became the patron saint of the fire- and epidemic-prone town. Long experience with corrupt administrators made the public realm a place of danger and uncertainty. Family connections were the best security. (The State has long been regarded as an enemy in Louisiana.) With the appointment of Pierre Cavagnal, marquis de Vaudreuil and a Canadian nobleman, as governor in 1743, New Orleans became a lively provincial social center. The city early acquired its reputation as a place where human foibles were not just tolerated but expected. Hard as it might be to define, a certain Creole temperament suffused New Orleanian society. As the historian Joseph Tregle wrote in 1952, the Creole was "provincial in outlook, style, and taste, the typical Latin Creole was complaisant, unlettered, unskilled, content to occupy his days with the affairs of his estate or the demands of his job. He lived in sensation rather than reflection, enjoying the balls and dances, betting heavily at table, or perhaps at the cockpit, endlessly smoking his inevitable cigar, whiling away the hours over his beloved dominoes, busying himself with the many demands of his close-knit family life." A perfumed myth of presumed aristocracy was later wafted over this provincial culture, one that clings to it still.

THE SPANISH CITY OF LA NUEVA ORLEANS: AN IMPERIAL BUFFER

The Seven Years' War between England and France, from 1753 to 1762 (known in the United States as the French and Indian War), was in part fought over the fur trade of the Mississippi River valley. It severely drained French resources and made worse the stagnation in French Louisiana. When the war was over, France had lost Canada and with it the will to hold on to Louisiana. Rather than see their indefensible colony fall to England in the next war that was bound to come, the French crown decided to cede Louisiana to Spain. In 1762, under the Treaty of Fontainebleau, Louis XV secretly gave Louisiana to Spain. The residents of New Orleans were unaware of the transfer for two years! From 1762 to 1768, as European powers clashed, mercantilist import and custom controls in New Orleans were not enforced, and the city became virtually a duty-free port. When Spanish governor Antonio de Ulloa attempted to assert Spain's authority over New Orleans, he was driven out by a revolt headed by Nicolas Chauvin de Lafrenière and Nicolas-Denis Foucault. But on August 18, 1769, General Alexander O'Reilly, an Irishman in Spanish service, took control of Louisiana for Charles III and executed the leaders of the Creole uprising. French culture, however, remained dominant in New Orleans. The Spanish were more changed by the city than they were able to change it. Because they saw Louisiana principally as a buffer for their rich Mexican colony they made little effort to transform the local culture, which, like theirs, was Roman Catholic in religion and Latin in temperament. During the Spanish period the population of New Orleans tripled. Most notably, with greater ease of manumission and self-purchase under Spanish law, and immigration of free people of color from Saint Domingue, the population of free people of color grew from only 165 at the end of the French period to almost 1,500 by the close of the Spanish era. New Orleans' free people of color matured as a cohesive community during the Spanish years.

Two great fires in 1788 and 1794 destroyed much of French New Orleans. The Spanish afterward imposed better building codes that mandated the use of fire-resistant roof tiles rather than flammable shingles. As the town rebuilt, two- and three-story masonry and stucco houses replaced the earlier one-story board-walled Creole cottages. But the Spanish city was not particularly Spanish in form. Its new buildings were actually a continuation of French colonial architectural development. There does not seem to have been a single Spanish architect working in the city during the entire Spanish period.

Space was at a premium on the narrow natural levee. Shops appeared along the ground floor, with living quarters above, on even the best residential streets, such as Royal, giving the town a more urban feel. Continuous galleries or balconies with spare, elegant hand-wrought iron railings were installed on street and courtyard walls. (Florid cast-iron did not appear until the 1840s.) The galleries provided light, air, views, and protection from the sun. The two- to three-story Creole townhouses, like the earlier Creole cottages, lacked interior hallways and their rooms tended to be multipurpose. Even bedrooms with imposing four-poster beds hung with mosquito netting might be used as sitting rooms. Slave quarters at the back of the new multistory houses were attached to, yet separate from, the dwellings. Common staircases were placed between the main house and its dependency.

The classic L-shaped French Quarter house plan was perfected toward the end of the Spanish period. It produced a patio or courtyard behind the house where household tasks could be accomplished in privacy and kitchen gardens could be planted. The courtyards also provided cool seclusion from the hot dusty streets. In a pretentious townhouse, a porte cochere, or exterior passageway, gave access to stables in the rear. A simple townhouse had a long interior passageway along one side of the ground floor that led to the back of the house (and lot) and to the backstairs. The Spanish imported oleander from Havana along with bananas and other showy tropical plants to cultivate in their back courtyards. Eventually many courtyards were landscaped with potted plants and *jars de Provence,* old olive-oil containers.

In 1778 Governor Galvez permitted Bostonian and other American merchants to trade freely in New Orleans. He also allowed the importation of slaves from any nation into the city, and slaves were brought in great numbers. Galvez drove the English from Baton Rouge and the Gulf Coast. In these years the French-speaking Acadians expelled by the English from Nova Scotia were encouraged to settle in the bayous southwest of New Orleans, in today's Cajun country. These farmers and trappers were culturally distinct from the urban and plantation Creoles.

At the close of the eighteenth century, New Orleans began to outgrow its original plan. Plantations upriver and downriver were subdivided for residential *faubourgs* (suburbs). In 1788 Carlos L. Trudeau laid out Faubourg Saint Marie upriver from the old city, today the site of the Central Business District. Growth, and almost annual summer epidemics, also demanded new burial grounds, and in 1789 Saint Louis Cemetery No. 1 was dedicated across Rampart Street. Because a grave could not be dug without filling up immediately with water, New Orleans required above-ground tombs built of stucco-plastered brick. Three kinds of tombs were constructed: two-space family tombs, large burial-society tombs, and niches (nicknamed "ovens") built into the walls enclosing the cemeteries. The family tombs are especially handsome. For many generations it has been the custom to visit cemeteries on All Saints' Day to repair and whitewash tombs, to decorate them with flowers, and to visit with friends.

THE CREOLE CULINARY HERITAGE

Louisiana's complex population produced a complex cuisine. Combining native and imported ingredients, a distinctive Creole cooking style evolved. From the Choctaws came *filé* powder, the dried leaves of the aromatic sassafras tree. The French brought their sauces, in particular the *roux* with which so many dishes begin, and traditional provincial stews. African slaves from Senegambia brought both rice, which became the local staple, and okra, which they used in *gumbo*. The Spanish introduced new spices including the fiery red Cayenne pepper that lingers on the palate after so many zesty Creole dishes. Simmered all together in a heavy, black iron skillet, the provincial French *pot-au-feu* became okra or *filé* gumbo. Rice became the basis of jambalaya, a version of Spanish *paella*. Italians later introduced andouille sausage, which became a flavorful addition to red beans and rice, the poor man's traditional dish on Monday washdays. The Sicilians introduced *muffulettas*, a soft, round bread sandwich with meats and cheeses spread with olive salad. Even the Americans contributed something; they brought Kentucky whiskey, bourbon, which became the preferred drink and the hard sauce for bread pudding.

Local game, venison, wild turkey, ducks, and geese were introduced to the table. Crawfish, oysters, crabs, shrimp, pompano, flounder, red fish, and catfish were also quickly assimilated into Creole cuisine. Shrimp Creole, and shrimp and crawfish étouffée (braised or smothered), became culinary specialties. Fried seafood has always been especially popular. Mark Twain remarked that seafood in New Orleans was "delicious as the less criminal forms of sin." The essential Creole spice rack came to include garlic; basil; tarragon; bay leaves; thyme; parsley;

oregano; Creole mustard; black, green, and Cayenne peppers; and *filé* powder. Fermented red peppers produced Tabasco sauce, a condiment that appears on virtually every table. Yellow onions, shallots, and celery are other culinary necessities. Yams, Creole tomatoes, peppers, and mirlitons are also local favorites. Louisiana cane sugar and molasses sweeten many dishes. The Creoles perfected the praline, an addictive confection made of pecans, brown sugar, butter, milk, vanilla, and a pinch of salt.

The Spanish introduced coffeehouses and New Orleans eventually became a great coffee importing port. Coffee with chicory (endive root), served with hot milk as *café au lait*, became a New Orleans tradition. The Creoles liked their coffee "black as the devil, strong as death, sweet as love, and hot as hell." Fine red Bordeaux wines, absinthe, and bourbon whiskey quenched more than thirst. Jambalaya, beer, and jazz eventually emerged as the perfect New Orleans picnic combination. Food and drink have always been favorite topics of conversation in New Orleans, and the city's flavorful cuisine is, like her population, distinctive and memorable.

NAPOLEONIC STRATEGY AND THE LOUISIANA PURCHASE

In 1795 the Pinckney treaty between Spain and the United States granted Natchez, Mississippi, and all the territory above it on the east bank of the Mississippi River to the United States. The treaty also gave American farmers in the upper river valley the right to use the port of New Orleans without paying duties. As American settlers began to fill the Ohio and upper Mississippi valleys, more and more flatboats piloted by *américains* began to appear on the quay at New Orleans. The infiltration of English speakers was slow but steady. By 1800 about a quarter of the city's population was English speaking.

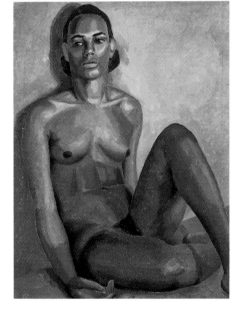

ALBERTA COLLIER, *Seated Mulatto*, 1938
New Orleans had the most complex society of any city in the American South. This studio portrait of a mulatto artist's model conveys something of the beauty of many of the city's people.
(Roger Houston Ogden Collection, New Orleans)

In 1801 Spain returned Louisiana to France in the Treaty of San Ildefonso. In 1802 Napoleon attempted to reconquer Haiti, which had been France's richest colony until a bloody revolution in 1791 expelled its Creole slave owners, many of whom had immigrated to Louisiana. Napoleon sent a large expeditionary force to retake the island, but Haitian resistance and deadly tropical diseases defeated it. In the same year, Spanish authorities at New Orleans attempted to close the Mississippi to duty-free American exports. To solve the crisis, the United States proposed the purchase of New Orleans and its immediate territory, the Isle of Orleans, from France. Without Haiti, Louisiana was of little value to Napoleon, and he decided to sell the entire territory for fifteen million dollars, or about four cents an acre. With this one move Napoleon not only raised money for France's oncoming war with England but helped to create a maritime power to rival his enemy. As Napoleon declared: "I have just given to England a maritime rival that will sooner or later humble her pride."

On November 30, 1803, France formally took possession of Louisiana from Spain. One month later, on December 20, 1803, William C. C. Claiborne and General James Wilkinson took possession of all Louisiana for the United States at a ceremony held in the Cabildo in New Orleans. Overnight the size of the United States doubled, and a distinct and foreign Catholic Creole population became encapsulated within an English-speaking Protestant nation. There were approximately eight thousand New Orleanians at the time of the Louisiana Purchase. President Thomas Jefferson predicted a great future for the acquired territory and thought that New Orleans might become the greatest city in the United States.

No Neutral Ground: Creoles and Americans Build Two Distinct Cities, 1803 to the 1850s

New Orleans was first linked to French Canada but soon turned toward the Caribbean, first Saint Domingue (Haiti) and the French West Indies, then Cuba and Mexico during the thirty-eight years of Spanish rule. After the Pinckney Treaty of 1795 opened the port to the Anglo-Americans upriver, the city's commerce was increasingly tied to them. The Louisiana Purchase cemented this link with the upper Mississippi valley and the rapidly expanding United States. Down the broad river came more and more flatboats loaded with pork, grain, corn, whiskey, and Protestant Anglo-Americans. Among the newcomers were the celebrated backwoodsmen from Kentucky who appalled the Creoles with their uncouth and violent ways. They came downriver to sell their produce, break up their flatboats to sell for timber, and have a rip-snorting time. Some built shanties in the Back-of-Town swamps behind the city. But other English speakers came as well — merchants, lawyers, doctors, and ministers looking for a foothold in the newly acquired trans-Appalachian empire.

The population boomed, and by 1810 the city could boast 17,242 residents, of whom 5,961 were African slaves and 4,950 were free people of color. It became, for a while, a black majority city, the oldest such urban concentration in North America and the most African-influenced city in the United States. New Orleans quickly became the fifth largest city in the United States, after New York, Philadelphia, Boston, and Baltimore. During the period from 1810 to 1840, New Orleans' rate of growth was greater than that of any other sizable American city. In 1812 Louisiana was admitted as the eighteenth state in the Union with New Orleans as its capital. In that same year the first steamboat descended the Mississippi River from Pittsburg. By 1830 some 989 steamboats were plying the Mississippi, depositing the wealth of a continent on the city's broad docks. Much of the historic fabric of the present-day French Quarter was built between about 1830 and 1860.

The French-speaking Creole population also grew during the early Federal period. A large influx of refugees from newly independent Haiti began life again in Louisiana and greatly stimulated its commerce. In 1809 some six thousand of them arrived in just two months. They were more sophisticated than local Creoles, and they enriched Creole cultural life by founding journals and elite social institutions. Many of the newcomers were free men of color, skilled craftsmen who emerged as important carpenters, furniture makers, and artisans in the booming city. They reinvigorated the city's traditional French assimilationist ethos. White French and Spanish Creoles tended to disdain manual work, allowing New Orleans' large, free colored population to secure a remunerative place in the city's expanding economy.

Anglo-Americans migrated to the newly-acquired city from the mid-Atlantic, upper South, and New England regions, especially New York, Pennsylvania, and Virginia. Despite the later impression that few Anglo-Americans resided in the old French city, the squares in the upper French Quarter between Canal Street and St. Louis Street were home to many English-speaking newcomers in the early years of the American city. Henry C. Castellanos, born in New Orleans in 1827, remembered that "many of the most enterprising American merchants and business men…had their principal establishments in the French Quarter." In the early 1820s, Bernard Marigny drew the line between the Anglo-American and the Creole communities at St. Louis Street, well inside the French Quarter. Conversely, many prominent Creole New Orleanians lived in the Faubourg Saint Marie in the early nineteenth century.

The rapid growth of both the French- and English-speaking populations led to the city's physical expansion. With no potential land enemy to confront, American authorities pulled down the decayed wooden fortifications around the old town and used the space to lay out three broad new streets: Canal Street upriver, Rampart Street lakeside behind the town, and Esplanade Avenue downriver of the old core. In 1807 the U.S. Congress reserved a 171-foot-wide swath of land for a canal. Although the canal was never excavated, the space became the location of the city's widest avenue, Canal Street. The street was broad enough that a median strip was left down its center. This strip became known as the "neutral ground" because it separated the existing French city from the new American city uptown. (Today, New Orleanians call all median strips in their many wide boulevards "neutral grounds." Apparently the term originally applied to all boundaries between faubourgs.) Seeking a modern "American" city, more and more of the English-speaking newcomers began to build shops and townhouses in the Faubourg Saint Marie, or Faubourg Saint Mary, as they called it, upriver from the Canal Street divide. They placed their important public buildings and Protestant churches around Lafayette Square, between St. Charles Avenue and Camp Street.

The French Creole elite also began to build outside the cramped French Quarter along Esplanade Avenue. The street was soon lined with large houses attractive to French-speaking merchants. Across Esplanade, Bernard-Xavier-Philippe de Marigny began subdividing his plantation to create Faubourg Marigny in 1806. He had grand intentions for his property and even named one major street the Champs-Elysées (today Elysian Fields). Other streets in his Creole subdivision were given such whimsical names as Rue de Craps (he introduced the dice game to

America), Rue des Grandes Hommes, Rue d'Amour, and Rue des Bon Enfants. While those names have been lost, the subdivision still exists and since the 1970s has captured the overflow from the now gentrified and high-cost French Quarter. In 1809 Faubourg Tremé was laid out by the municipal authorities to expand the city lakeside across Rampart Street. It, too, attracted Creole house builders, including many free Creoles of color. A great building boom occurred in the French Quarter itself during these heady years.

The "growing apart" of the expanding city was part of a deeper estrangement that developed in multicultural New Orleans. Creoles resented the upstart go-ahead Americans, and Anglo-Americans looked down on the tradition-minded Creoles. In 1835 the Americans opened a new canal linking their uptown sector with Lake Pontchartrain to compete with the old Creole-dominated Carondelet Canal behind the French Quarter. On March 8, 1836, the long-standing animosities between the Americans and Creoles resulted in the American-dominated state legislature imposing a new charter on New Orleans. It divided the city into three "municipalities," each with its own board of aldermen and control over its internal financial affairs. The reason for the division of the city seems to have been the reluctance of the Creole-dominated municipal government to make sufficient investments in the wharfs in the growing upriver American sector. Under the new system the Creole French Quarter became the First Municipality; the growing American sector upriver became the Second Municipality; and the lightly populated, swampy, and truck farming area downriver became the Third Municipality. During the years of division, the Americans taxed themselves to improve their docks, streets, and public facilities. The Creole section, however, stagnated, and the Third Municipality also fell behind. By 1840 New Orleans, with 102,193 people, was the fourth largest city in the United States. Her port was second only to that of New York City. In 1852, when the English-speaking population clearly dominated, the city was reunited under American leadership and the former uptown suburb of Lafayette was annexed as well.

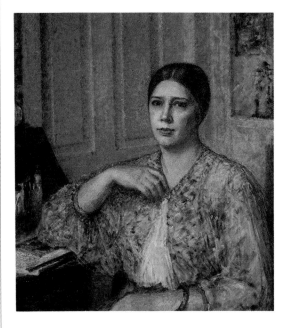

HELEN M. TURNER,
Portrait of a Lady, 1938
New Orleans is famous
for its attention to the
rituals of high society.
This portrait, probably of
an Uptown lady, radiates
the sophistication of the
city's old guard.
(Roger Houston Ogden
Collection, New Orleans)

The twenty years before the Civil War saw New Orleans enter her golden age. Cotton, sugar, rice, cypress, and other agricultural products poured into the city and out to the world. Manufactured goods and luxuries came to her from New England and Europe along with a great wave of Irish, German, and other European immigrants seeking economic opportunity. By the late 1850s the Germans and Irish held the political balance of power between the Creoles and the Anglo-Americans. Religion and outsider status tended to ally them in city elections with the Creoles. So many Irish immigrants settled near the docks upriver that the area became known as the Irish Channel.

This new working class created a demand for simple, inexpensive houses. New Orleans' solution was the "shotgun" house, which remained popular into the early twentieth century. These one-story, frame cottages consisted of three or four interconnecting rooms set in a row with no hallways. Wits claimed that the pellets of a shotgun fired through the front door would exit the back without hitting anything. These long, narrow buildings could be built singly or as "double shotguns." Wooden shotgun houses replaced older cottages in the French Quarter and spilled out into new working-class neighborhoods all over the city.

The antebellum boom also created great fortunes whose owners built large freestanding houses in spacious gardens uptown, away from the bustling core. Most of these great houses were built by merchants engaged in banking and commerce. Many were New Englanders and Englishmen who came to the city when its English-speaking elite was still open and receptive to new men. The area in which they settled, known as the Garden District, was linked to the Central Business District by the St. Charles horsecar line, and later by an electric streetcar. The Garden District reflected the Anglo-American preference for bucolic settings removed from the city. The Greek Revival style was favored, and many houses, filled with costly furnishings and lavish appointments, were almost palatial in scale. Often boasting monumental white columns, these great houses epitomize the architectural ideal of the American South. Many survive today as testimony to the palmy days "before the war" and the glittering entertainments that earned New Orleans its reputation as a city of lavish hospitality.

The new Victorian industrial technologies of the 1840s and 1850s made cast-iron building elements both available and affordable. Cast-iron columns, railings, brackets, fences, and ornaments were imported from New York City, Philadelphia, and Baltimore. Irish, German, and English iron masters established foundries in New Orleans. Lacy cast-iron galleries were attached to the facades of new and old buildings. The old French Quarter's stern masonry blocks were overlaid with a filigree of fanciful iron galleries that completely transformed the appearance of the city. These modern additions turned house facades into box seats and the streets below into theater stages. The new material resisted rot and could be cast into almost any form—geometric, Gothic, neoclassical, or romantic. Naturalistic motifs were especially popular, including roses, fuchsias, morning glories, oak leaves and acorns, trailing vines, and even cornstalks. This mid-century innovation helped establish the distinctive look still associated with New Orleans.

Protestant Americans were uncomfortable with the frank pursuit of pleasure among Latin Catholic Creoles. In 1804 William C. C. Claiborne wrote to James Madison, the secretary of state, about a "fracas" between some young Americans and Creoles over whose dances should have preference at a public ball. Claiborne ended his report apologetically, "I fear that you will suppose that I am wanting in respect in calling your attention to the Balls of New Orleans, but I do assure you, Sir, that they occupy much of the Public mind, and from them have proceeded the greatest embarrassments which have heretofore attended my administration." The next year Auguste Tessier began advertising dances on Wednesdays and Saturdays for white men and free women of color which became known as quadroon balls. But in 1806 the new American city council prohibited all masking in the city, public or private, and the following year prohibited interracial marriages. Later, in 1817, the city council attempted to limit prostitution in the seaport city.

In 1827 some elite young men recently returned from Europe, members of the local *jeunesse dorée,* celebrated the first recorded Mardi Gras on Shrove Tuesday, the last day before the Lenten fast. In the early 1830s Bernard Marigny, a wealthy Creole, seems to have been the first to make Mardi Gras a regularly celebrated event. Prince Achille Murat, passing through New Orleans in 1832, noted that intellectual conversation was rarely met with, but that there were "ample means for eating, playing, dancing, and making love." The first reports of street masking, as distinct from private ball masking, appeared in the press in 1837.

The Carnival season, of which Mardi Gras is the climax, was embraced by the Americans in 1857. In that year six young Anglo-American men, disappointed that New Orleans did not celebrate Carnival with an annual parade as in their native Mobile, organized a parade and ball. Calling themselves the Mistick Krewe of Comus, they borrowed their central figure, the god of sensual pleasure, from Milton's *Paradise Lost.* This set the pattern for future Mardi Gras krewes, as Carnival organizations are known, and Creole dominance of Mardi Gras began to wane. The Anglo-American adoption of Carnival is a key sign of how New Orleans' Creole culture influenced Anglo-American culture. There were marriages across the cultural boundaries as well and this also led to the creation of a distinctively New Orleanian culture. Assimilation was a two-way street in New Orleans. Carnival and all its rituals became ever more important after the Reconstruction decade of the 1870s. New Orleans' American high society adopted and elaborated the pre-Lenten Carnival season as a round of dinners, parades, and balls for the debut of young women into society. Krewes proliferated to include every sector of the city's population, and eventually Carnival became a major citywide celebration, the pivot on which the New Orleanian year now revolves.

THE CRESCENT CITY:
THE ONLY METROPOLIS IN THE DEEP SOUTH

As long as riverboats were the dominant form of fast transportation, New Orleans was supreme. But in the 1850s Chicago and Saint Louis began developing railroad networks that eventually siphoned off trade from the upper Mississippi River valley. Hardening attitudes in the North and South during the tense 1850s led to deep changes in easy-going New Orleans. A demographic revolution took place in the 1840s and 1850s as more and more white European immigrants poured into the city. The great flood of Irish and German immigrants displaced African-American workers on the docks and in the skilled trades. The city's sizable population of free people of color found themselves ever more constrained. In 1859, 281 New Orleanian free men of color immigrated to independent Haiti to escape the mounting economic pressure and increasing racial repression.

When the Civil War came, Louisiana seceded from the Union and joined her sister states in the Confederacy. In May 1861 the Union navy blockaded the port of New Orleans, and trade was cut off. The following year Admiral Farragut captured the city, and federal agents confiscated the property of Confederate supporters. Hard times fell on the once-rich city. The public celebration of Mardi Gras, for example, did not resume until 1866. Then came the 1870s and Reconstruction, a decade of polarization. The bitterness of the defeated New Orleanians burst out in biting satires in the Carnival parades of the 1870s. In 1877 the theme "Hades, A Dream of Momus" was a slashing attack on President Grant and his Republican administration. In that year federal troops were finally withdrawn from Louisiana, and the South erected its system of modern racial segregation.

In 1872 painter Edgar Degas visited his brothers Achille and René, prominent cotton brokers who lived on Esplanade Avenue. He painted an interior scene of his family's business, perhaps the most famous work of art to be created in the city. He also made a masterful portrait of his sister-in-law, Estelle Musson deGas, arranging flowers (today the jewel of the New Orleans Museum of Art collection). Another visitor in the 1870s was journalist Lafcadio Hearn, who wrote sketches in the local newspapers between 1877 and 1887. His 1878 sketch "The Glamour of New Orleans" evocatively described the fairest city of the South:

> [New Orleans] the far-off Southern city, whose spell is so mystic, so sweet, so universal. And to these wondering and wandering ones, this sleepy, beautiful, quaint old city murmurs: "Rest with me. I am old; but thou has never met with a younger more beautiful than I. I dwell in eternal summer; I dream in perennial sunshine; I sleep in magical moonlight. My streets are flecked with strange sharp shadows; and sometimes also the Shadow of Death falleth upon them; but if thou wilt not fear, thou art safe. My charms are not the charms of much gold and great riches, but thou mayest feel with me such hope and content as thou hast never felt before. I offer thee eternal summer, and a sky divinely blue; sweet breezes and sweet perfumes, bright fruits, and flowers fairer than the rainbow. Rest with me. For if thou leavest me, thou must forever remember me with regret.

Hearn loved the faded elegance and seductive decadence of the old city and found in its arrested and declining state a world removed from the stresses of nineteenth-century Progress. In his eyes New Orleans became romantic, remote, and strangely important. He was among the first writers to forge the modern view of New Orleans as a refuge from modernity, important to romantics for its human qualities of age and a certain perhaps feminine softness that the Industrial Age lacked. The old Creole French Quarter so admired by Hearn owes its preservation to the Sicilian immigrants who crowded into the area at the end of the century. Their poverty, ironically, saved the Quarter from change, leaving it to be rediscovered by bohemians in the early 1920s.

But while Hearn was casting his literary spell, Progress was nonetheless making headway in the New South. In 1880 the federal government and Captain James B. Eads completed the jetties at South Pass at the mouth of the Mississippi and deepened the river's channel to thirty feet, permitting large steamships to reach New Orleans' docks. Railroads also thickened their iron network, better connecting the city with its hinterland. Cotton, sugar, and rice flowed downriver to the South's busiest port and then out by steamship to the world's markets. New Orleans remained the only cosmopolitan metropolis in the South, a cultural position she maintained until after World War II even though Atlanta saw more bank clearings as early as the 1920s. The brokers, bankers, and merchants conducting New Orleans' wholesale and retail operations amassed great fortunes. With them they built large commercial buildings, sturdy warehouses, and grand late nineteenth- and early twentieth-century showplace houses along St. Charles Avenue. Many of these opulent mansions survive today.

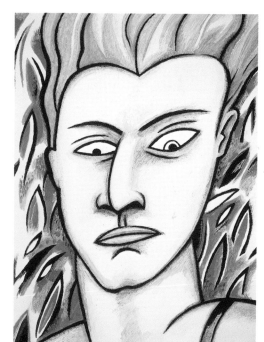

ROBERT GORDY, *Yellow Queen in the Fires of Hell*, 1983
This monotype captures something of the love for the eccentric that is so much a part of New Orleans.
(Roger Houston Ogden Collection, New Orleans)

RAGTIME AND JAZZ: THE GREAT MUSICAL FLOWERING FROM THE 1890s TO 1917

The musical history of New Orleans, like her culinary history, is long, rich, and exceedingly complex. Perhaps only the theological arguments over the nature of the Holy Trinity match in contentiousness the history of music in New Orleans. This introduction can only touch on one moment in this imperfectly documented and still-living aspect of the city's culture. Many different elements have gone into the creation of New Orleans music and dance. Dancing was a passion in the French city. As one early traveler put it, "in the winter they dance to keep warm, and in the summer they dance to keep cool." French gavottes and quadrilles were early imports. Dances and masked balls created a steady demand for musicians. Opera appeared in the city as early as 1796, and for many years New Orleans had America's only resident opera company. In 1822 the first regular ballet troupe appeared in the city. Parades were another local mania; militias, volunteer fire companies, fraternal lodges, all had their uniformed marching bands. In 1819 architect Benjamin Henry Latrobe commented that burial parades were "peculiar to New Orleans alone among American cities."

African slaves brought their music from West Africa, which they conserved and embellished. Forbidden so many other cultural expressions such as reading and writing, Afro-Americans found music to be a powerful outlet for cultural creativity. In 1817, even under the repressive Anglo-American municipal government, African slaves were permitted to dance at the circus grounds and market across Rampart Street from the old city. Soon dubbed Congo Square, Afro-Caribbean music and dance flourished there every Sunday until sundown. Here the bamboula and other dances were performed to drums and rattles. (Today Louis Armstrong Park and the Municipal Auditorium, scene of many Mardi Gras balls, occupy this historic spot.) European fifes, fiddles, banjoes, triangles, and tambourines were also adopted. Influences as varied as French dances, Spanish songs, Caribbean rhythms, Anglo-Saxon hymns, and African chants are all part of New Orleans' polyglot musical heritage. Creoles of color formed a Philharmonic Society in the late 1830s with more than one hundred members.

After the Civil War Afro-Americans were able to express their musical tastes more freely. Black musicians and music teachers composed everything from songs to symphonies in late nineteenth-century New Orleans. The melding of African rhythms, European instruments, and local social functions produced a great musical flowering at the end of the nineteenth century and the dawn of the new one. In the 1890s "spasm bands" formed by young Afro-American boys began to appear on the city streets. Dance halls flourished. In 1898 the city council passed the "Storyville ordinance," named after the councilman, Sidney Story, who proposed it, and which in effect created a thirteen-block brothel district along Basin Street. The madams of these fancy houses hired piano "professors." In these establishments Uptown blacks and downtown Creoles of color made music together for white patrons. As musician Paul Dominguez commented, "See, us Downtown people…we didn't think so much of this rough Uptown jazz until we couldn't make a living otherwise." By 1899 a new syncopated musical style among piano players known as ragtime was at its peak. Ferdinand "Jelly Roll" Morton, a Creole of color, and Tony Jackson were among its great exponents. Ragtime music became the first nationally accepted Afro-American cultural expression. In the late 1890s, Charles "Buddy" Bolden put the new ragtime piano rhythms in the context of a dance band.

In the early 1900s hot jazz began to emerge in New Orleans. (The word is said by some to be derived from a slang word for sexual intercourse.) Joseph "King" Oliver moved to the city about this time and began to play piano in the Storyville brothels. In 1909 the Zulu Social Aid and Pleasure Club began its tradition of King Zulu and black Mardi Gras parody parades. The next year Edward "Kid" Ory moved to New Orleans and developed his quintessential New Orleans–style trombone playing. By 1912 the blues, another musical style, emerged from the city's fertile subculture. In 1914 fourteen-year-old Louis Armstrong was released from the Municipal Home for Colored Boys where he had been sent for firing a pistol on New Year's Day. He had learned to play the trumpet while in the home's band. In 1915 Jelly Roll Morton's "Jelly Roll Blues," composed about ten years earlier, was published. And in 1917 Nick La Rocca, son of a Sicilian New Orleanian shoemaker, made the first jazz recordings in New York City with his Original Dixieland Jazz Band.

But in 1917 the United States entered World War I, and the secretary of the navy ordered closed all brothels in cities with naval bases. Storyville emptied out and jobs for musicians evaporated. The innovative, bright, brassy, happy, musical flowering of New Orleans faded. Many of her best musicians moved on to larger markets in Saint Louis, Kansas City, Chicago, and New York City. New Orleans music did not disappear, of course, but the most innovative years were over. In 1919 the Original Dixieland Jazz Band took jazz to Europe for the first time. Sadly, in that same year, the historic French Opera in the French Quarter burned and never reopened. It marked the end of an era for the city's Creole elite, just as the closing of Storyville ended a key chapter in the history of American popular music.

Music and dancing continue to change and to delight in contemporary New Orleans. By turns witty, joyful, sexual, sorrowful, and spiritual, the musical culture of New Orleans is vibrantly alive. The annual Jazz & Heritage Festival at the old Fair Grounds has provided the modern city with a world-famous showcase for all the many kinds of Louisiana music. As Gwendolyn Midlo Hall has written, New Orleanians "tore down the barriers of language and culture among peoples throughout the world and continue to sing to them of joy and the triumph of the human spirit through the sounds of jazz."

SINCE WORLD WAR II: THE CITY IN DECLINE

The first half of the twentieth century was a paradoxical time for New Orleans. On the one hand, she finally managed, in the early 1900s, to conquer the constraints of her swampy site with a modern drainage system, and the threat of spring floods diminished after the U.S. Army Corps of Engineers took over responsibility for the Mississippi levees after 1927. Modern drainage and sanitation made 1905 the last year that yellow fever—"bronze John"—struck the city. New pumps and drains finally permitted the city to expand lakeward into the Back-of-Town swamps. A new Central Business District also sprouted between 1900 and 1929. Bank and office buildings along Carondelet and other financial district streets gave the city a modern office core. On the other hand, her regional dominance went into eclipse after World War II.

In contrast to this city-wide structural decline was the rediscovery of the historic French Quarter. After a long interval as an immigrant slum, New Orleanians began to prize the long-neglected Vieux Carré. In 1911 the State of Louisiana designated the historic Presbytère, located on Jackson Square, as the Louisiana State Museum. Things had reached a nadir in the French Quarter by the late 1910s. The Roman Catholic archbishop briefly closed Saint Louis Cathedral to the public because of its deteriorated condition. William Ratcliff Irby anonymously made a substantial donation for its repair in 1918. A new theater group, Le Petit Theatre du Vieux Carré, opened a small theater in the Upper Pontalba Building and, in 1922, built its own hall near the corner of Chartres and St. Peter streets. Designed by Richard Koch, it was the first new building in the Quarter to reflect the architectural character of the district. A woman's club restored an 1838

Greek Revival townhouse at 620 St. Peter Street and christened it Le Petit Salon. William Ratcliff Irby restored other important French Quarter landmarks including the Seignouret-Broulatour house and the old Banque de la Louisiane. Irby also bought the Lower Pontalba Building from Baroness Pontalba's heirs and willed it to the Louisiana State Museum. These creative investments saved the core of the French Quarter.

The low rents and European ambience of the Quarter attracted writers and artists to the district in the years after World War I. Sherwood Anderson lived on Governor Nicholls Street, and William Faulkner rented rooms behind Saint Louis Cathedral. Edmund Wilson, Oliver LaFarge, and Lyle Saxon were among those attracted to the affordable, exotic French Quarter. Nightclubs and art galleries popped up and began to draw New Orleanians to the narrow, historic streets. Royal Street emerged as "antique row" and drew more attention to the Quarter.

The Depression years were hard on New Orleans, but under the Works Progress Administration streets and parks were improved, and historic buildings including the French Market and the Pontalba Buildings were restored. Artists and writers were employed by New Deal programs, and New Orleanians became more aware of their historical legacies through books published with W.P.A. support. The Depression, and then World War II, halted most new construction, but the core of the city remained lively.

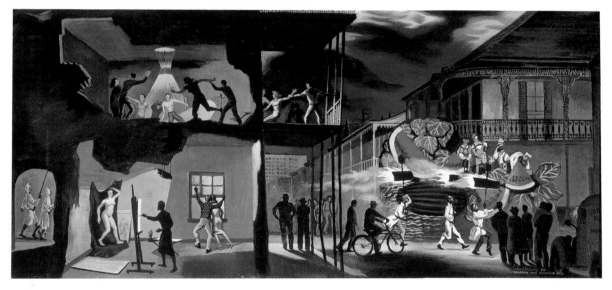

JOHN McCRADY,
The Parade, 1950
This panoramic painting weaves together many of the essential qualities of New Orleanian culture: her many peoples, the historic French Quarter, a Carnival parade, music, dancing, and, in the far left corner, the artist at work painting a sensuous nude.
(Roger Houston Ogden Collection, New Orleans)

Suburbanization came a bit late to New Orleans, but when it did, in the 1960s, the city began to lose its middle-class population, both white and black. The spread of the automobile, the decay of public transit, a new interstate highway, and a causeway across Lake Pontchartrain made it possible to leave Orleans Parish for cheaper suburban land. Integration of the public schools induced white flight. The city's tax base began to drain away alarmingly. Growth continued in the very core of the commercial city, but many residential neighborhoods began to decay. A brief oil and natural gas boom in the 1970s changed the city's skyline with a spine of high-rises along widened Poydras Street. In 1971, after a long battle, citizen protest stopped a destructive riverfront superhighway that would have disfigured the French Quarter. Construction of the gargantuan Louisiana Superdome in 1975 and a turn toward tourism and high-rise hotels stimulated parts of the city's economy, but did not stem the steady loss of residents and jobs. New housing in East New Orleans, a previously undeveloped swampy area technically within the city limits but actually far from the old neighborhoods, drew families out of the historic city. Between 1960 and 1990, the population of New Orleans fell by 20.8 percent, from 627,525 to 496,938.

ELEGANCE AND DECADENCE: NEW ORLEANS' DISTINCTIVE STYLE ENDURES

To look only at recent trends would be to fail to see the vitality of this distinctive city. Just as character and soul are the most important qualities in people, so character and soul are what make New Orleans not just a decadent city, but a still stylish one. In fact, the recent economic decline has had a paradoxically invigorating effect on the city's contemporary artistic life. Low living costs have drawn artists, writers, sculptors, furniture designers, and other creative people to the Crescent City. They are comfortable with the active music scene and the open spirit of the place. The visual arts are especially alive in New Orleans in the 1990s.

Some New Orleanians make a distinctive art form out of living with things the way they are. They don't fight the decadence of their city—they embrace it. Fussy wallpaper is stripped from old rooms to reveal the stained plaster underneath. Carpets are taken up to reveal the pine floors. *Faux* graining is sometimes stripped from cypress mantles to reveal this now-rare native wood. Instead of doing over old houses in a single contemporary mode, furniture and finishes from many different periods are mixed and mingled. Rooms in old houses are encouraged to speak of all the generations that have lived in them, changed them, and loved them. New Orleans pursues a way of living that is both decadent and elegant.

NEW ORLEANS

Elegance and Decadence

CHAPTER ONE
Urban Fabric

Sensitive to the beauties of Nature...the Devil could not suppress a sigh of regret as he gazed with far-reaching eyes along the old-fashioned streets of the city, whose gables were bronzed by the first yellow glow of sunrise. "Ah!" he exclaimed, "is this, indeed, the great City of Pleasure, the Sybaris of America, the fair capital which once seemed to slumber in enchanted sunlight, and to exhale a perfume of luxury even as the palaces of the old Caesars?"

LAFCADIO HEARN, "A Visit to New Orleans," *Item,* 1879

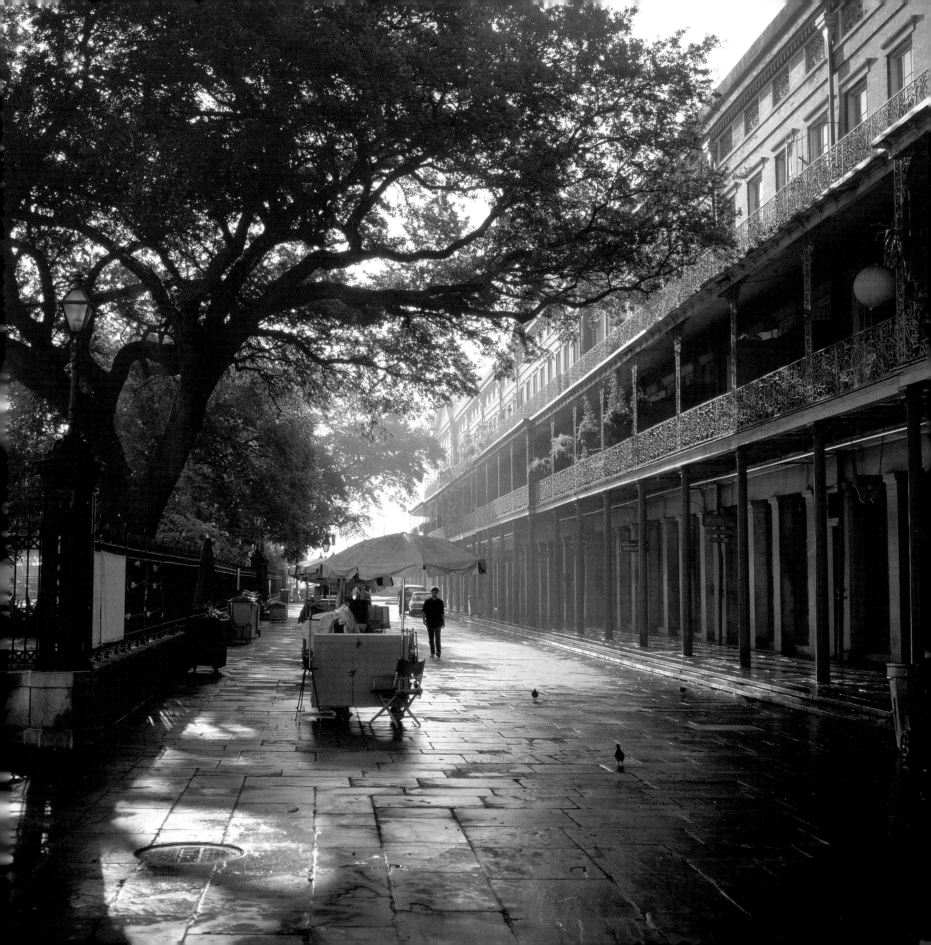

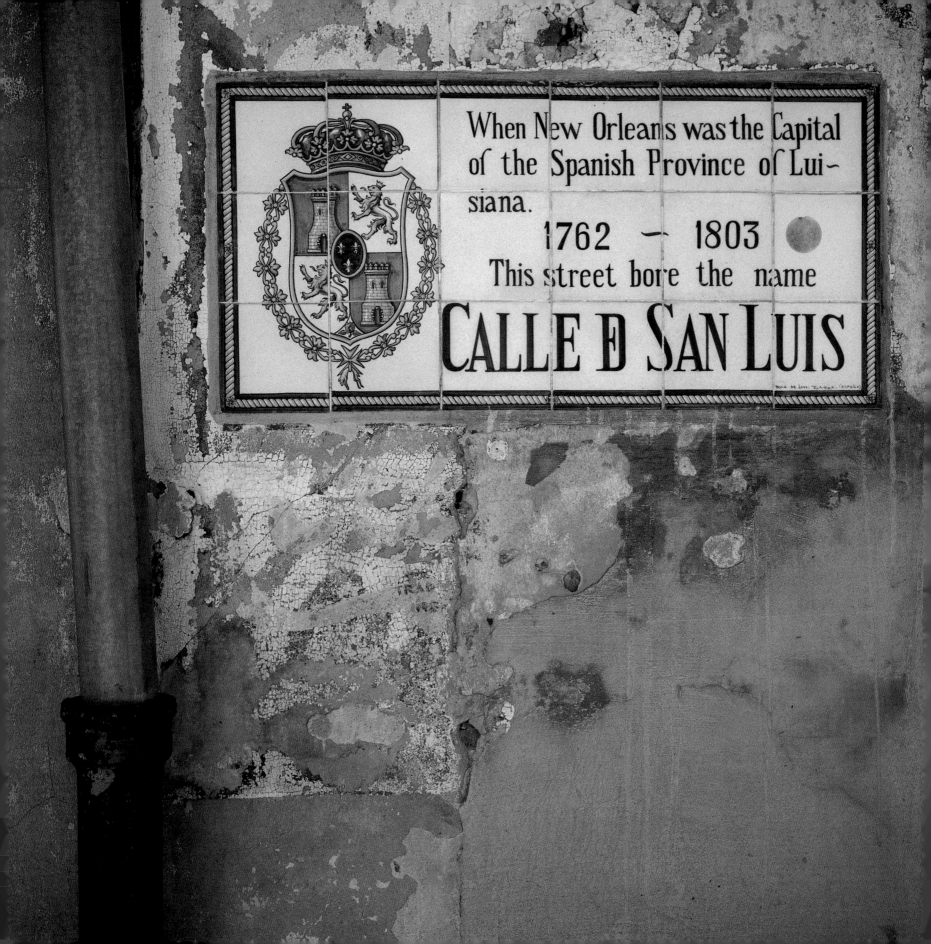

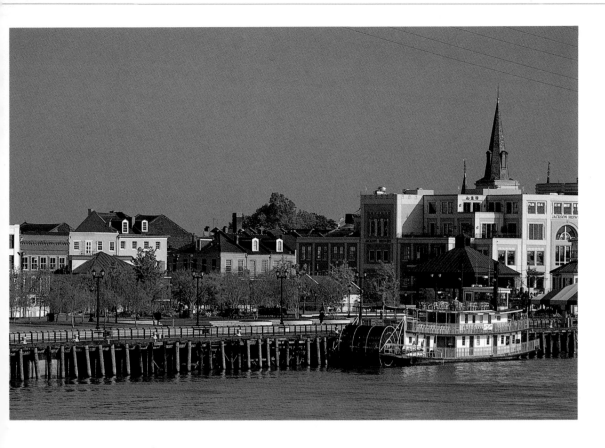

New Orleans exists because it lies athwart the shortcut between the Gulf of Mexico and the Mississippi River that allowed water traffic to bypass the river's bewildering delta. Bayou Saint John was the easiest portage for small boats traveling from the gulf up the Mississippi via Lake Pontchartrain. In 1718 the Company of the Indies, a private French enterprise (and the S&L scandal of the eighteenth century), established the town on a natural levee of the Mississippi. After long giving over all its river frontage to wharves and shipping, New Orleans has recently made a park out of part of its river frontage. Here the sternwheeler *Creole Belle* lies next to Wollenberg Park and the converted Jax Brewery. Old buildings to the left line Decatur Street; the central spire of Saint Louis Cathedral pierces the horizon.

This view from Canal Place looks out over the rooftops and trees of the French Quarter, where the city preserves its low-rise profile. Saint Louis Cathedral was rebuilt in 1849–51 by J. N. B. de Pouilly on the site of an earlier church, designed in 1724 by Adrien de Pauger. In 1721 de Pauger laid out the sixty-four blocks of the Vieux Carré (old square), more commonly known as the French Quarter, or "the Quarter" to New Orleanians.

Opening Photograph:
Early in the morning, while it is still cool and the riverine fogs still hug the swampy city, portraitists set up their easels along the St. Peter Street mall in the Vieux Carré (French Quarter). Today more than ever, artists and writers are drawn to this atmospheric city. To the left is Jackson Square, still the emotional and spiritual heart of New Orleans. To the right is the upper Pontalba Building built in 1849–50 for Micaela Almonester, the baroness de Pontalba. The fine red brick, granite, and cast-iron Pontalba Buildings flank the upriver and downriver sides of Jackson Square, thus they are designated as "upper" and "lower." Sixteen row houses share a continuous arcade of shops on the ground floor of each building. Commercial and residential spaces were layered one over the other in the traditional Creole city.

This ceramic street sign marks the 1814 Napoleon House at the Downtown-riverside corner of Chartres and St. Louis streets. The flaking and stained wall displays the special quality of antiquity cultivated in New Orleans.

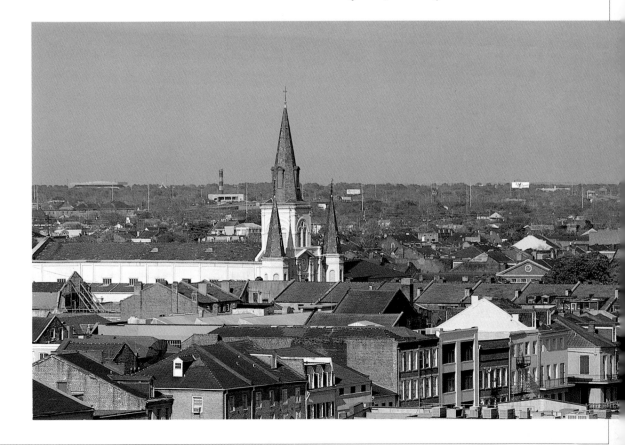

The heavy rains and intense sun of southern Louisiana quickly age her buildings while stimulating her lush vegetation. The rusted *abat-vent* (wind breaker) on this French Quarter house protects the brick walls from heavy rains. Iron galleries over the sidewalks were often later additions to houses. They provide cool, shaded upper porches for residents while sheltering pedestrians below from the hot sun and sudden showers. Galleries make the street a theater, with the pavement the stage and the galleries the dress circle.

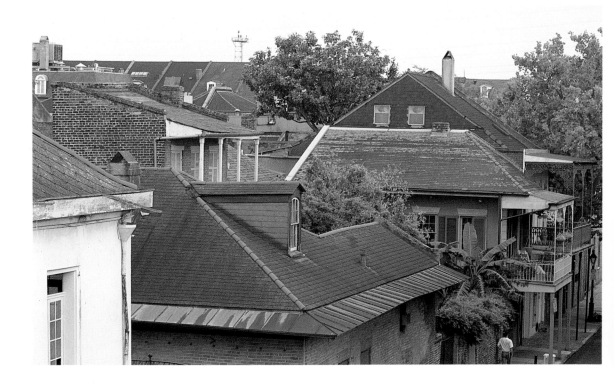

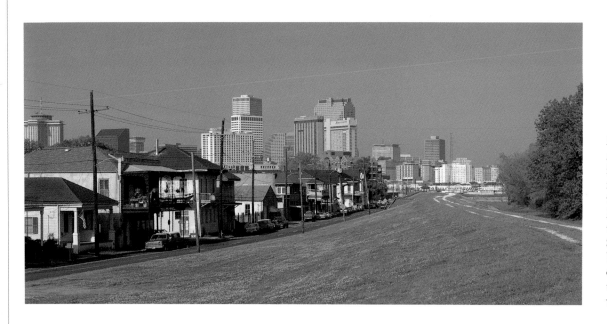

Most of New Orleans is below the level of the river. A great system of levees, embankments that prevent flooding, was begun in 1723 and must be continually maintained. The grassy slope of the levee slopes down to the old residential area of Algiers on the west bank of the Mississippi. In the distance, on the river's east bank, is the modern city with its high-rise skyline. One Shell Square (left) and Place St. Charles (right), the tallest buildings in New Orleans, are monuments to the booms of the 1970s and 1980s. Even though the great river is usually not visible from the city because of levees and wharves, its presence is always felt.

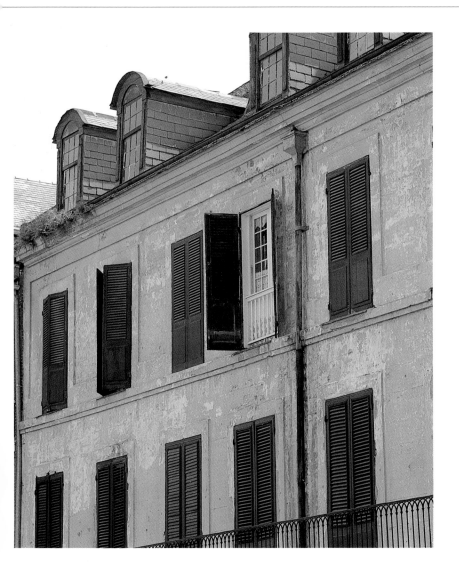

Europe in the Americas. The abstract pattern created by the casement windows and louvered shutters of the Nicholas Girod house, better known as the Napoleon House, looks like Mediterranean Italy or France.

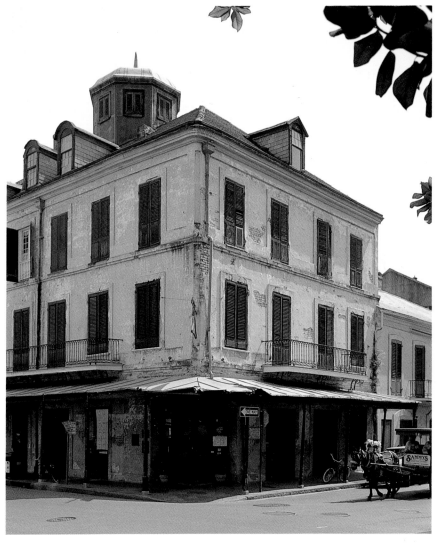

The Girod house was designed by Hycinthe Laclotte, an architect from Bordeaux, and built in 1814 for Nicholas Girod, mayor from 1812 to 1815. The covered sidewalk provides shade from the sun, and tall rooftop dormers increase ventilation upstairs. It is one of the few buildings in the city with its original tile roof. Tradition has it that Girod offered his house as a refuge for Napoleon Bonaparte in a plot to rescue him from exile. Today the Napoleon House Bar & Cafe occupies the ground floor. Classical music and local flavor heighten the effect of its dark, cool, ancient-seeming interior. The owners, the Impastato family, have wisely refrained from over-restoring it.

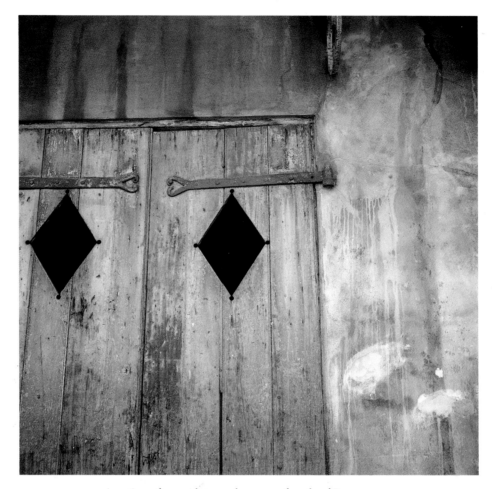

A patina of age enhances the stucco facade of Preservation Hall on St. Peter Street in the French Quarter. Old forged-iron strap hinges secure the shutters. "Spasm bands" formed by young Afro-American street musicians began appearing in the city in the 1890s. By the end of the decade, ragtime, a new syncopated musical style, was at its peak. It was the first Afro-American cultural expression to find national acceptance. In 1961 the Society for the Preservation of Traditional New Orleans Jazz was formed, and live jazz continues to pour from this music-soaked building.

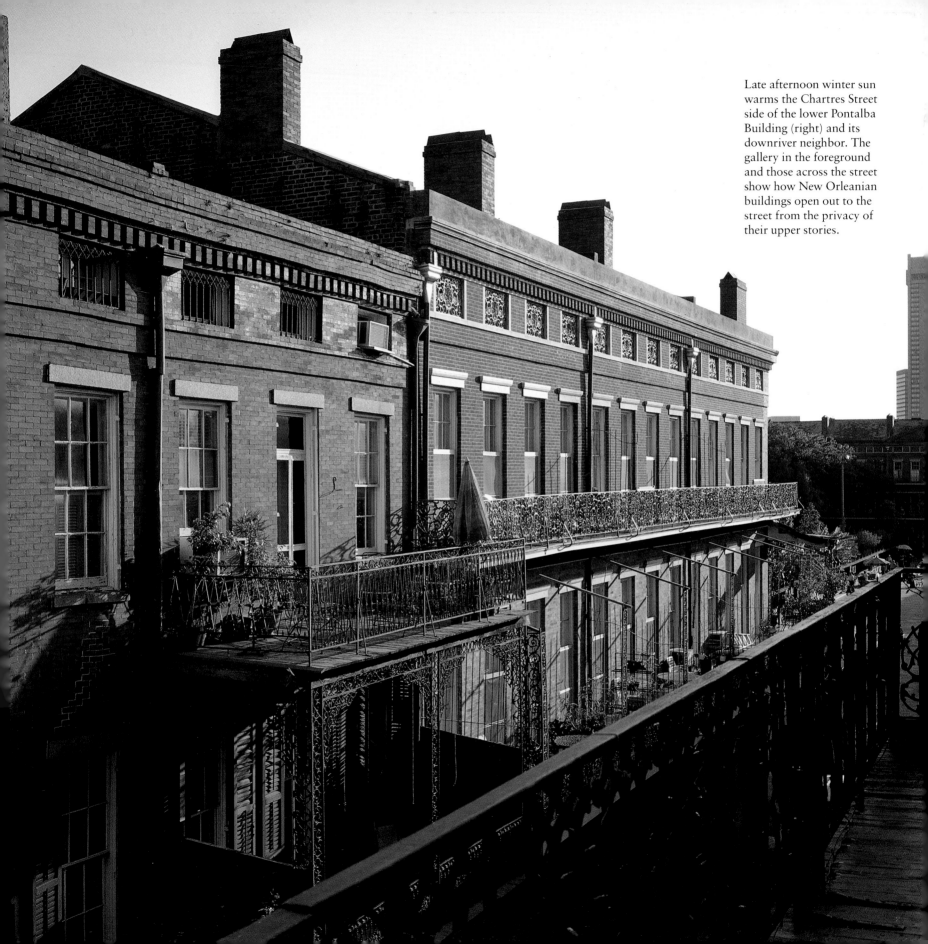

Late afternoon winter sun warms the Chartres Street side of the lower Pontalba Building (right) and its downriver neighbor. The gallery in the foreground and those across the street show how New Orleanian buildings open out to the street from the privacy of their upper stories.

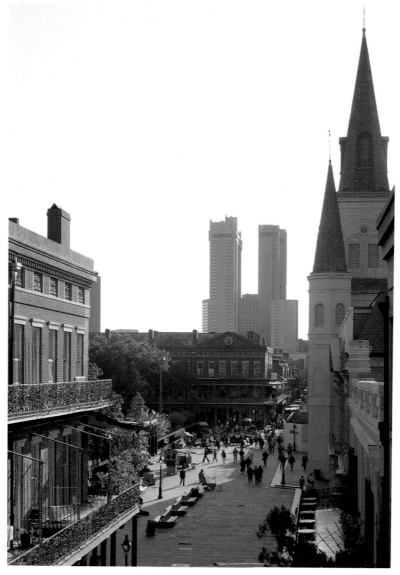

The Creole and American cities meet in this view looking up Clinton Place in the French Quarter toward the back of the monumental United States Custom House. Begun in 1848 with Alexander Thompson Wood as architect, the building had many other designers before its completion thirty-three years later. This structure is the fourth custom house to occupy the site. The sober exterior, of Quincy granite, is embellished with colossal columns with Egyptian lotus capitals. Inside is the vast and stately Marble Hall ringed by Corinthian columns, one of the finest late Greek Revival rooms in America.

Spires old and new. Jackson Square is the site of one of the greatest urban ensembles in North America. Laid out in 1721 by Adrien de Pauger as the French city's *place d'armes* (parade grounds), it achieved its present appearance in the early 1850s. To the right are the sharp spires of J. N. B. de Pouilly's Saint Louis Cathedral. Barely visible next to the cathedral is the columned facade of the Presbytère, begun in the 1790s and converted into the Louisiana State Museum in 1911. The upriver and downriver sides of the square are framed by the elegant Pontalba Buildings of 1849–51. In 1972 three of the streets surrounding the square were closed to traffic, creating a lively, people-filled place. Looming in the distance are the modern Marriott and Sheraton hotel towers on Canal Street.

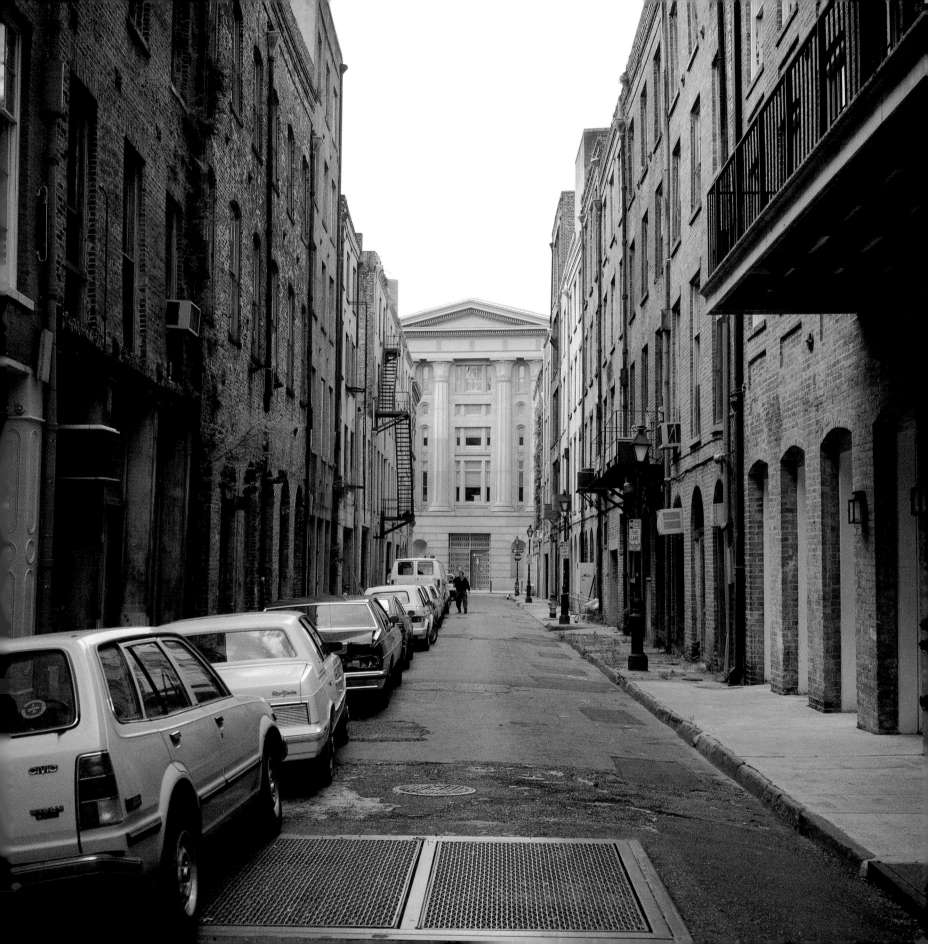

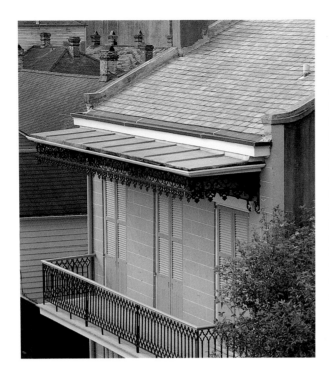

The simple beauty of a Creole townhouse on Governor Nicholls Street epitomizes the architectural sobriety of the French Quarter. This brick structure is stuccoed, scored, and painted to look like stone. Elegant cast iron decorates its gallery and the edge of its *abat-vent*. Its fine slate roof is a warm gray. In the distance are characteristic old New Orleans brick chimneys.

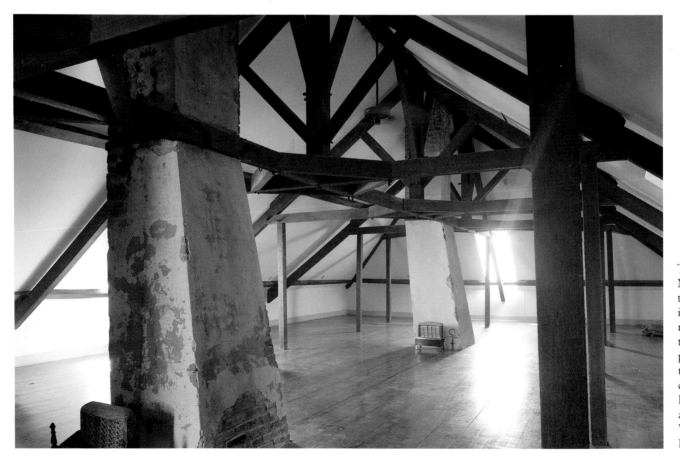

The cypress-timber Norman truss system in the 1826 Lombard House in Bywater is a fine and rare example of traditional colonial French plantation roof construction. Building techniques came to Louisiana from France via French Quebec and also from the French West Indies and Saint Domingue (Haiti).

A Creole-period color scheme of French red, mustard yellow, putty, and Egyptian blue enlivens the rusticated facade of the circa 1836 Nathan-Lewis-Cizek house in Marigny. (American Greek Revival houses had uniform white walls with dark green shutters.)

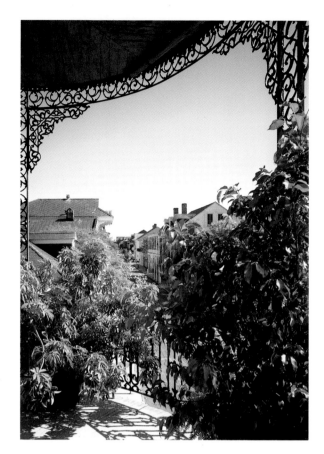

Nineteenth-century cast-iron galleries and contemporary potted plants frame a view looking down Barracks Street in the lower French Quarter. Gallery gardens are increasingly popular in contemporary New Orleans.

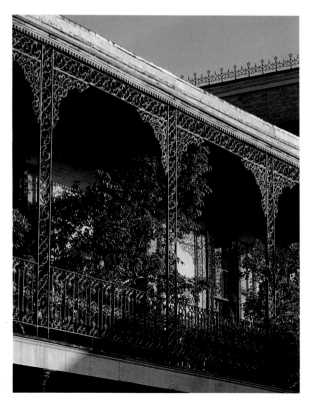

The same second-story gallery as seen from the street displays the lacy cast iron for which New Orleans is famous.

An old 12-over-12 sash window with a few panes of handmade glass looks out from the 1824 Erard-Espy house in the lower French Quarter into the rear courtyard garden next door. The tall trees with leathery, dark green leaves are magnolias. Private hidden views like this are typical of the old Creole city's modern gardens.

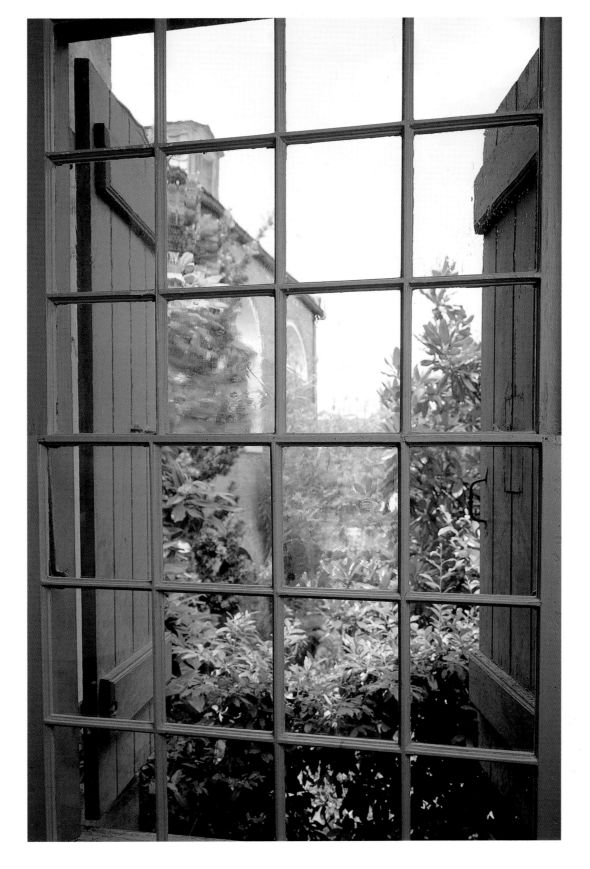

The white painted dormers of a French Quarter house on Bourbon Street are characteristic of old New Orleanian neighborhoods.

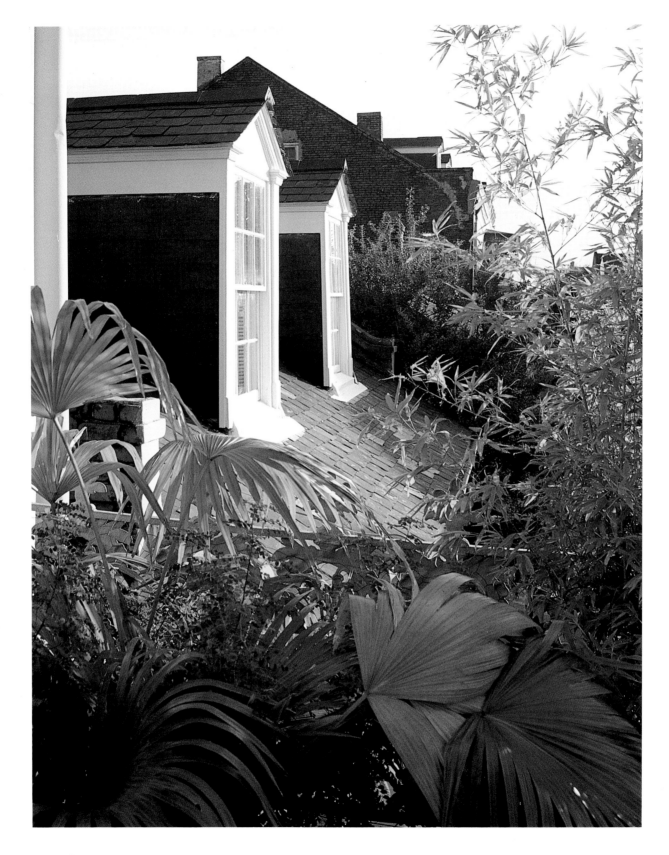

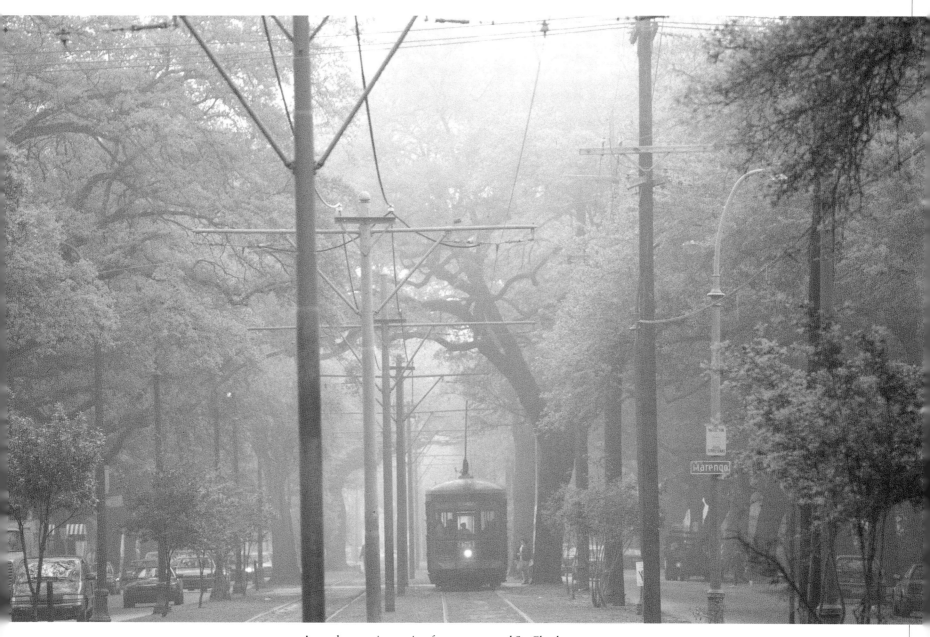

An early morning spring fog wraps grand St. Charles
Avenue and its old oaks in a soft, dreamy atmosphere. St.
Charles Avenue Uptown may be the grandest street of
old houses in the American South. Opened on September
26, 1835, the New Orleans & Carrollton Railroad Company is considered the oldest continuously operating
streetcar line in the world. Originally horse-drawn, it
was electrified in 1893. The olive green cars in use today
were designed by Perley A. Thomas, built in 1922–24,
and recently refurbished.

Grand hundred-year-old live oaks embrace St. Charles Avenue where a fruit vendor has set up her truck stand. "Creole tomatoes" are grown in Louisiana's dark, rich soil under its hot, intense sun. They are as flavorful as everything Creole.

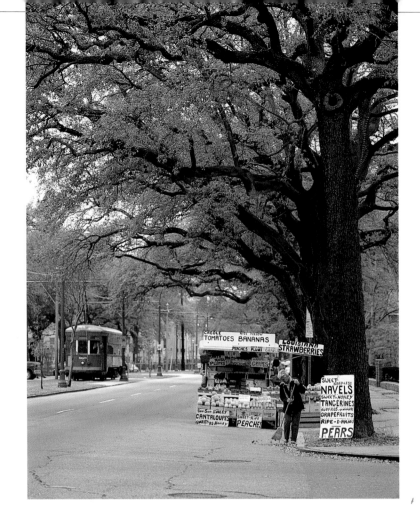

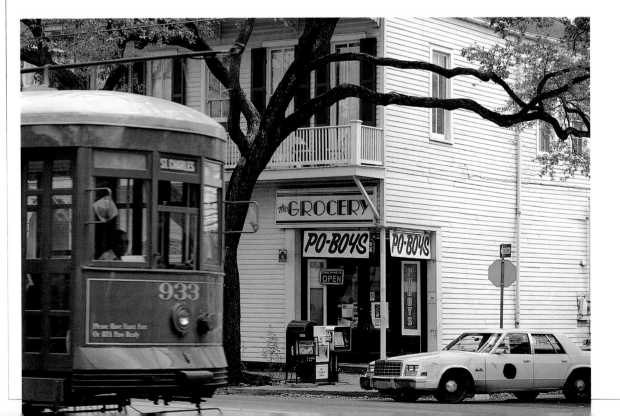

A corner grocery at St. Charles Avenue and Sixth Street, on the edge of the Garden District, features "po-boys," generous sandwiches on soft French bread said to be enough for a poor man's meal. New Orleans is, of course, famous for its foods. It is probably the only American city where homemade meals in mom-and-pop restaurants can be memorable experiences.

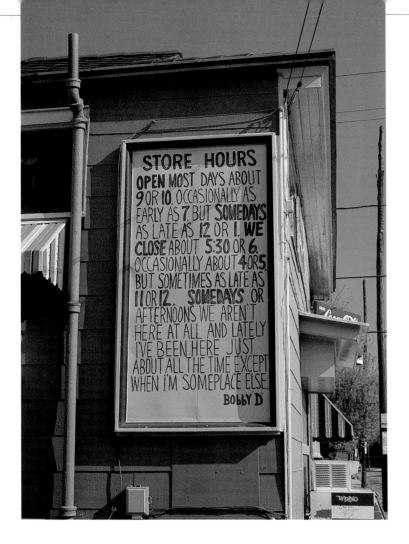

Bobby D's grocery store in Algiers keeps its own hours.
Let the buyer beware!

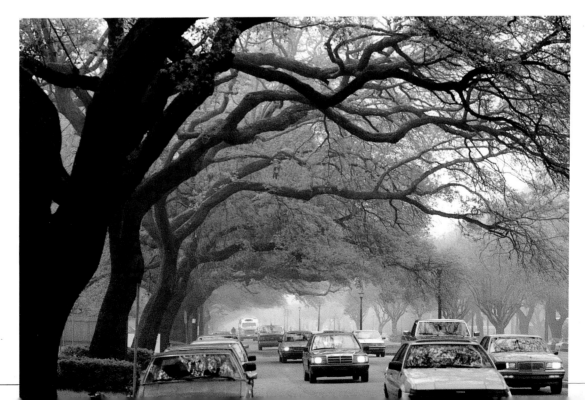

Great live oaks form a living canopy over Napoleon
Avenue as cars stream by during morning rush hour.
This part of Faubourg Bouligny, originally a plantation,
was subdivided in 1834 by Laurent Millaudon and
Samuel Kohn. Even years after Napoleon's exile,
enthusiasm for the French emperor survived among
Creole New Orleanians. Other streets flanking the wide
avenue were named after famous Napoleonic victories:
Milan, Austerlitz, Berlin (renamed General Pershing
during World War I), Marengo, and Constantinople.

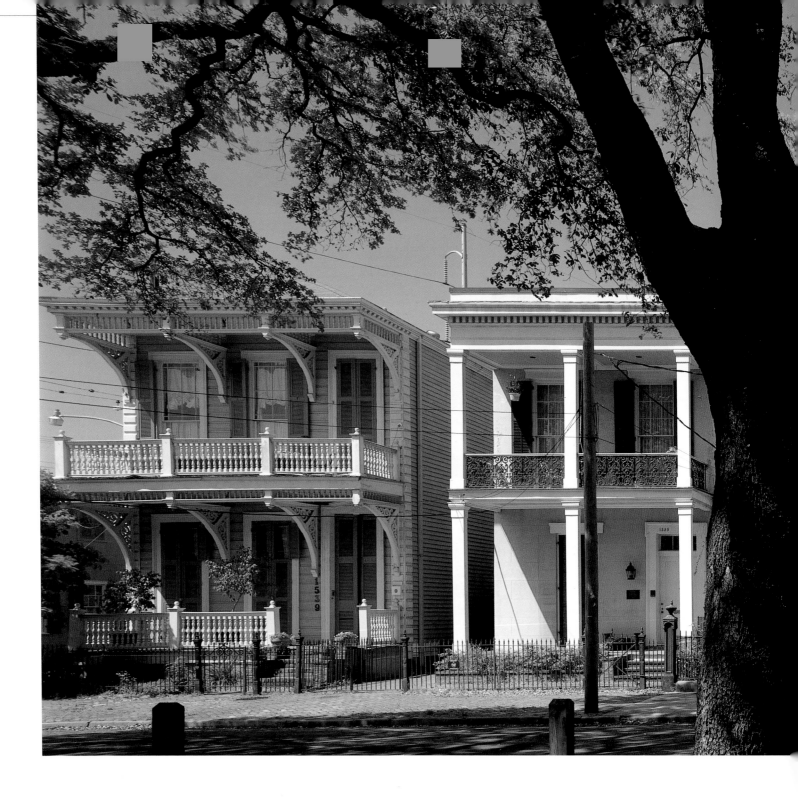

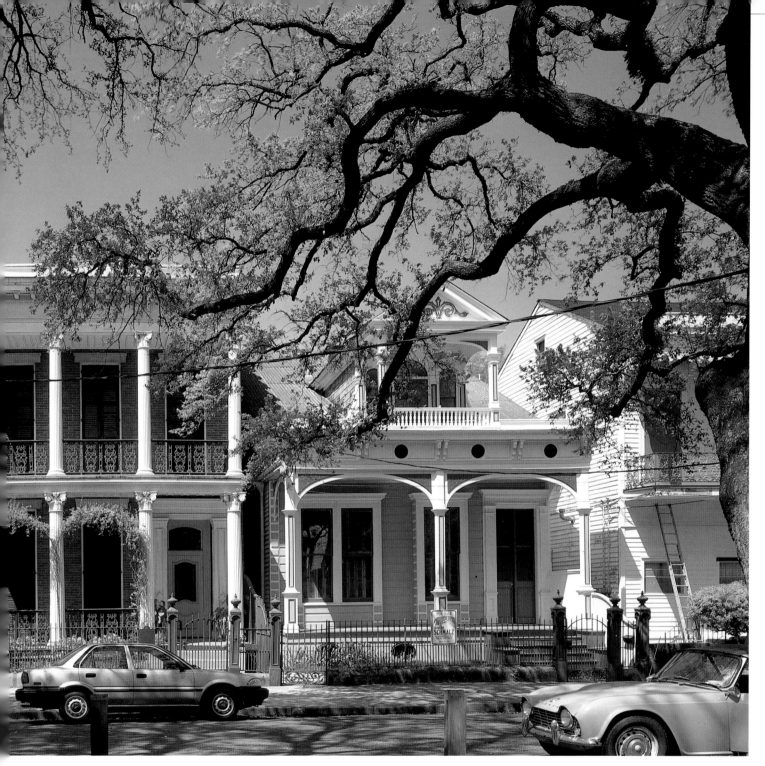

Unity and variety mark the characteristic galleried houses of New Orleans. This row faces Coliseum Square in the Lower Garden District. Architect and surveyor Barthelemy Lafon platted the area in 1806 for Madame Delord-Sarpy and named nine cross streets after the Greek muses: Calliope (heroic epic), Clio (history), Erato (lyric poetry), Thalia (comedy and pastoral poetry), Melpomene (tragedy), Terpsichore (dance), Euterpe (music and lyric poetry), Polymnia (sacred poetry), and Urania (astronomy). These most felicitous street names display the love of classical learning so much a part of high Creole culture. Although the houses were built at different times, they all employ the covered gallery so useful in this hot, rainy climate.

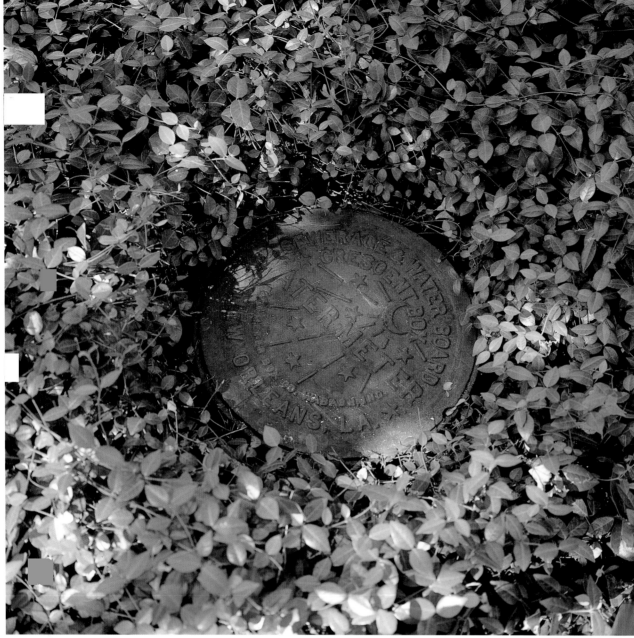

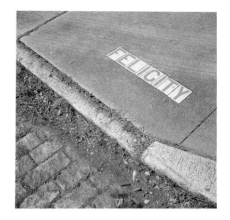

Blue and white turn-of-the-century street tiles survive here and there at intersections in old parts of the city. Felicity Street was named by Barthelemy Lafon in 1810 for Sister Saint-Felicitée Alzac, assistant to the Ursuline mother superior, when he subdivided the Faubourg des Religieuses, Uptown land owned by the Ursuline nuns.

Nothing is more important in New Orleans than the Levee Board, which protects the swampy, low-lying city, and the Sewerage and Water Board, which drains it. Under most of the city's wide avenues and planted "neutral grounds" (medians) are miles of covered canals leading to pumping stations that lift rainwater from the shallow saucer of the city and into Lake Pontchartrain. Started in 1896, and reorganized as the Sewerage and Water Board in 1903, the system is an invisible marvel; it can drain the city of the heaviest downpour in a matter of hours. Cast-iron water-meter covers are decorated with stars and a crescent for the Crescent City.

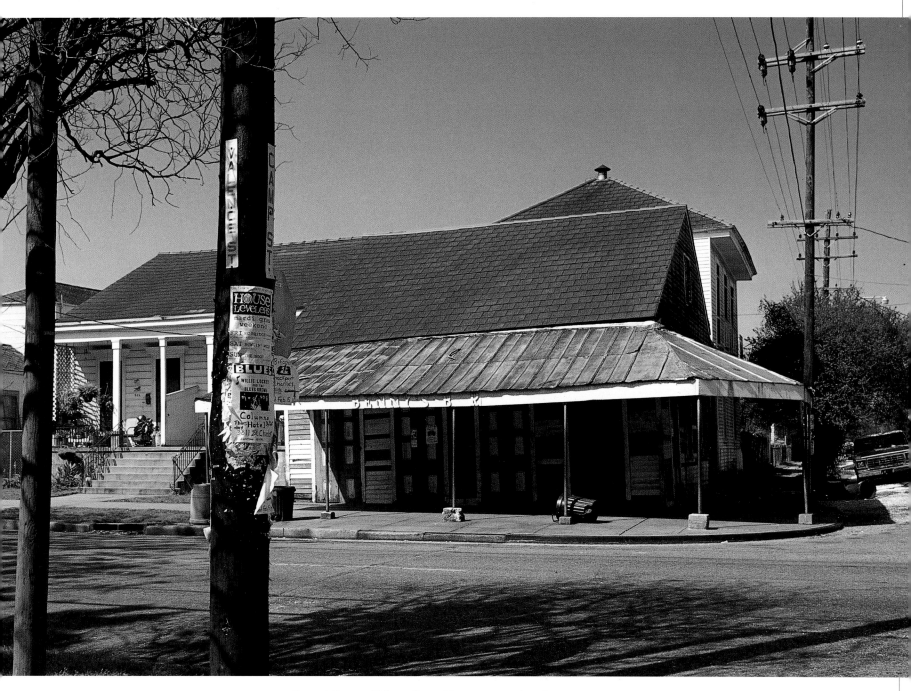

Benny's Bar on Valence Street Uptown occupies what
was probably once a corner grocery store. These corner
buildings with covered sidewalks are typical of the city's
complex prezoning urban fabric.

A great papier-mâché and clay Muse presides over one room in Villa's gallery. All the furnishings in the foreground, including the *faux-marbre* table, are his work. Atop the mantle is an old mirror from a plantation, its silver backing tarnished and peeling. It offers a melancholy reflection on the Deep South's lost grandeur, while Villa's contemporary work continues the long tradition of fine furniture making in Louisiana.

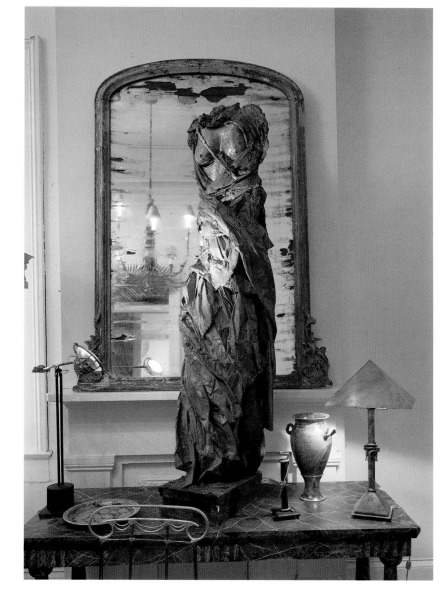

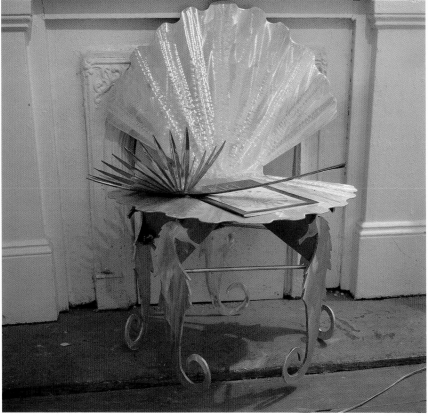

Villa's whimsical Shell chair with seahorse legs was envisioned as the Mardi Gras throne for Rex or Comus, or for the Queen of the Ocean. The copper palmetto frond is a tribute to the fecund Gulf Coast environment.

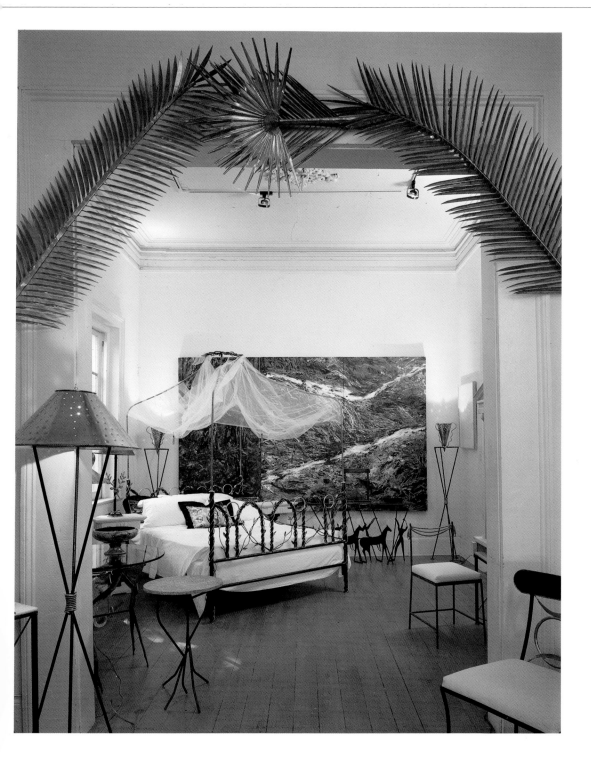

Mario Villa is a fervent believer in the ability of New Orleans to enrich one's life. Even the decayed aspects of the city are fertile ground for his art. The building that houses his gallery was left in the state in which it was found "to show people that ruins can be beautiful." The pine floors were pickled to further age them. All the furnishings shown here are Villa's work. The bed with gauzy canopy is called the Gothic bed; the chair in the lower right is the Crescent chair, named for New Orleans, the Crescent City. The great copper palm and palmetto fronds, important motifs in Villa's art, are symbols of the celebration of life. Over time the copper fronds will take on a rich green patina.

The artisan, the epicurian, and the antiquarian are woven through New Orleans' urban fabric. Music, art, food, and antiques are all things New Orleanians love and do so well.

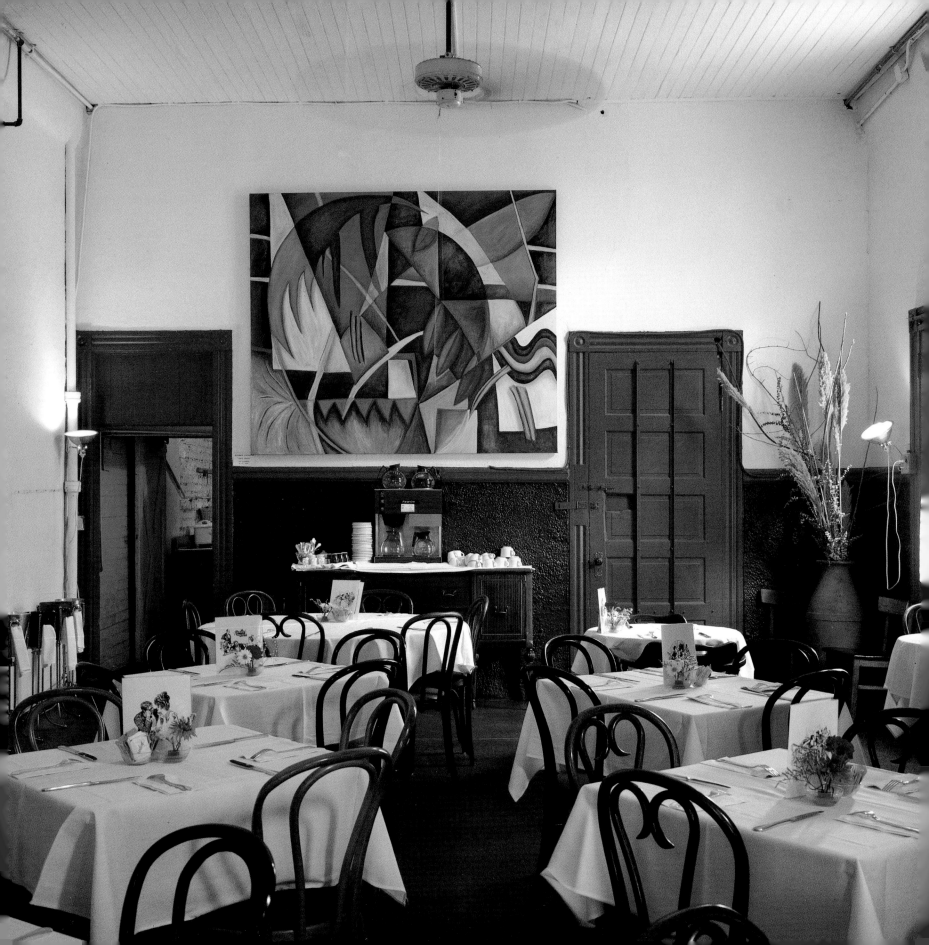

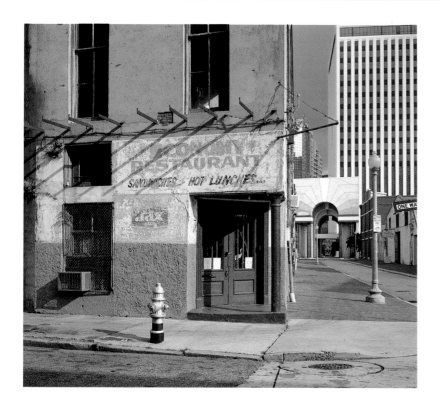

Wonderful surprises are tucked all over New Orleans. L'Economie restaurant at Girod and Commerce streets, at the edge of the warehouse district, opened in 1989. Because its owners, Hubert and Nina Sandot, want to "impress at second sight," they left the facade as they found it, filled the interior with art, and concentrated on light French cuisine with a Creole influence. The restaurant's kitchen has no freezer; most ingredients are purchased fresh each day. Hubert Sandot, whose father was from Martinique and his mother French, was born in Madagascar and raised in Paris.

The fading archway down the street leads to Charles Moore's postmodern Piazza d'Italia, a grand folly with a fountain built from 1976-79 and already a nonworking, neon-trimmed ruin. Things age quickly in New Orleans!

L'Economie restaurant is a moved-into space, not a million-dollar renovation. Traditional bentwood furniture and white tablecloths welcome the diner to a room that is, as the chef describes it, elegant but not stuffy. The colorful painting by Elizabeth Polchow Livingston is entitled *Tropical Freeze* (1990). Her works are influenced by her Zen practice and her tropical garden Uptown.

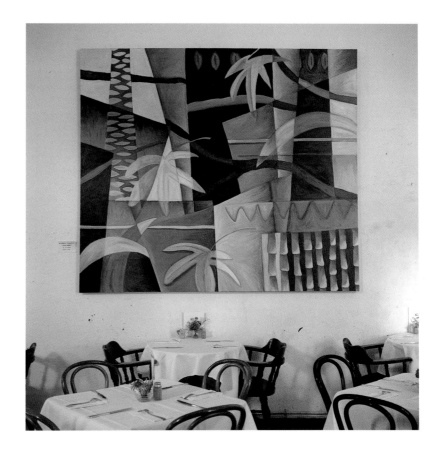

Another work by Livingston, *Samba Hubert* (1990), fills the side wall of the restaurant with vibrant color. Food and art are natural partners in New Orleans. Even down-home places are often decorated with lithographs and mementos.

A. Oakley Hall's *The Manhattaner in New Orleans, or Phases of "Crescent City" Life* (1851) observed that "Emperor Appetite and King Alcohol hold their court in a most recherché style" in New Orleans. Votaries of the table still thrive in the Crescent City. *Antiquaire* Patrick Dunne's shop, Lucullus, is filled with fine old things associated with cooking, dining, and drinking, all of which can be used and enjoyed. An *antiquaire,* Mr. Dunne notes, is someone who deals in old things but who brings an intellectual dimension to the process. The shop is named for Lucullus, a Roman general famous for his banquets. His palace had many dining rooms evoking different themes, but the most famous was a room for one where he could dine in solitary splendor. A Parisian red front with gold lettering has been simply and artfully applied to the facade of this characteristic Spanish-era building built about 1800 on Chartres Street.

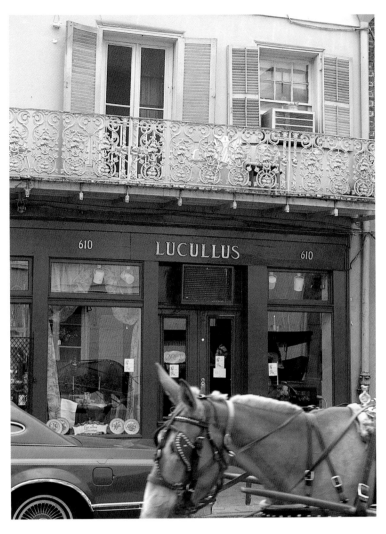

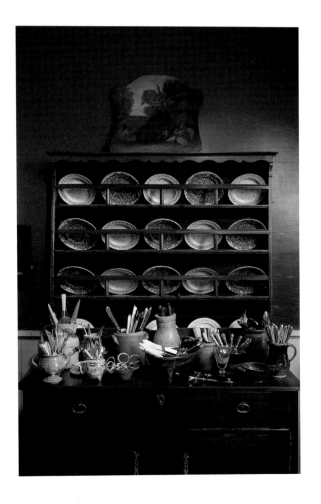

Frank and sophisticated in its enjoyment of pleasure, New Orleans has always reached out to the world for its luxuries. In Lucullus objects have been gathered from many nations and ages to enhance the enjoyment of food and drink. The newest things in the shop are from the 1920s, the oldest go back to 200 B.C.E. Here a tall, cherry wood French *directoire vaissilier* holds two collections of plates. The white-and-blue Chinese export ware with cornflower decorations was made for the French market. The green "leaf" plates are nineteenth-century English. French provincial pottery on the countertop holds dining accoutrements including ivory-handled oyster forks, melon and salmon forks, table and dessert knives, and a *manche gigot* (leg-of-lamb holder); a silver spoon rests across a conical absinthe glass. Propped atop the *vaissilier* is a French painting of a bear breaking into a beehive.

Under a nineteenth-century Venetian glass chandelier is a stripped table displaying chaste nineteenth-century soft-paste Luxembourg porcelain and Louis Philippe (1830s) champagne flutes. The silver French Empire flatware (early 1800s) has a filet pattern. Atop the commode to the right is an ivory-and-ebony inlaid Louis Philippe–era *cave des liqueurs*.

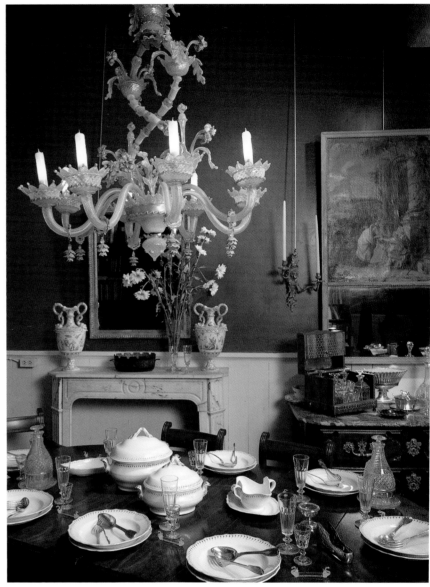

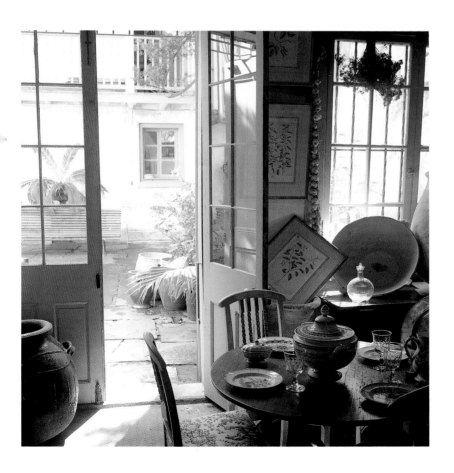

French doors at the rear of the shop open onto a hidden courtyard. Flagstone paving and movable potted plants make the space both a garden and a work area. The green oil jug to the left is from the Auvergne region of France. The courtyard houses French glazed pottery and a white *saloir*, a salting jug. On the window ledge is a yellow-glazed olive oil jug from Provence. (*Jars de Provence* are traditional French Quarter garden ornaments.) The round pine and walnut table was made for wine tasting. The clear glass globe on the table by the window, a fly catcher, would have once been filled with sugar water to attract and trap flies.

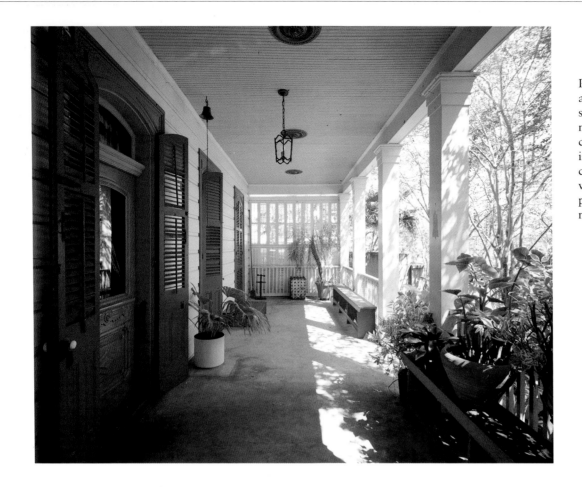

Paul Poché's Creole cottage in Bywater is enlivened by a distinctive, untraditional color scheme. Louvered shutters are painted the bright pink of flowering crepe myrtle. The yellow and green were inspired by the house colors of Oaxaca, Mexico. At the far end of the porch is an old, white-painted iron safe found, locked, in a creek. Poché and his friends opened it, imagining they would find riches, but the safe was empty. They put plastic Mardi Gras beads inside and locked it for the next safecrackers.

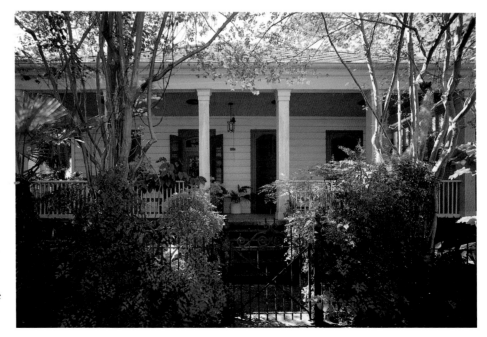

From the sidewalk, Paul Poché's Creole-plan cottage seems embowered in plants. The wrought-iron fence is almost engulfed by nandina bushes. At the far left is a bright green windmill palm. The taller trees are Chinese paper plants grown from slips from the Magnolia Mound plantation upriver.

Four French doors, a Greek key doorway, and two pedimented dormers produce an unusual rhythm in this Bywater house, which combines a Creole facade with an American center-hall plan. New Orleanian architecture was shaped by the cultural complexity of this riverine *entrepôt*.

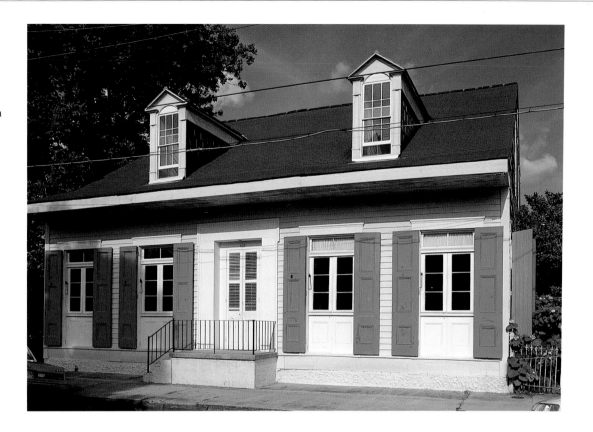

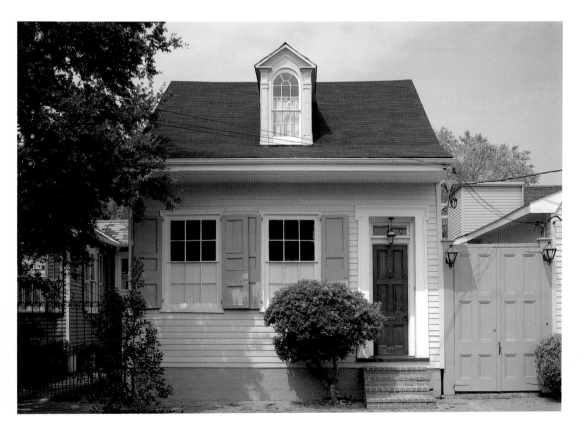

This trim Creole cottage with shutters and Greek Revival detailing was built for a free woman of color in the Marigny district in 1833. Before the Civil War, New Orleans had the largest community of *gens de couleur libres* in the South. Free men of color were prominent among the city's carpenters, painters, plasterers, and furniture makers. Many free women of color owned their own homes in the early nineteenth century. The white Greek key door surround is a characteristic and elegant New Orleans touch.

"The heart of New Orleans is its old neighborhoods. I like living in the Creole section," says antique dealer Marcus Fraser. Raised in suburban Metairie, Fraser discovered this late 1890s Victorian cottage in Bywater after it had been condemned by the city. He bought the house because it was a challenge. "I found something that no one else appreciated," he recalls. "I thought I could make it beautiful." His dog, Bessie, watches the street. The old semaphore flags are a tribute to the Mississippi riverboat captain who once lived here.

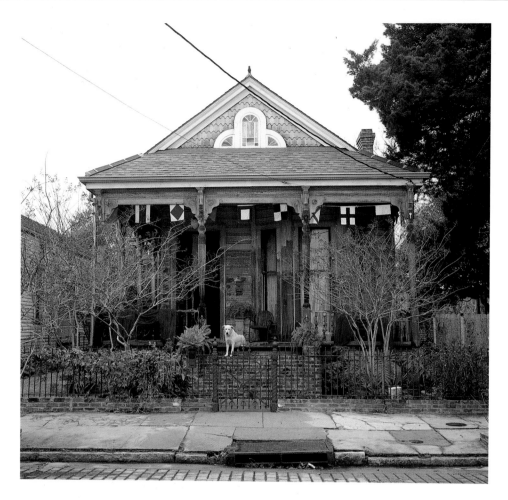

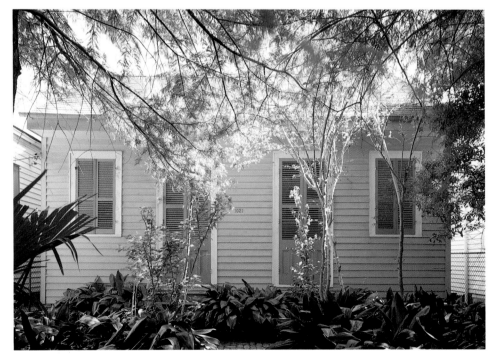

This circa 1845 four-bay Creole cottage in Bywater is built from thick planks recycled from flatboats that made one-way trips down the Mississippi River. Two front doors serve the single dwelling. The owner, Henri Schindler, art director for the Comus and Rex krewes (parading clubs), used the house's unusual setback to plant a buffering front garden of dark green aspidistra. He painted the originally white house a golden yellow, a color that reminds him of Rome, and used Chinese green for the shutters. Altogether this gives the modest cottage a secluded setting and a cheery aspect.

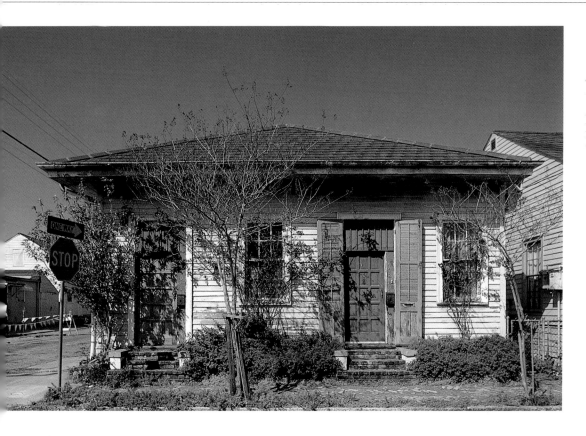

This Bywater double-shotgun house, owned by English-born "artist of the applied arts" Ken Reynolds, probably dates from the latter part of the nineteenth century. Preferring to maintain the home's unremarkable facade, Reynolds reserves a fanciful dimension for the interior.

Using trompe l'oeil murals and various *faux* finishes, Reynolds has created an elegant neo-Palladian world inside his working-class cottage. This mural is based on a portrait by Titian with a Palladian rotunda in Florence in the background. Another mural in the house depicts a bacchanalia, a Roman festival celebrated with frenzied dancing, singing, and revelry.

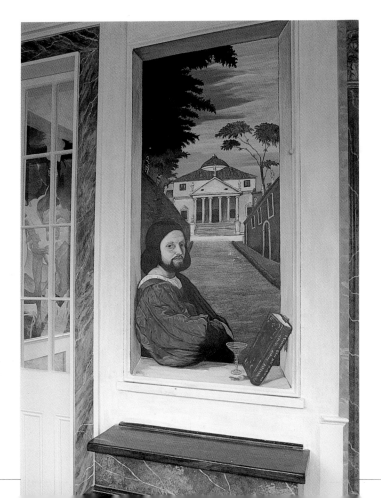

Like a bijou classical temple set on a wildflower-strewn riverbank, artist Mario Villa's house happily weds a classical Greek Revival colonnade to a modest frame house. Probably built during the second half of the nineteenth century as a working-class shotgun house, it has been reconfigured with a central pedimented entrance and double parlors. With his house tucked between older and grander plantation homes, Villa feels himself to be "next door to the beauty I like the most." He wanted not grand formality in his garden but rather the sweetness of an old flower-embowered cottage.

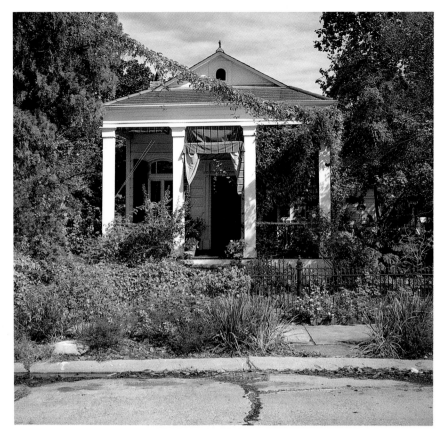

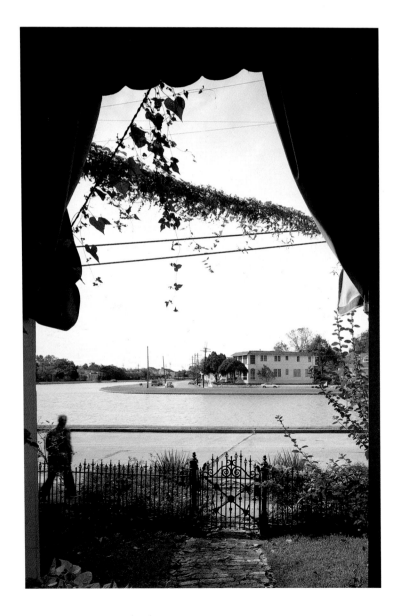

When Mario Villa was a young man, he saw Bayou Saint John and told himself that someday he would live there. Raised in Nicaragua overlooking broad Lake Managua, he values a water view. Here, where the bayou bends toward Lake Pontchartrain, was the Native American trail and portage between the Gulf Coast and the Mississippi. The French crown granted plantations in this area before the founding of New Orleans. On even the sultriest days, a light breeze off the water cools the Bayou Saint John neighborhood. A Clematis montana rubens vine reaches out from the house to the utility pole.

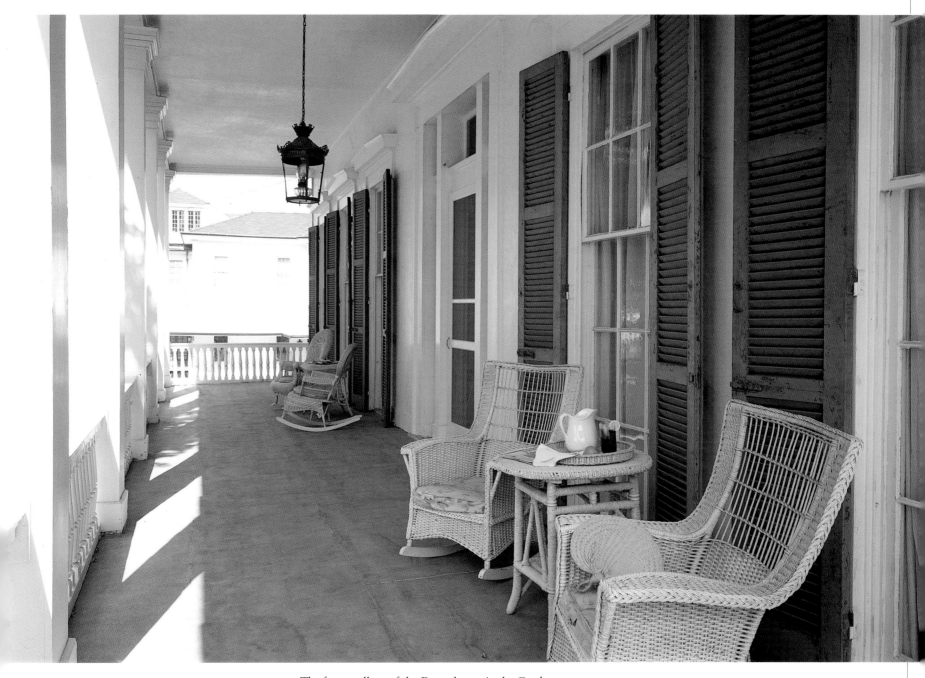

The front gallery of the Freret house in the Garden District is hospitably furnished with old wicker rocking chairs. The owner, a writer, works here when it rains; children also like the wide verandah. This raised, center-hall Greek Revival cottage was built for the parents of the Freret brothers, famous New Orleans architects.

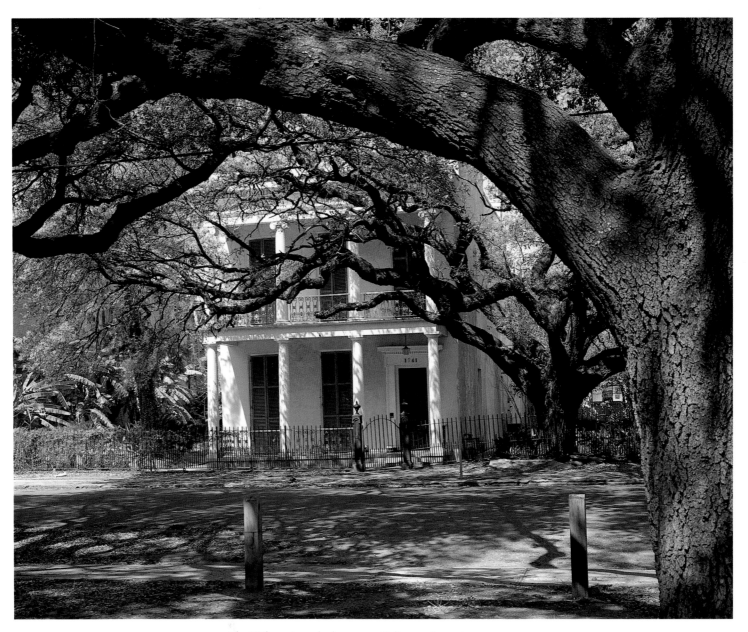

The Wilson-Josephs house on Coliseum Street is
glimpsed here through magnificent live oaks. The
suburban, almost "oak alley" feel of this American
neighborhood with its great, gnarled trees and spacious
yards is in sharp contrast with the urban European
density of the older Creole French Quarter. This fine
brick house has double wooden galleries. The restrained
columns are properly Doric on the first floor and Ionic
on the second. The elegant house also displays a Greek
key door surround and cast-iron balustrades.

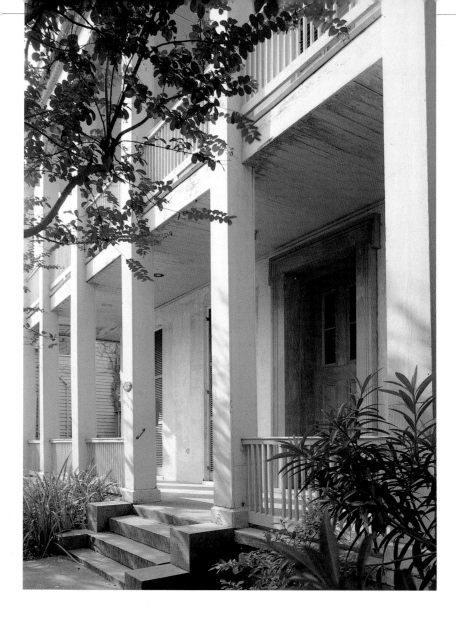

This Greek Revival house on Euterpe Street Uptown was built in 1847–48 with simple wooden galleries that entirely encircle the masonry building. Originally the brick walls were stuccoed, scored, and painted to look like stone. A Greek key design frames the *faux-bois* front door. A crepe myrtle at the upper left and an oleander to the right frame the view.

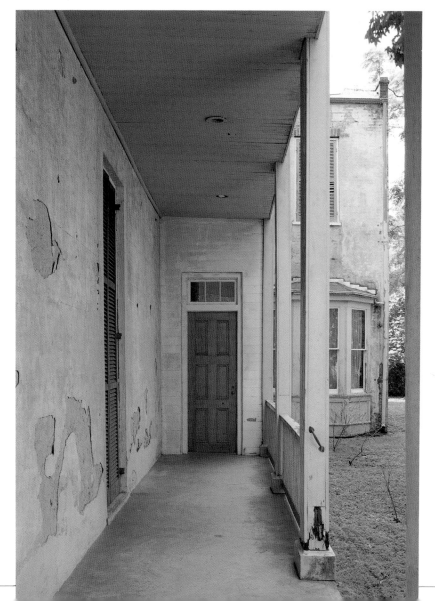

The side gallery of the house ends in a door and hallway that were added later. The simple box columns show how elegantly proportioned Greek Revival houses can be.

The simplest houses in New Orleans are working-class shotgun cottages, with rooms lined up one behind the other, front to back, with no internal hall. Because the interior doors also align, it was claimed that a shotgun discharged through the front door would send its pellets straight through and out the back door. This bracketed Victorian shotgun cottage on Foucher Street, in Bouligny Uptown, has an open side gallery on the right. The shotgun, which first appeared in New Orleans in the 1830s, is common in the southern Louisiana countryside as well. Its popularity lasted into the early twentieth century.

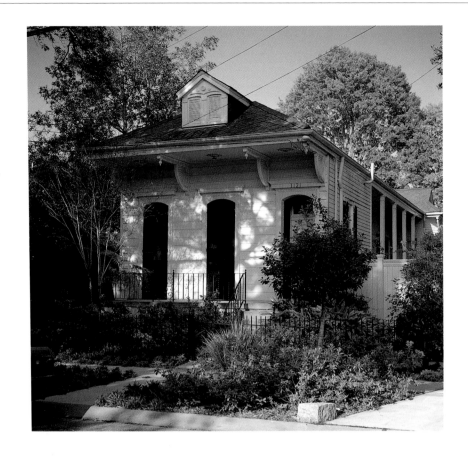

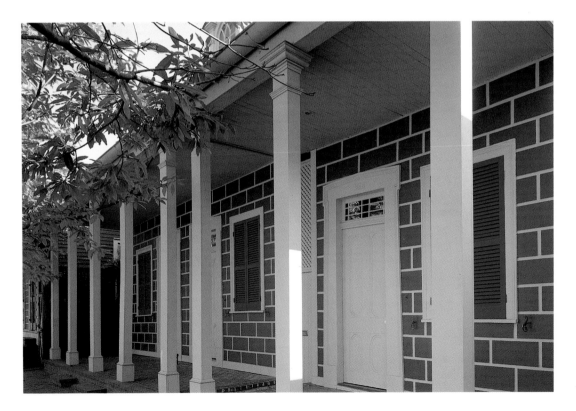

This unusual Greek Revival triple cottage with a rusticated facade and slender Doric box columns, on Burgundy Street in the Faubourg Marigny, has been artistically painted by its architect and artist owners, Eugene Cizek and Lloyd Sensat. They employed a Creole color scheme of French red "stones" with yellow "mortar" for its wood facade, a putty color for the trim and columns, and Egyptian blue for the louvered shutters. Now known as Sun Oak, it is a combination home, house museum, and guest house.

Faubourg Marigny, across Esplanade Avenue from the French Quarter, was developed by Bernard-Xavier-Phillipe de Marigny in 1808 when he subdivided part of his plantation downriver from the old city. He named one street in his new subdivision Rue de Craps after the dice game he is said to have introduced to the city. (It was renamed a then more respectable Burgundy Street in 1850.) Other original names in Marigny included Rue d'Amour, and, only a block away, Rue des Bons Enfants. Marigny became home to many free people of color in the early nineteenth century. The area was also favored by wealthy Creole and American men who set up houses for their quadroon mistresses and mixed-race children.

Americans built light cypress-wood buildings and, following the style of early Creole plantation houses, raised them on six-foot-high brick piers. They introduced a center hall for easier social separation and better ventilation, and built a colonnaded gallery across the front and, often, the back of the house. The Cooper house is a circa 1885 raised American cottage that faces the levee and river in Bywater. When it was moved in 1907 because of levee improvements, it was again set up high to ride out floods and to catch the constant, cooling river breeze. The house has no air conditioning. The tall dormer was destroyed by hurricane Betsy in 1965, but in 1990 owner and restoration carpenter Marc Cooper replaced the dormer using recycled sash and shutters.

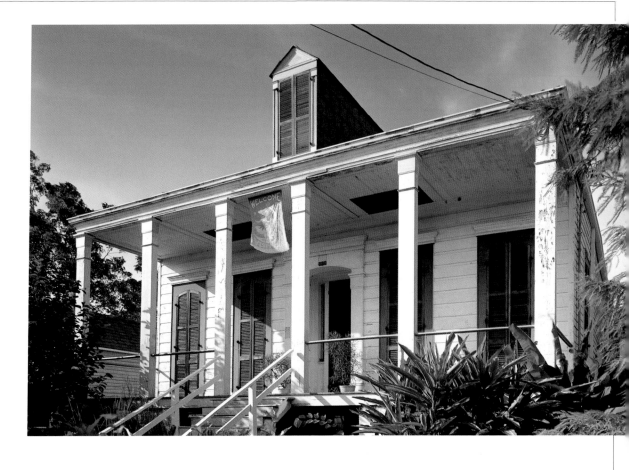

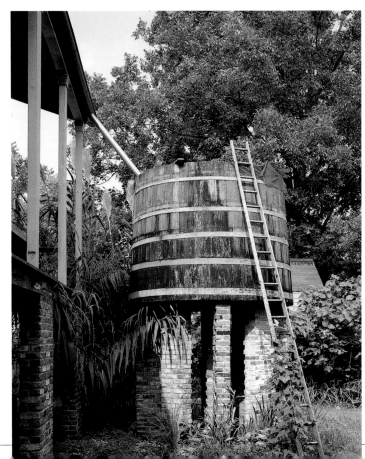

A rare old-fashioned cypress cistern made about 1940 in Reggio, Louisiana, was moved and resited by Marc Cooper in the backyard of his Bywater house. The fifteen-hundred-gallon tank catches rainwater from the roof for garden irrigation. To the left of the cistern is striped cane, a loofah vine climbs the ladder, and at the lower right is a fig tree. Looming in the background is a mature pecan tree. The Coopers work with southern Louisiana's subtropical environment by respecting the traditional gardening solutions of the past. When asked to characterize New Orleans, Marc Cooper notes that it is a city with a more European than American attitude toward waste. Just as the string on a package should be untied and not cut, he observes, friends should share cuttings for the garden. This traditional point of view is environmentally forward-looking and an approach to gardens, houses, furnishings, and living that is quintessentially New Orleanian.

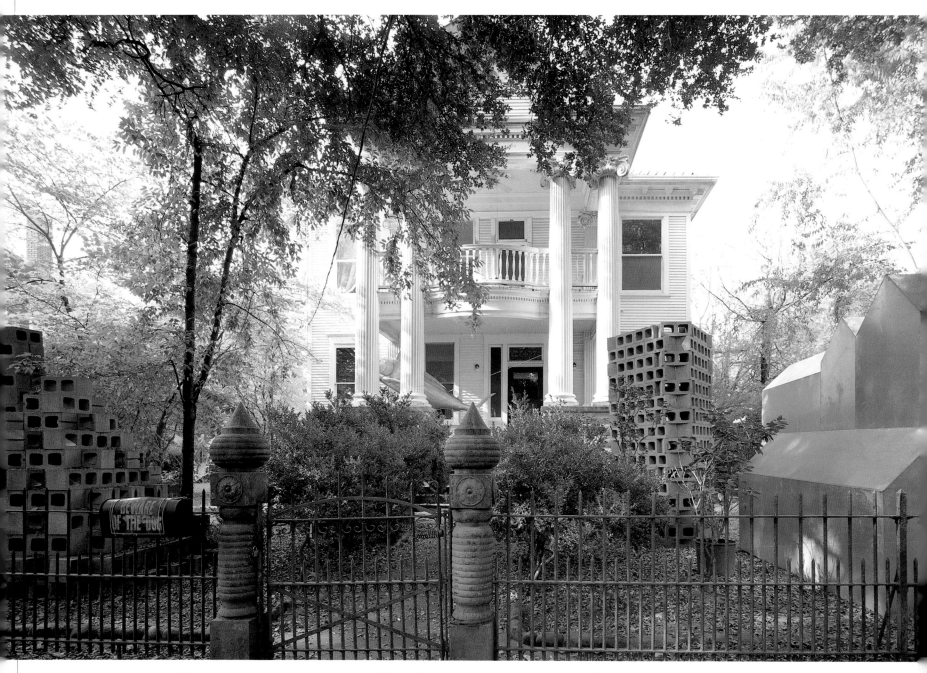

The early twentieth-century Georgian Colonial Revival house of artist and urban planner Robert Cary Tannen and Jeanne Nathan stands behind bold, cast-iron Victorian gateposts. Tannen's Archisculptures, *Stacked Shotgun Houses* (1979) and *Concrete Block Towers* (1979), flank the entrance path. The configuration of the concrete blocks can be changed, making this, in the artist's words, "temporary art." Tannen cast the gold-colored fiberglass piece partially visible on the porch from the largest marlin caught by a fisherwoman in the Gulf of Mexico. Tannen's is an ethic of assemblage, of making something new out of old things. Even though Tannen's unexpected front yard appears very different from what most people think of as New Orleanian, it could be regarded as the city's varied urban fabric in microcosm: a place of high-rises and "shotguns." "What will the neighbors think?" doesn't seem to bother some New Orleanians.

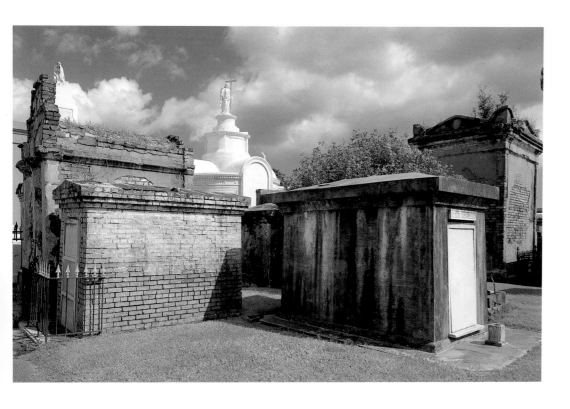

Frequent epidemics made death a too-familiar presence in old New Orleans. Elegant, walled cities with above-ground tombs were a practical response to the city's swampy site. Creole, American, and immigrant families built stuccoed brick tombs; mutual aid societies built "society" tombs; and individuals could lease wall vaults known as "ovens." Bodily corruption comes quickly in Louisiana; a family tomb is designed with a *caveau*, a sepulchral cavity in the base like the ash pit of a fireplace. When a family member dies, the remains of a predecessor are swept into the *caveau* to make room in the vault for the newcomer. Like the houses of the city itself, families are kept apart and yet together in these stately final dwelling places.

The architectural dignity of old New Orleanian cemeteries is evident in Saint Louis Cemetery No. 1, opened in 1789. An unusual, tall decayed tomb (far left) has five levels. Next to it, an iron fence, like a front yard's, guards a family tomb whose sloped walls have lost their stucco covering. The fine tomb with superb classical proportions (right foreground) was built by the Société Hospitalière. The resplendent white marble society tomb on the horizon, crowned by a woman holding a cross, was erected by the Italian Mutual Benevolent Society in 1857. The large decayed tomb (far right) with a fine cornice and plants sprouting on its roof is the Portuguese society tomb.

Cast-iron angels are silhouetted against the weathered marble of the Famille Medelice Thomas tomb in Saint Louis Cemetery No. 1.

The tombs in Lafayette Cemetery No. 1 in the American Garden District Uptown are also noteworthy. In some of the inscriptions there, Victorian sentimentality finds its best monuments. The tomb of Samuel Jerome Bennett, who died at the age of twenty-six years and two months on November 13, 1859, has this sad epitaph:

> The light of other days have faded,
> And all their glories past;
> For grief with heavy wing hath shaded,
> The hopes too bright to last.
>
> Erected by his bereaved mother

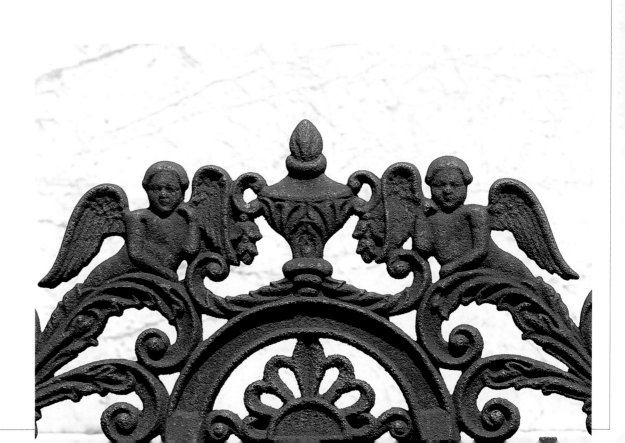

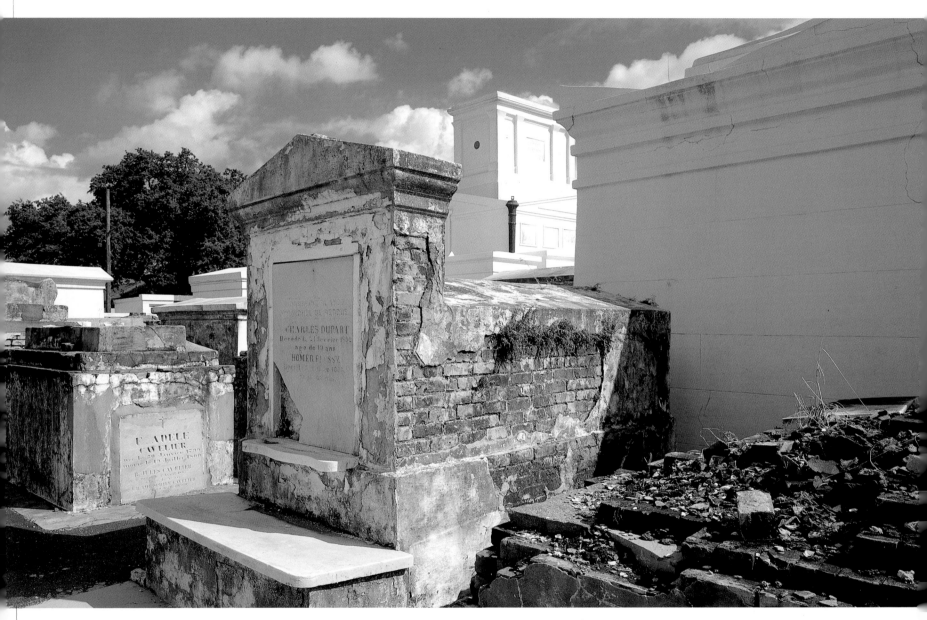

History ultimately sifts the heroes from the villains, though the process takes much longer than one man or woman's lifetime. Saint Louis Cemetery No. 1 is honored to have the tomb of Homer Plessy, "décédé le 1 Mai 1925 age de 63 ans." It was this proud New Orleanian of color who pursued for four years, and lost, the case of Plessy v. Ferguson whereby, in 1896, the U.S. Supreme Court sanctioned a half-century of racial segregation.

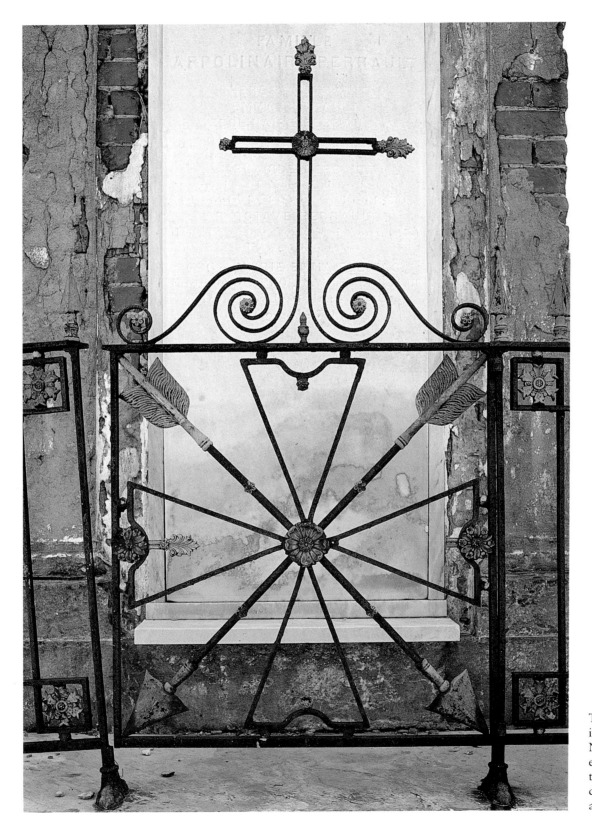

This wrought-iron gate in Saint Louis Cemetery No. 1 shows just how elegant New Orleanian taste can be. The downward-pointing arrows signify death.

CHAPTER TWO
Inward Views

A courtesan, not old and yet no longer young, who shuns the sunlight that the illusion of her former glory be preserved. The mirrors in her house are dim and the frames tarnished, all her house is dim and beautiful with age. She reclines gracefully upon a dull brocade chaise-longue, there is the scent of incense about her, and her draperies are arranged in formal folds. She lives in an atmosphere of a bygone and more gracious age. And those whom she receives are few in number, and they come to her through an eternal twilight.

WILLIAM FAULKNER, "New Orleans Sketches" *Times-Picayune,* 1925

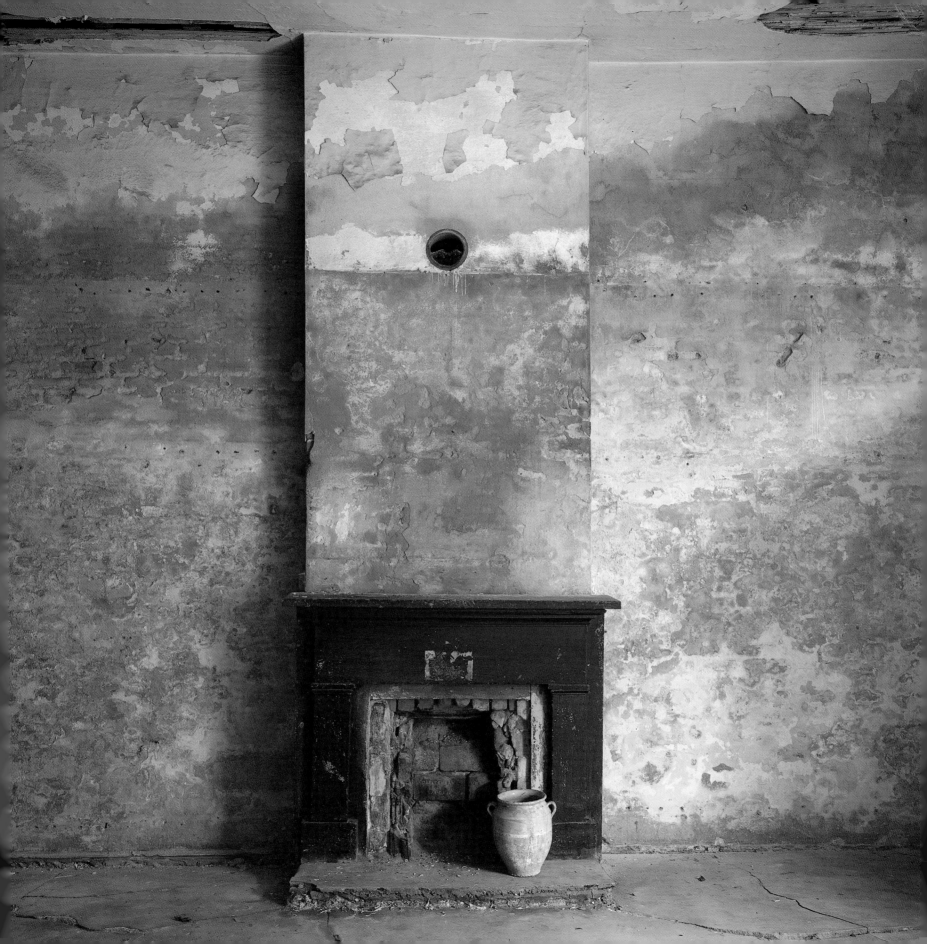

Preceding Page:
The once genteel salon of this 1832 Creole townhouse in the lower French Quarter displays the patina of age and the elegance of decay. The two-story brick house was bought in 1915 by a family that occupied only the upper floor, leaving this room to slowly discolor. Today new owners are only gingerly settling into the old house, letting it speak to them before changing it too much. They use this time-painted room for Thanksgiving and other large gatherings.

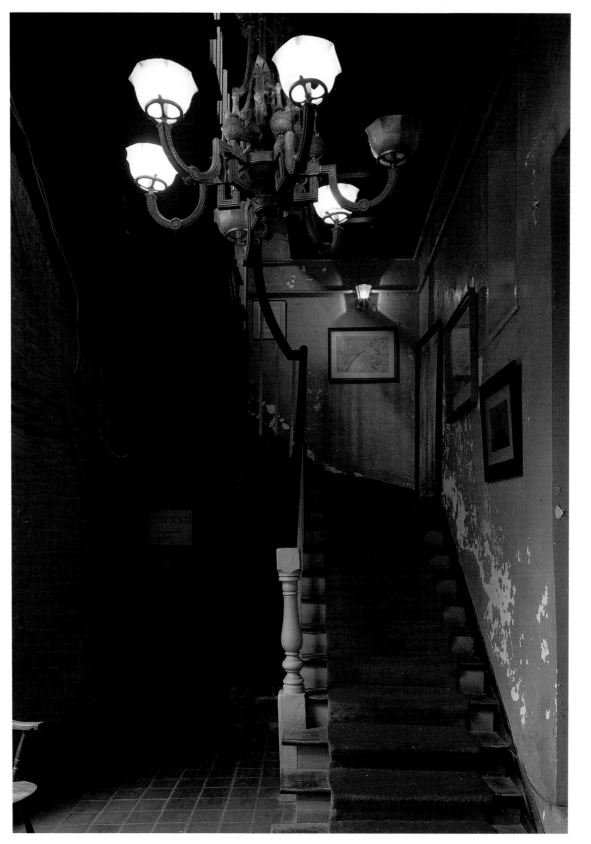

The moody and mysterious rear-stair hall of the Casa Hinard on Toulouse Street leads to living quarters over a ground-floor shop in this old Creole porte-cochere townhouse. A pewter and brass chandelier from the Orleans Ball Room, site of the famous quadroon balls, dimly lights old maps that line the walls. In 1939 Mrs. Alvin Hovey-King moved the family's Hové perfume shop to this site. Today her grandson, Peterson Moon Yokum, lives and paints in this elegantly decayed French Quarter relic.

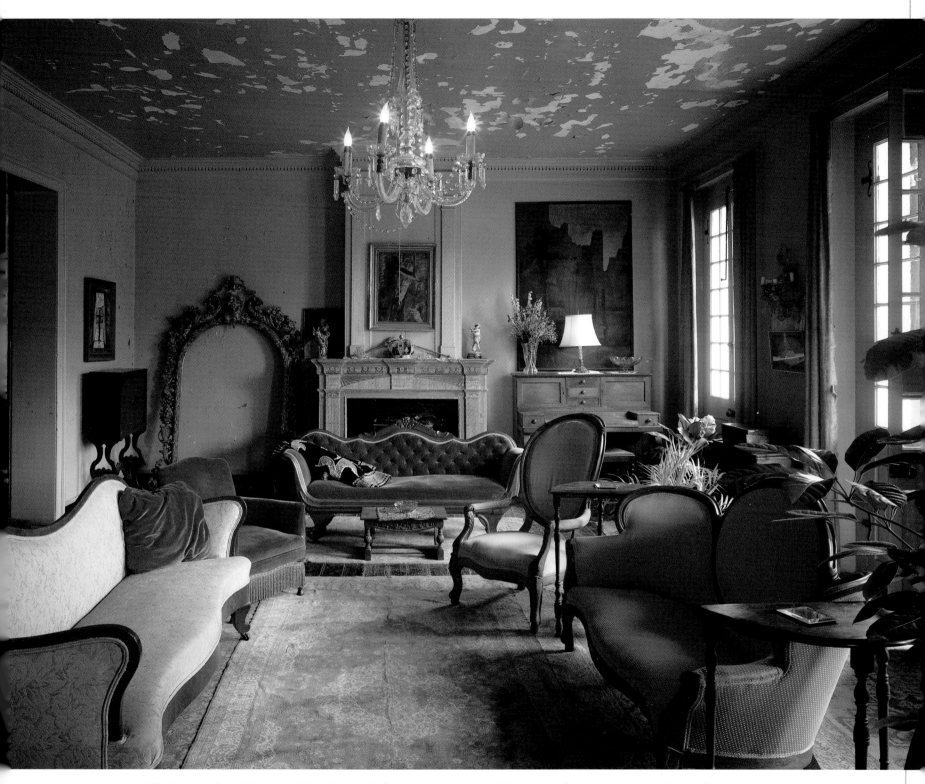

The front parlor of the Casa Hinard is presided over by a portrait of Peterson Moon Yokum's father, painted by his mother in the 1930s. Titled *The Bon Vivant*, it looks down on the family's antique Spanish and French fur- niture. The cape on the rococo sofa and the regalia on the mantel are finery that belonged to the Royal Street Rounders, the Mardi Gras krewe of the elder Yokums. A mood of faded glory pervades the old Creole parlor.

A rich patina lends an aura of antiquity to this corner of the bedroom. A portrait of a woman in deshabille by Rita Elizabeth Hovey-King hangs on the wall. Heirloom toilet articles rest on the bureau.

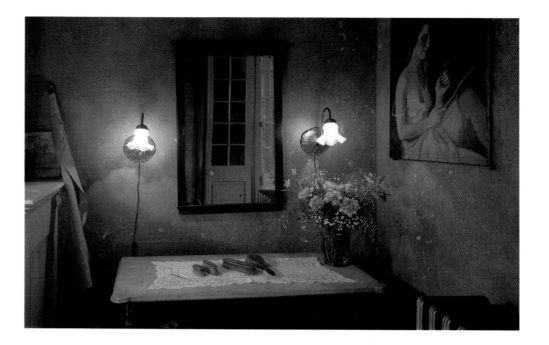

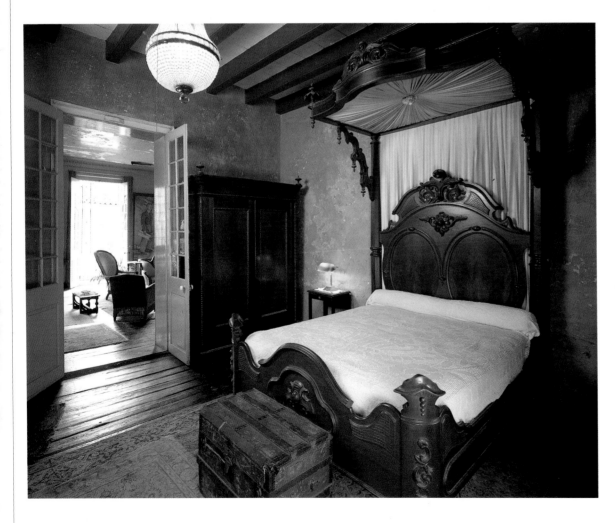

Fine Louisiana furniture fills the bedroom with its stately presence. The bed, inherited from Mr. Yokum's grandfather, may be the work of master furniture maker François Seignouret. The armoire is credited to Prudent Mallard, another furniture maker who came to New Orleans from France. French doors open into the parlor and out to Toulouse Street.

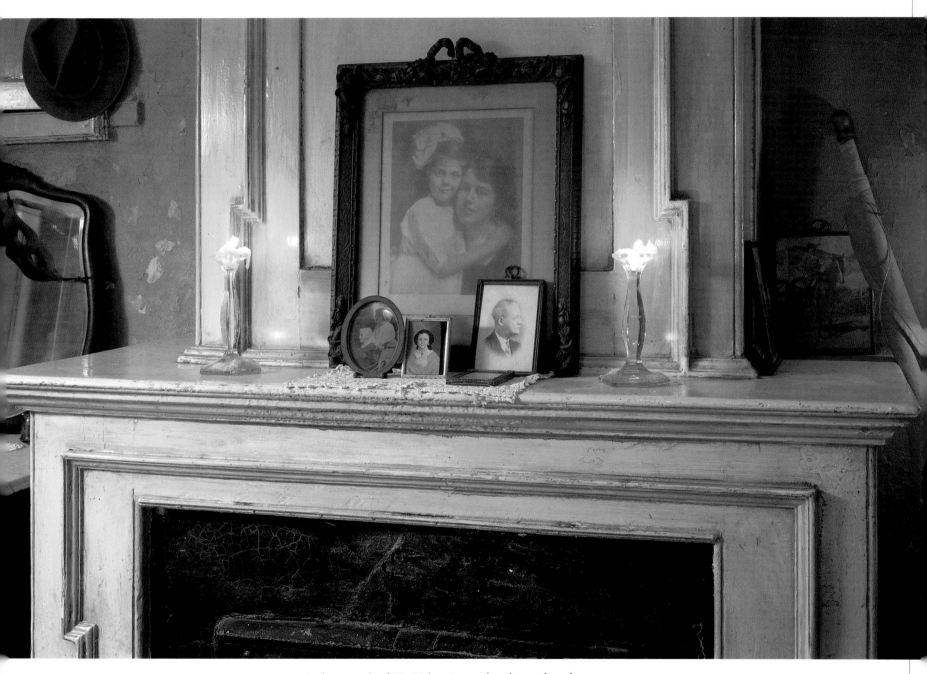

A photograph of Mr. Yokum's grandmother and mother stands with family mementos on the bedroom mantel. New Orleanians live in resonant continuity with their past.

An antique statue of a
Spanish warrior-saint
presides over the dining
room. Behind him are
paneled French doors with
wrought-iron hinges. The
first house on this site was
built by Don Geronimo
Hinard, a Spanish banker.

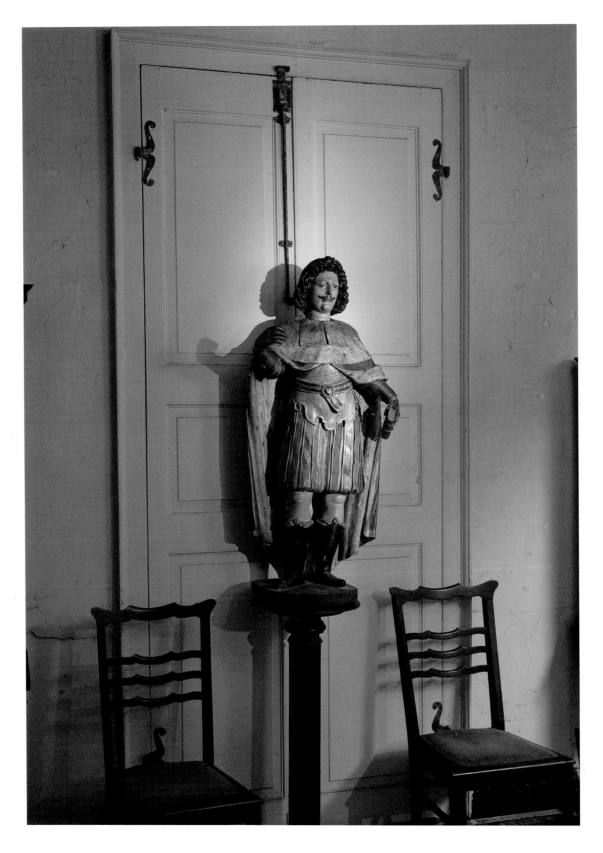

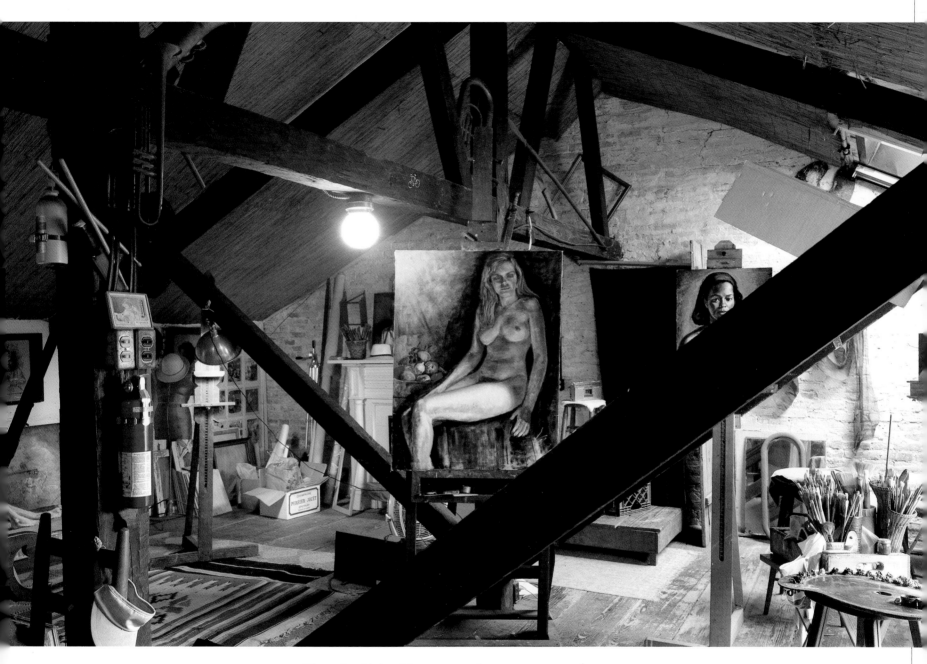

The attic with hand-hewn cypress beams was converted into a painter's studio for Peterson Moon Yokum's mother in the 1930s with the addition of two north-facing skylights. Today it is her son's studio. The painting on the easel is titled *Blue Nude*.

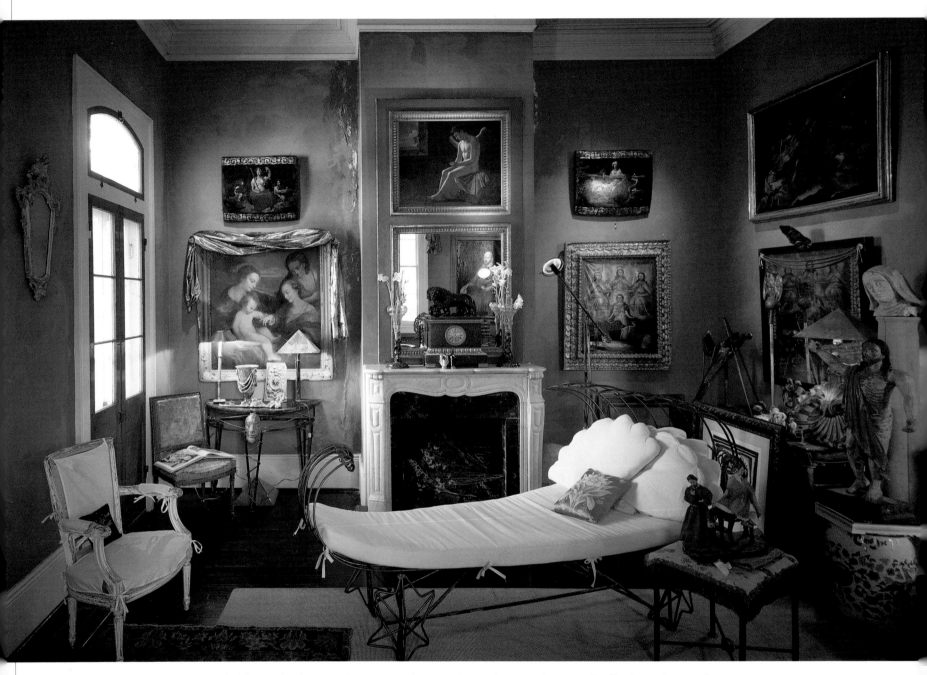

Mario Villa likes to daydream in this room, to be carried away by a reverie: "I am a gentleman. I love life and romance. Sometimes at night I like to open the front door onto the bayou while the music plays." The rich reddish color of the walls was achieved by "ragging," rubbing color into the plaster and then coating it with a clay slip. Seen here during the day, the room has a warm glow at night. One of Villa's lamp designs illuminates a French neoclassical picture, *Eros in Chains*. To the lower right of *Eros* is a Peruvian ex-voto, painted in 1802, depicting the Trinity crowning the Virgin. In the center of the parlor is Villa's Shell daybed. Peeking from behind the bed is Rouault's *Veronica*.

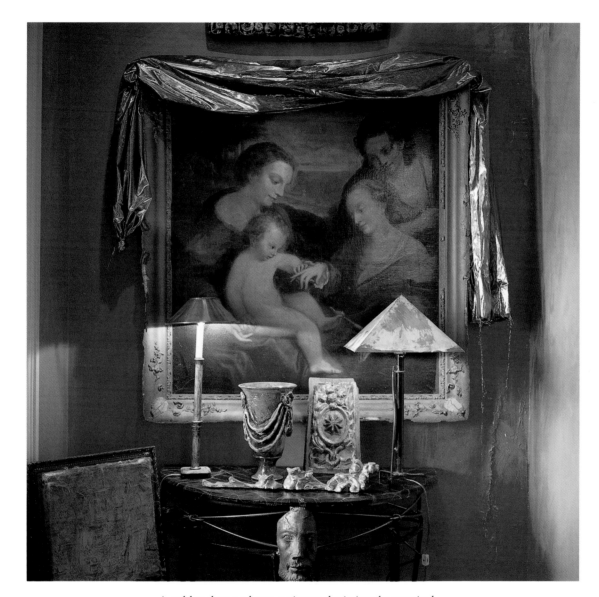

A golden drape adorns a picture depicting the mystical marriage of Saint Catherine and the Christ Child. Atop Villa's Mars console table is a draped raku urn and two Villa-designed lamps. The eighteenth-century French chair to the left has its original, if tattered, covering. The painterly texture of the rubbed walls can be seen clearly here.

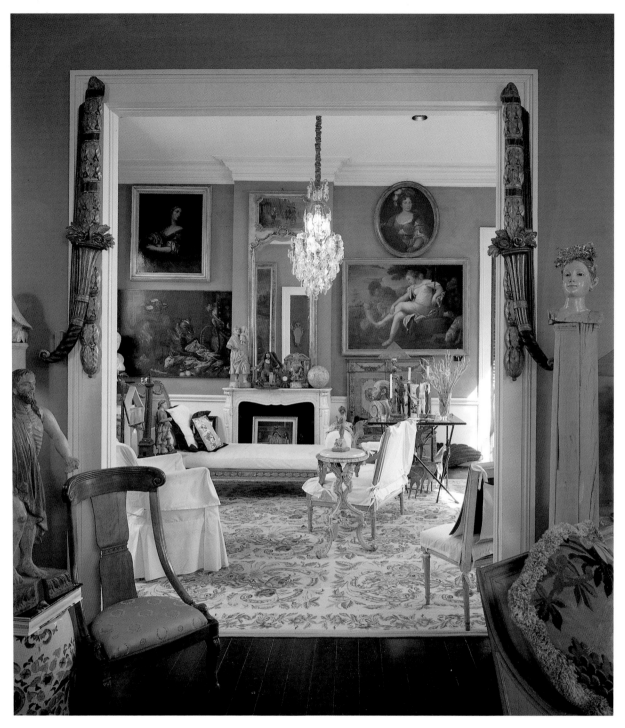

In what is actually a very small house, Mario Villa has created the opulence and visual richness of a Venetian palazzo. The provenance of individual pieces is not as important as the magnificent effect that their juxtaposition creates in the second parlor. A large painting of Venus presides over the room. The daybed is Second Empire; the rug, needlepoint. The eighteenth-century French and Italian furniture is in its summer dress of white muslin. Light streams into the room from both sides. Religious and mythological art fills the room, making the parlor a grand salon. To the far left, standing just inside the front parlor, is a rare statue of Saint John the Baptist carved in Portuguese Goa in the eighteenth century. Atop a column to the far right is a smiling Neapolitan wood-and-gesso head with a starry tinsel crown.

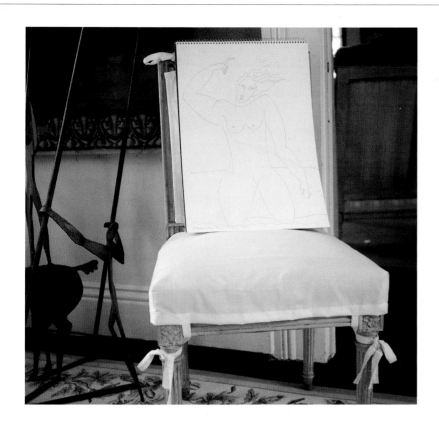

New Orleans provides a fertile ground for Mario Villa's art. Here his drawing *Woman Playing at the Beach* (1991) is propped against a muslin-covered chair.

The library has marbleized walls and opulent purple drapes. The catacomb-like room is conducive to contemplation, fantasy, and literature. The white sculpture to the left is Arthur Kearn's *The Abduction of the Queen* (1979). To the far left is Villa's Nefertiti lamp.

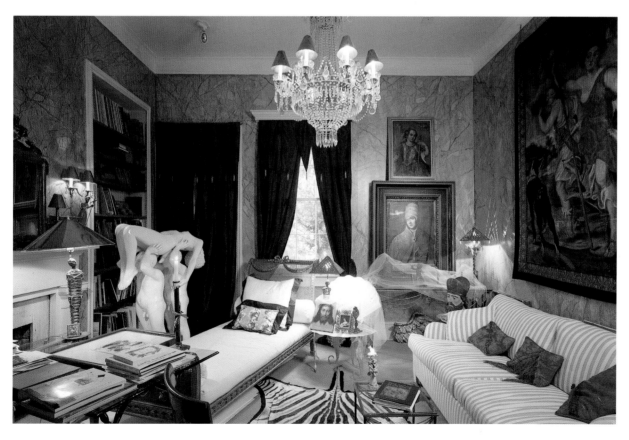

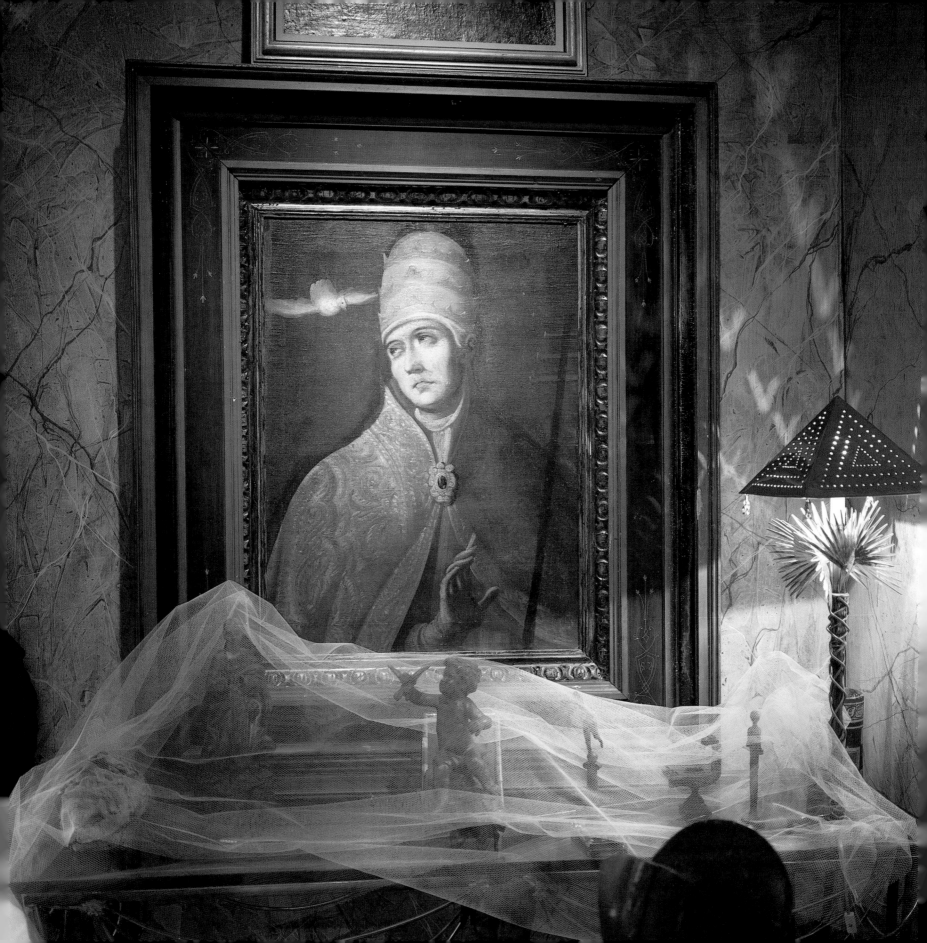

In a corner of the library is
an old portrait of Pope
Gregory with the dove of
the Holy Ghost hovering
beside him. To the right
is Villa's Palmetto lamp.
The gauze draped over the
table envelops a saint,
Cupid, figurines, and an
antique lamp in a cloud
of mystery.

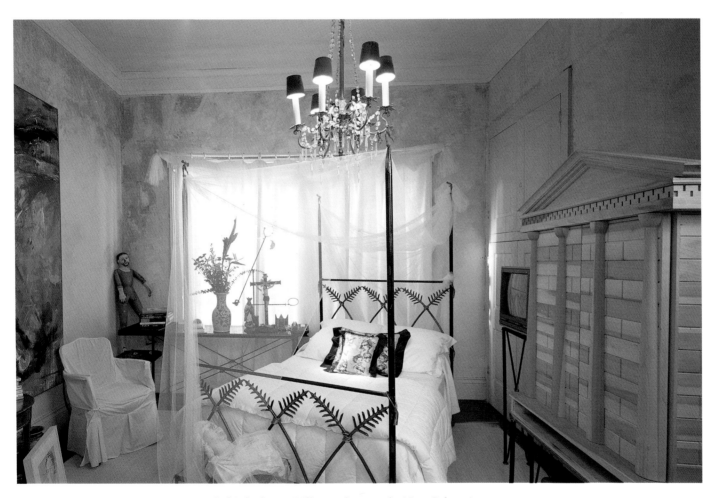

In his bedroom Villa sought to evoke New Orleans'
semitropical atmosphere of humidity and decay. The
walls were stripped down to the bare stained plaster. "I
love ruins," says Villa. The bed is called Winged Victory,
the cabinet to the right holds a personal computer and is
dubbed the Temple of Knowledge. In the far left is an
antique Guatemalan Good Friday figure.

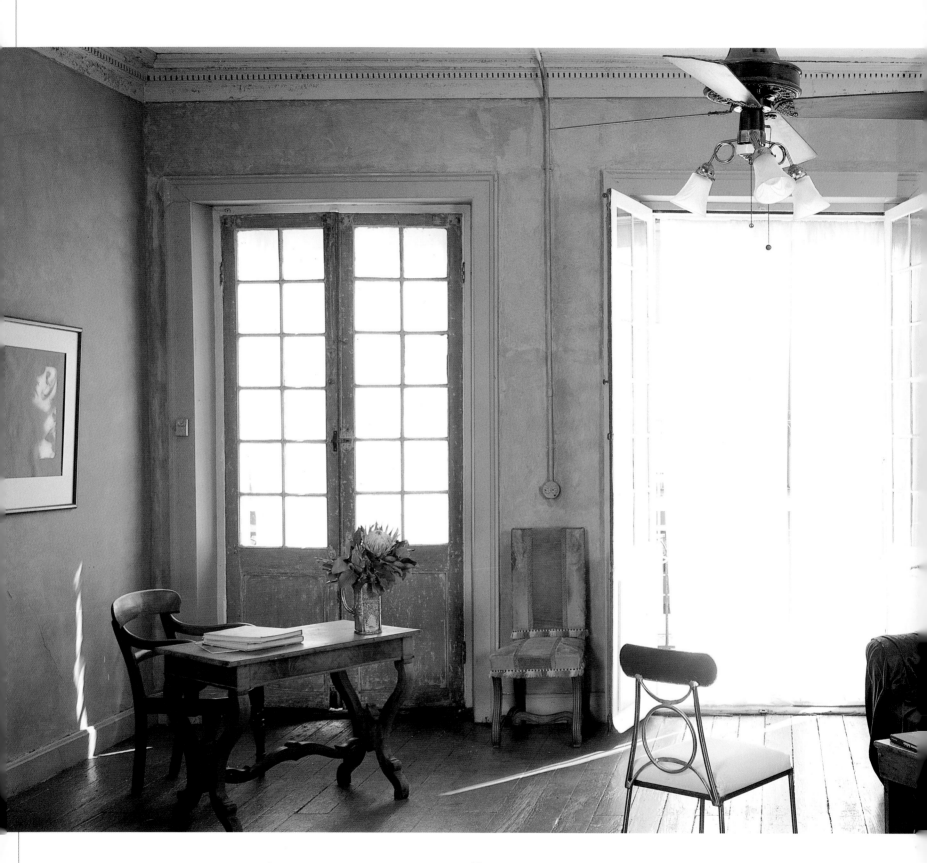

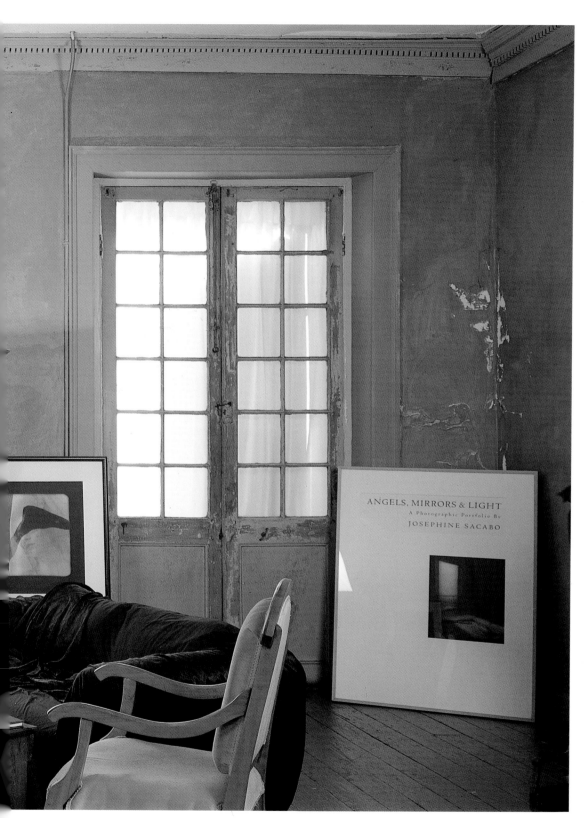

ANGELS, MIRRORS & LIGHT
A Photographic Portfolio By
JOSEPHINE SACABO

Photographer Josephine Sacabo's French Quarter studio is sometimes the subject, and often the background, for her evocative studies and portraits. Located on the second floor of a Creole porte-cochere townhouse, she has sparsely furnished the airy, light-filled room with a mélange of pieces given, bought, and found, along with examples of her own work. The table to the left came from a Canal Street secondhand shop; atop it is a silver pitcher given to her by her mother. The 1920s Hollywood Spanish high-backed chair against the patinated wall has a theatrical, honestly bogus look. The contemporary iron chair in the center foreground is by Mario Villa. Sacabo threw a black sheet over a nondescript couch; the armchair was inherited from a friend. The three photographs are, from left to right, two pieces from Sacabo's *Une femme habitée* series (1991) and, to the far right, a photograph of the empty studio entitled *Angels, Mirrors, and Light* (1988).

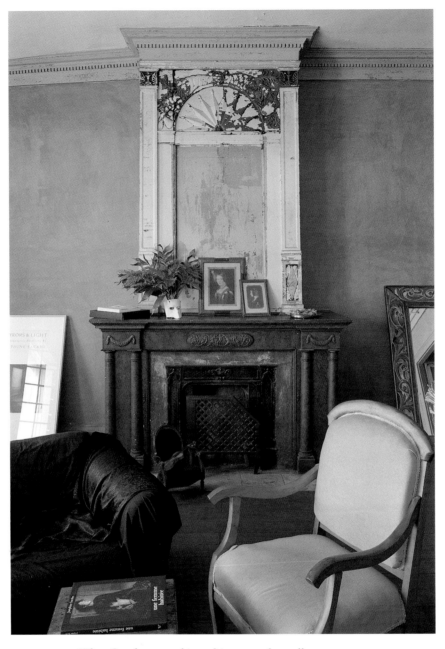

Sacabo found these two dried palm fronds one morning on her way to her darkroom. The rich red and mauve fabrics came from a secondhand store on funky Decatur Street. Together they create a still life evocative of the faded tropical splendor of old New Orleans.

When Sacabo moved into this space, the walls were white. To better complement her black-and-white work she darkened the walls with rubbed bluish paint. She left as she found them the *faux-marbre* mantelpiece and the distressed woodwork with the sunburst design. Like many sensitive New Orleanians, Sacabo accepts the accidental and chooses to live in a place as it is. This respectful aesthetic embraces rather than denies history. On the mantel are prints of Italian Renaissance portraits from her mother's antique store in Laredo, Texas, and a rare white Venetian *bauta*, or mask. A child's chair holding a violin stands in front of the hearth.

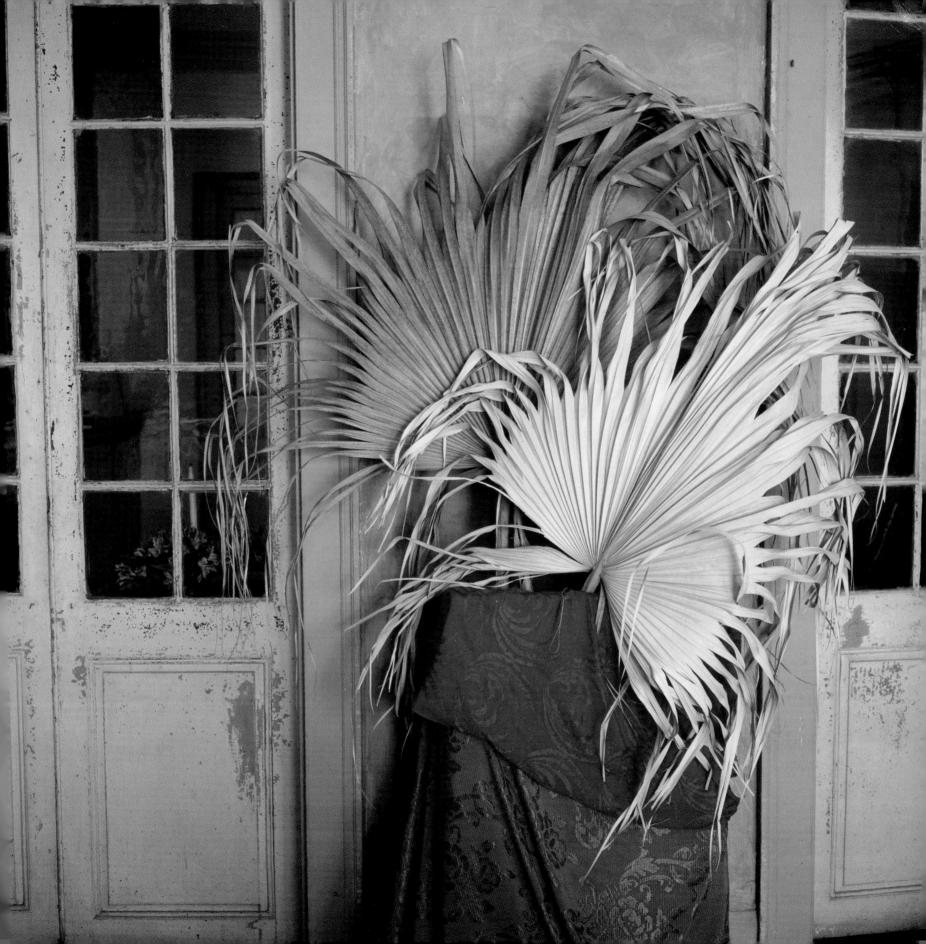

French doors opening onto the gallery facing St. Louis Street are hung with unbleached muslin to diffuse the sunlight. Sacabo likes to use natural light for her portraits.

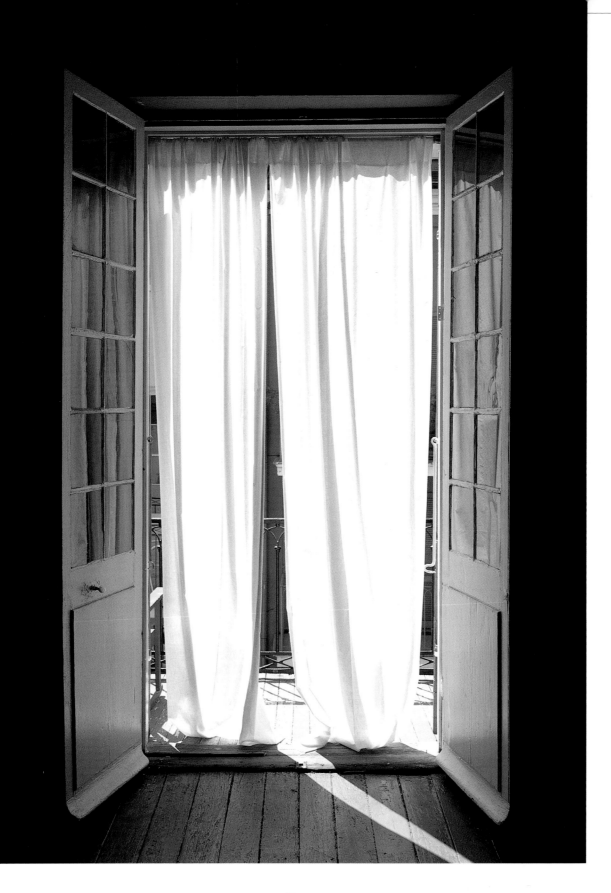

Hanging over an old iron bed is an untitled photograph from Sacabo's *Une femme habitée* series (1991). The lithograph by the open door was left behind by a previous tenant and discovered in a closet. New Orleanians treasure found objects that offer continuity and carry traces of previous inhabitants. A weaver who once lived here started to strip the paint from the cupboard but gave up. Sacabo liked the unfinished effect and left it alone.

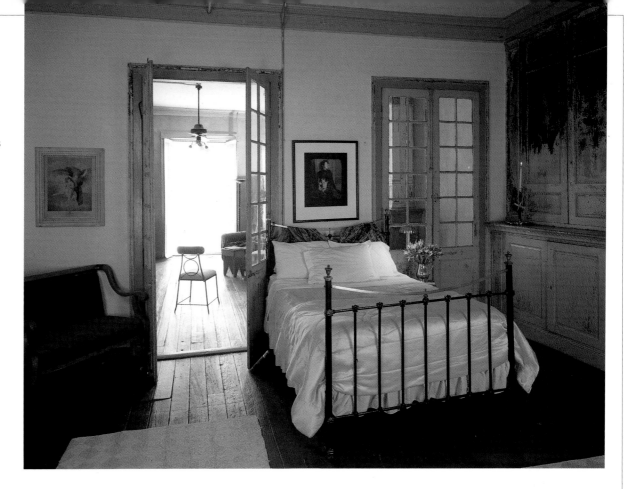

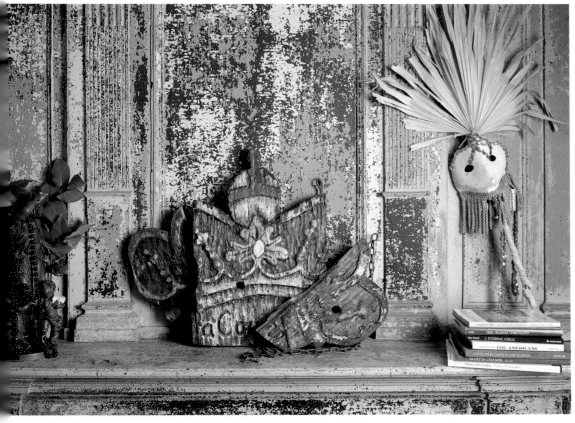

The elegance of decay is clearly evident in this detail of the bedroom mantelpiece. The textured, painterly effect of layers of peeling paint shows a reverence for time's ability to slowly transform things in a way that no deliberate intervention could. The statue to the left, draped with black Mardi Gras beads, came from Sacabo's mother's shop. A broken, crown-shaped sign from an old antique store stands in the center. The Mardi Gras mask to the right was made by Dawn Dedeaux, a friend of Sacabo's.

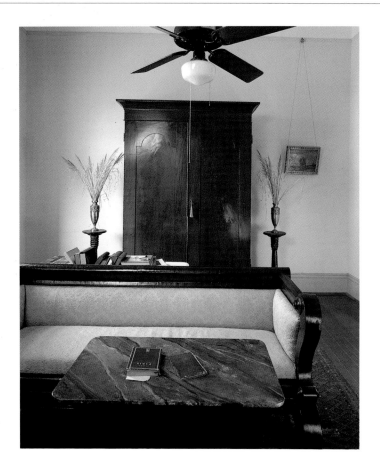

Mary Cooper painted the *faux-marbre* tabletop in the back parlor. The box sofa, upholstered in Belgian linen and jute, came from Natchez, Mississippi, and dates from about 1840. The monumental Empire-style mahogany linen press was a birthday gift to Mary from Marc Cooper, who fashioned a replacement for its missing crown moulding. Two funerary urns typical of those once used in old cemeteries hold vetiver plumes. The Creoles used aromatic vetiver root to scent their linens and to repel insects.

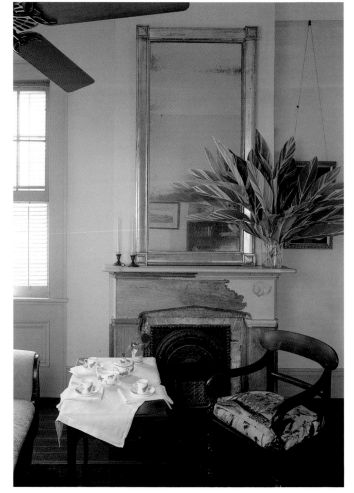

The 1885 Cooper house assembles the past and present of Louisiana in a living home that is gracious, elegant, simple and hospitable. The raised American cottage faces the levee and the Mississippi, catching the river's constant breeze. Louvered cypress shutters and old-model Hunter fans keep the high-ceilinged house cool on the hottest afternoons. The mirror was made in New York City about 1820. Variegated ginger leaves adorn the partially stripped cypress mantel. The antique armchair was refinished by Mary Cooper and uphol-stered in documentary toile. A red Louis Philippe rose stands in an 1830s French mustard jar dug up at the site of the privy of the neighboring 1826 Lombard house.

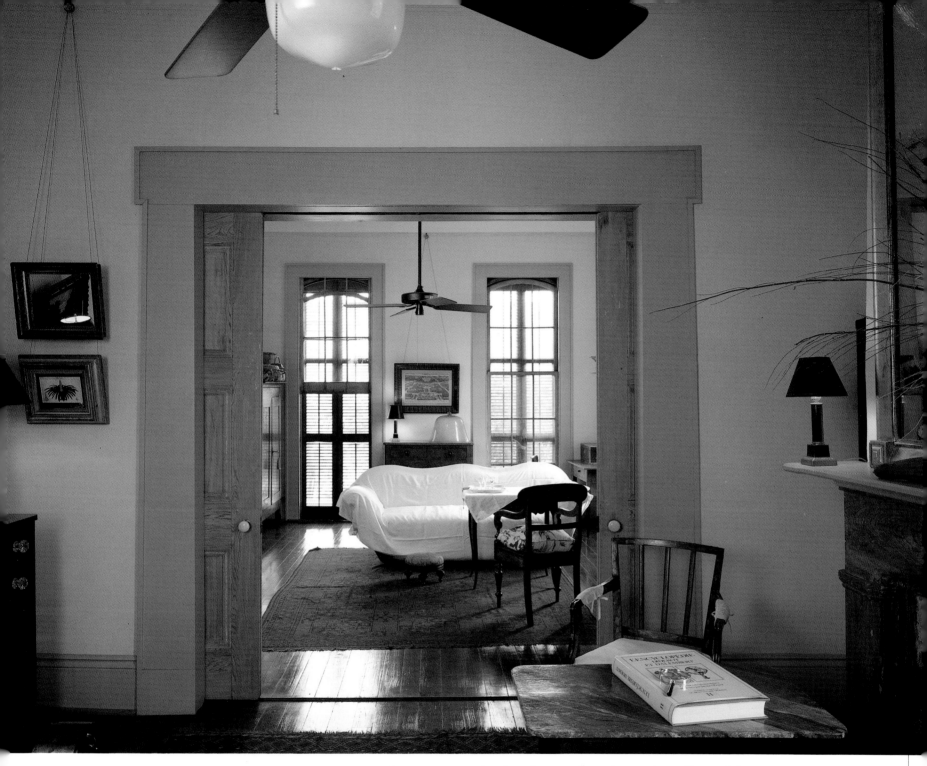

This Cooper house view looks from the rear to front parlor and toward the river. The sofa is in summer dress. New Orleanians have long rolled up carpets, covered upholstered furniture with white muslin slipcovers, and virtually stripped rooms during the hot summer months. This helped preserve good furniture from perspiration and insects and also made rooms feel cooler. The cypress pocket doors between the parlors are framed by a subtly battered Greek key doorway painted in a warm Creole mustard. The small botanical print hanging to the lower left depicts a sago palm, a showy Japanese ornamental that thrives in New Orleans. Its fronds are cut and brought into churches on Palm Sunday to recall Jesus' triumphal entry into Jerusalem.

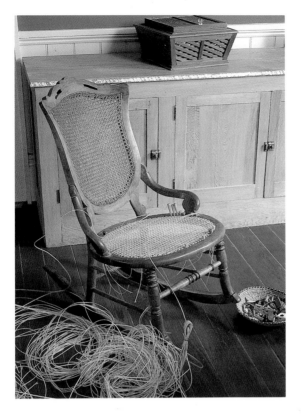

Mary Cooper is a chair caner, weaving seats and backs that "breathe" during the sticky summer. Her tools lie on the floor beside a recaned Victorian bedroom rocking chair. The cypress sideboard was made by a student at the Delgado Trade School in the 1930s. Atop it sits a *garde-manger*, a small hamper that protects food from flies.

The austere kitchen preserves the simple country feel of a house on the city's edge. Marc Cooper prefers to keep old floor plans intact, working with, not against, them. "It meant something then," he says, "and it can mean something today." The vintage Chambers stove was manufactured in Indiana. Over the raised-hearth wood-burning fireplace is a pecan sack found in an Uptown shed. Cayenne peppers grown in the garden festoon the edge of the mantelpiece. Recycled marble was used to make the tabletop.

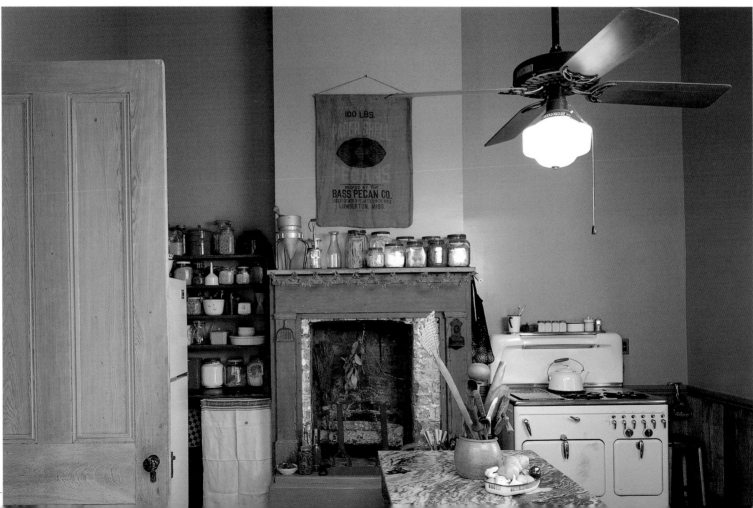

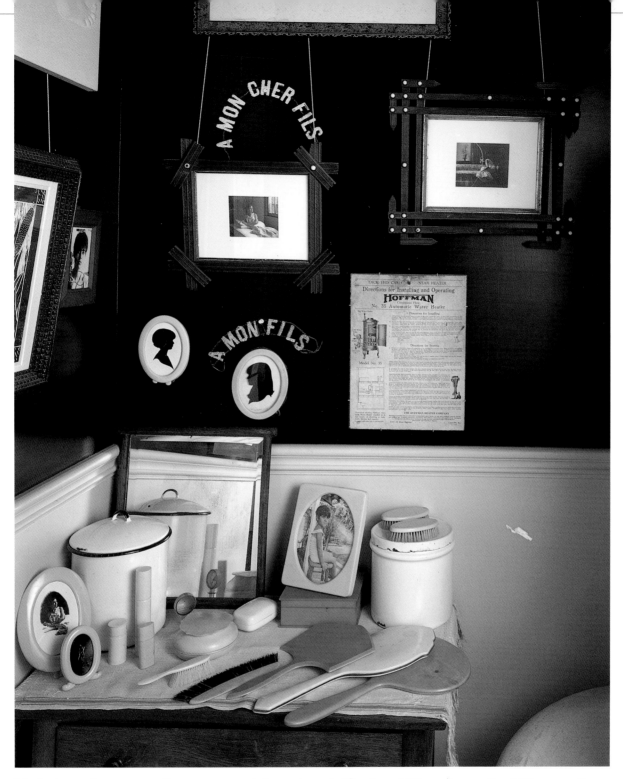

The bathroom has creamy yellow wainscot and almost black walls. On the countertop is a collection of old "French ivory" (celluloid) toilet articles. The two center pictures are in walnut Arts and Crafts frames dating from about 1870. The most unusual items are the wire and black-and-white glass bead *immortelles*, which in French read "To my dear son" and "To my son." Permanent funerary art such as these, found in a Magazine Street antique shop, were placed on tombs instead of perishable flowers on holy days and personal anniversaries.

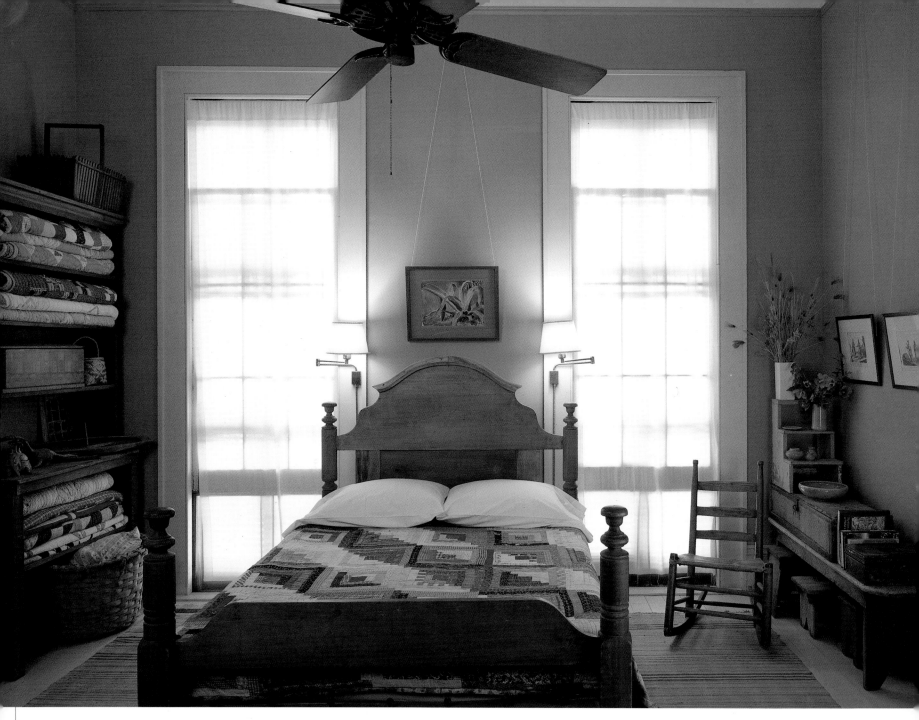

The fresh Paris green of the bedroom makes this river-facing room seem cooler. The bottom sections of the tall guillotine sash windows rise up six feet into pockets over the window frame, allowing access to the front gallery. Here the open louvers allow fresh air into the room. The turned post rope bed, made in the 1850s, is covered with a log cabin quilt. More old quilts are stacked on shelves which once held paint cans. On the floor underneath is a cotton picking basket. Mary Cooper, who rotates her quilts and uses them all, notes that nothing is so fine, or so plain, that she won't use it. Next to the bed is a southern ladderback rocker with a cowhide seat. Mary Cooper grew up in nearby Ocean Springs, Mississippi, across the street from the Shearwater pottery works, whose blue wares line the stepped shelves in the corner. Over the pottery are dried weeds gathered from the margin of the belt line railroad across the street. Over the bed is a watercolor by Lee Tucker, a Jackson Square artist and a defender of French Quarter sidewalk painters.

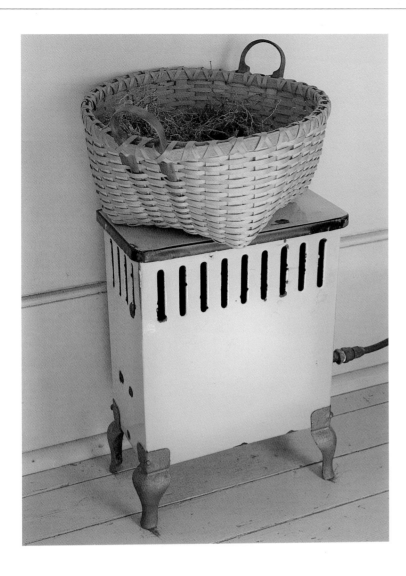

The cream-and-green bathroom gas heater dates from the 1920s or 1930s and sports a favorite color scheme of the time. The split ash basket was made in Oregon.

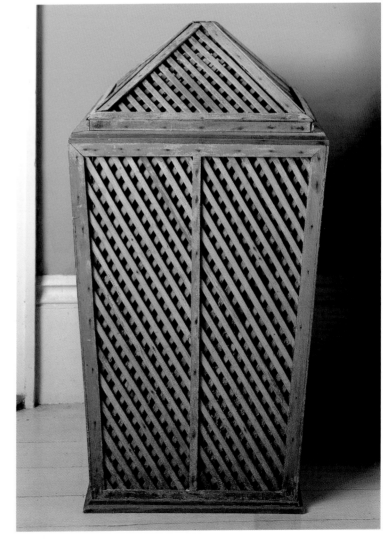

Master carpenter Marc Cooper collects old lattice clothes hampers. This monumental example of West Indian Spanish cedar probably dates from the early twentieth century. It was found in a dumpster, repaired, and now is appreciated for the work of art it is.

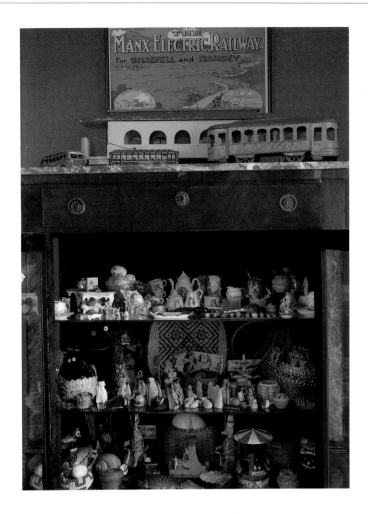

The child of the household christened this breakfront crammed with bibelots the "precious cabinet." "If it looks like it might break or be eaten by insects, we put it in the precious cabinet." Here are displayed a child's tea service, Spanish-moss dolls, Coushatta, Chitamacha, and Houma Native American dolls and basketwork, Carnival mementos, and fragile old Christmas ornaments. In the center of the bottom shelf is a toy Rex float from Gambino's bakery, guarded by a tin alligator. On top of the cabinet are toy streetcars.

Over the American Empire sofa in the front parlor is a portrait of Laure Livaudais, painted in 1834 by J. F. Feuille. Classical nineteenth-century Italian paintings and engravings bought in Paris flank the old portrait. The round table (left) came from Saint Joseph's Convent in Gretna across the river. The Egyptian Revival English side table (right) holds family photos including one of the owner's mother dressed as Columbia.

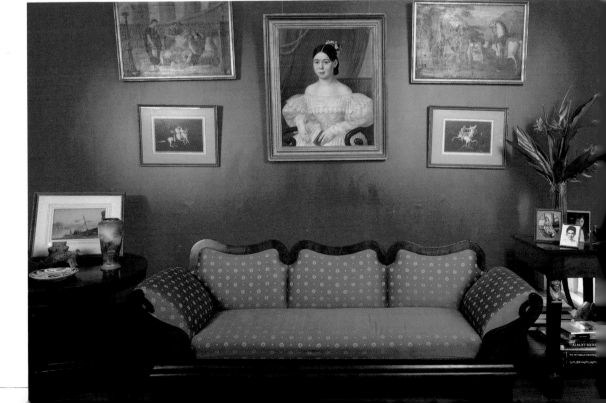

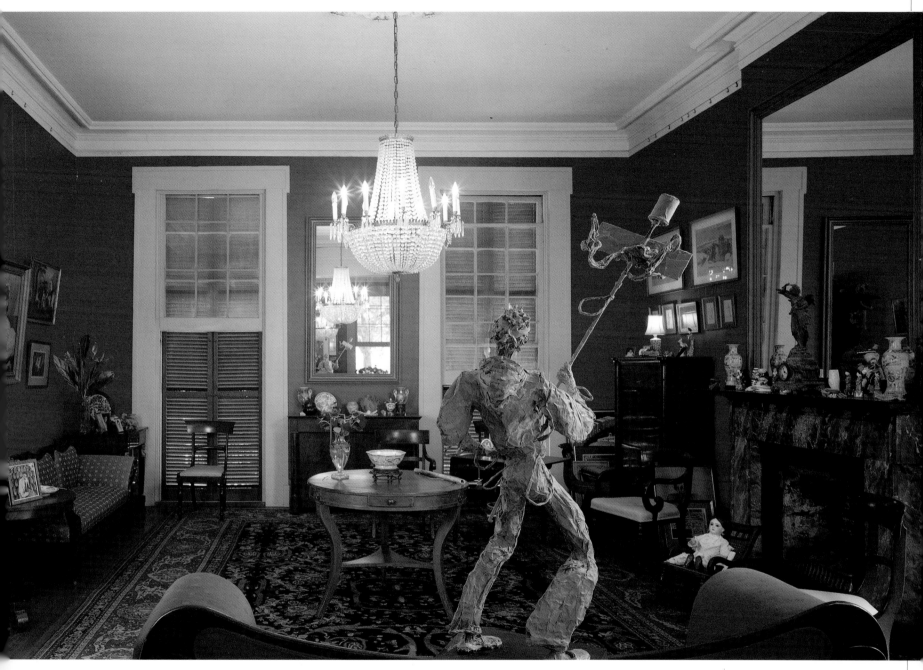

This house on Euterpe Street, near Coliseum Square, was built in 1847–48 in the Greek Revival style. After the Civil War the building was confiscated by the federal government to house the U.S. Bureau of Refugees, Freedmen, and Abandoned Lands, and in the 1940s it was divided into small apartments. It was restored as a single-family home in 1971. The walls of its spacious front parlor are painted a rich Pompeiian red and the elegant Greek key window mouldings are ivory. The louvered, peacock blue shutters of the double-hung slip-

head windows screen the front gallery beyond. The gray marble fireplace continues the Greek key motif. The room is eclectically furnished with a Melayer rug, a round Biedermeier table from a French Quarter antique shop, and a crystal chandelier from the D. H. Holmes department store on Canal Street. The *flambeaux* carrier in the foreground is a maquette for a life-sized papier-mâché statue made by Joe Barth, a Carnival float designer and builder.

New Orleans-born artist George Dureau comes from an arts and crafts family of "indefatigable doers." His spacious studio is a true "live-work" space. Dureau's paintings line the walls, and sometimes tattered but always treasured possessions animate the sunny space. Most items in the house are heirlooms, hand-me-downs, found objects, or the results of swaps with friends; very few are purchases. French Quarter furnishings migrate from household to household, outlasting their "owners." The canopied 1840s Louisiana bed, set like a stage or pavilion in the airy room, came from Dureau's grandmother's house. Paintings-in-progress fill the room. From left to right, they are: *Constitutional Melee* (1988), *Troy Bound* (1992), *Street Dancer at Carnival* (all in working state), and *Ganymede and Jupiter* (1991).

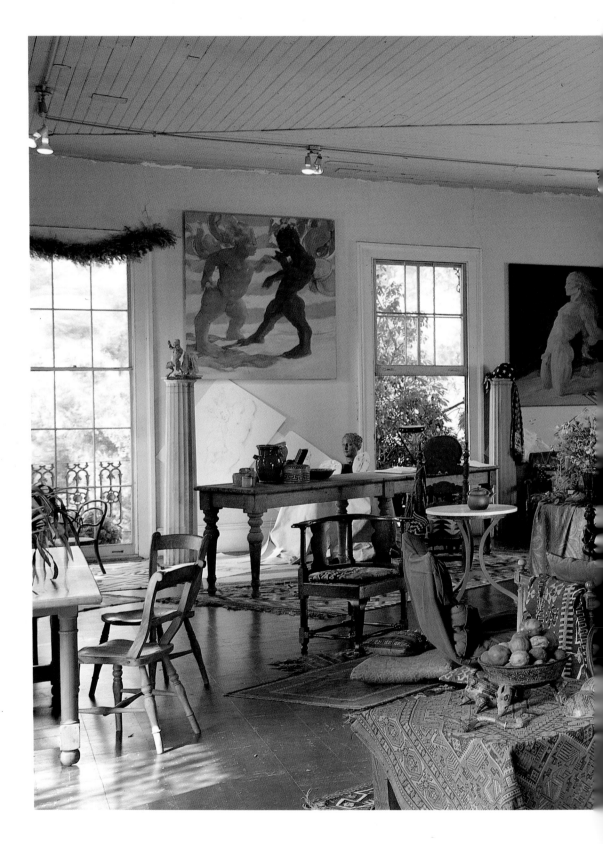

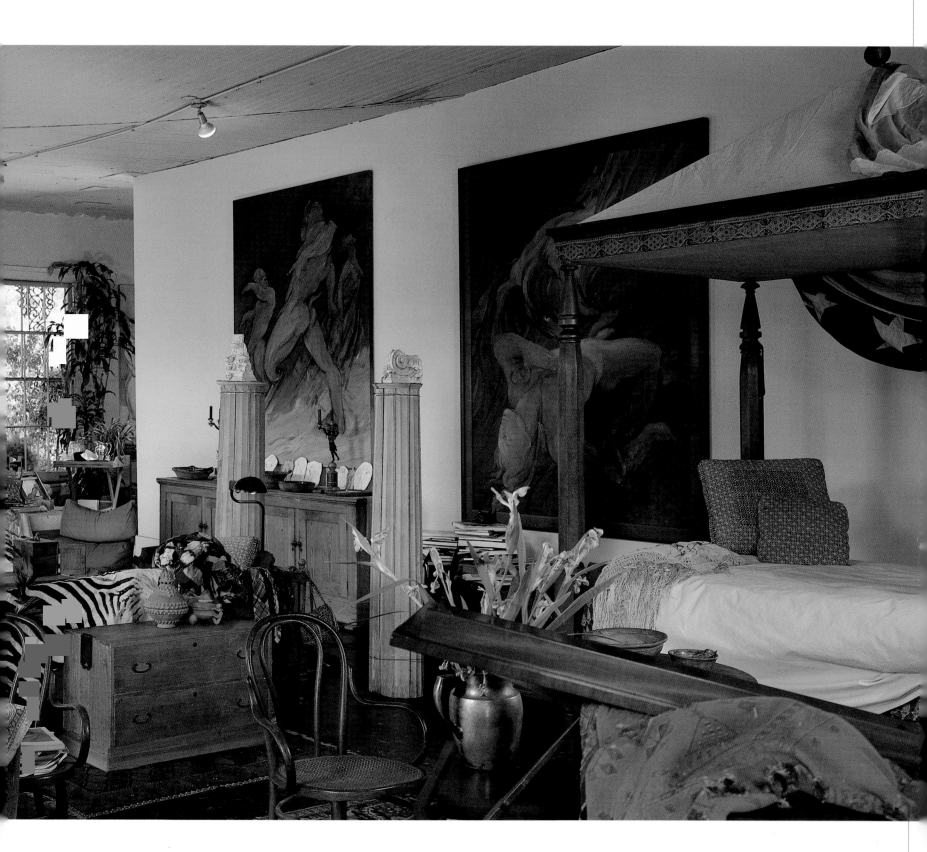

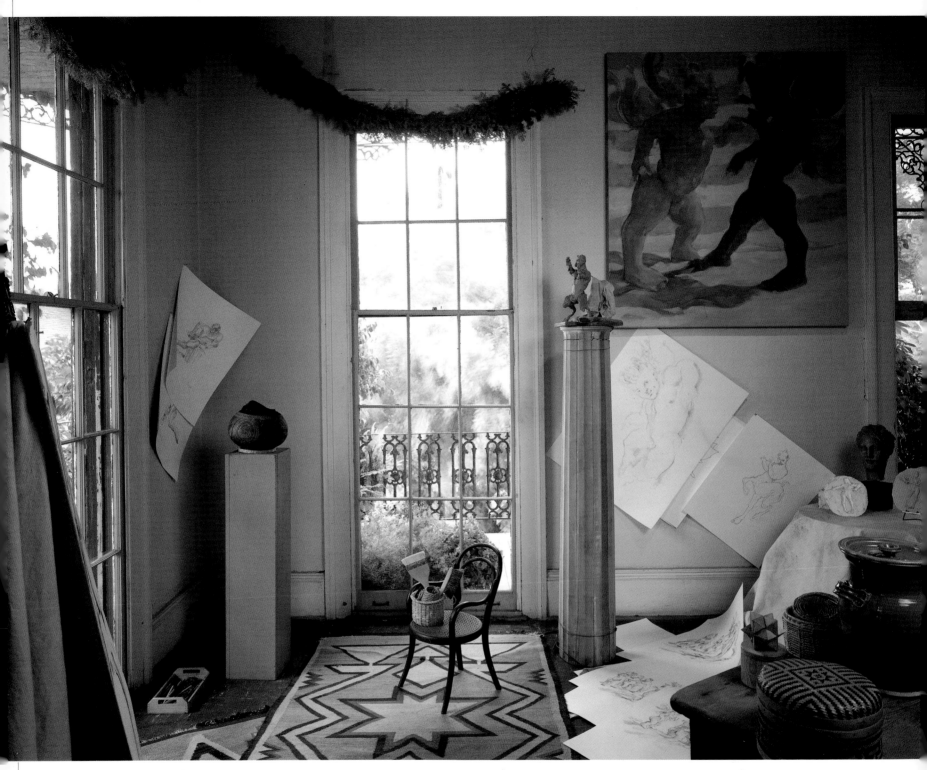

The south corner of Dureau's home-studio gets light from sunrise to sunset, and the artist often sketches here in the early morning. A child's chair and ten-foot-tall windows play tricks with one's sense of scale. One of Dureau's sculpted sketches atop the column to the right faces a New Guinea cooking pot on the square pillar in the corner. Sketches are pinned to the walls, where one of the artist's allegorical paintings, *Constitutional Melee* (1988), hangs.

A tabletop still life set on a paisley shawl assembles objects from many times and places. Under a bouquet of dead flowers is an invitation to the Rex Carnival ball. The wooden bowl is from New Guinea; the two pottery figurines are from Costa Rica. The cross to the right is paved with ex-votos.

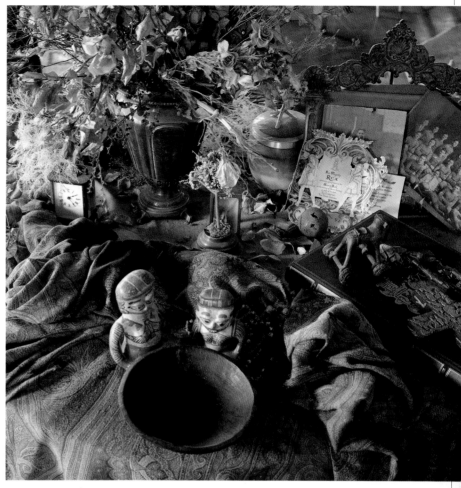

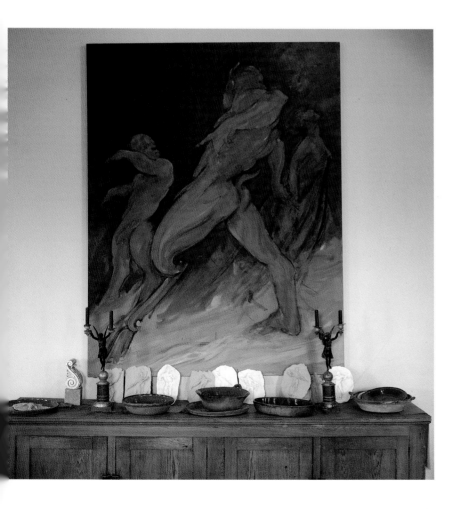

Street Dancer at Carnival, a work-in-progress, shows the vital influence of New Orleans on Dureau's work. Small plaster molds for the artist's great bronze gates to a new wing of the New Orleans Museum of Art lean against the painting. The shallow bowls are everyday pottery from Central America.

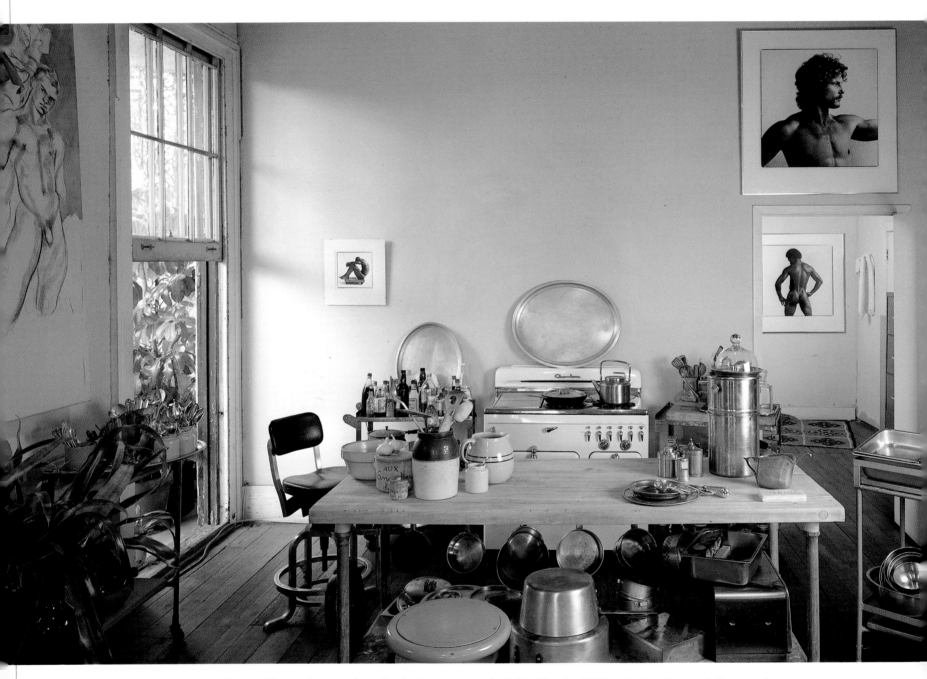

George Dureau likes to draw, cook, and paint in one space. Most items in the kitchen section of his house-studio are restaurant equipment. The tables on casters to the right and left were discarded by the Charity Hospital. But it is, of course, Dureau's sketches and photographs that make the space. The drawing to the

far left is *Sketch of Wilbur* (1983), the small photograph near the window is *Emmett Johnson* (1986), the large photograph in the upper right is *Troy Brown* (1979), and the photograph beneath it is *Glen Thompson* (1981). Many of the artist's models are New Orleanians.

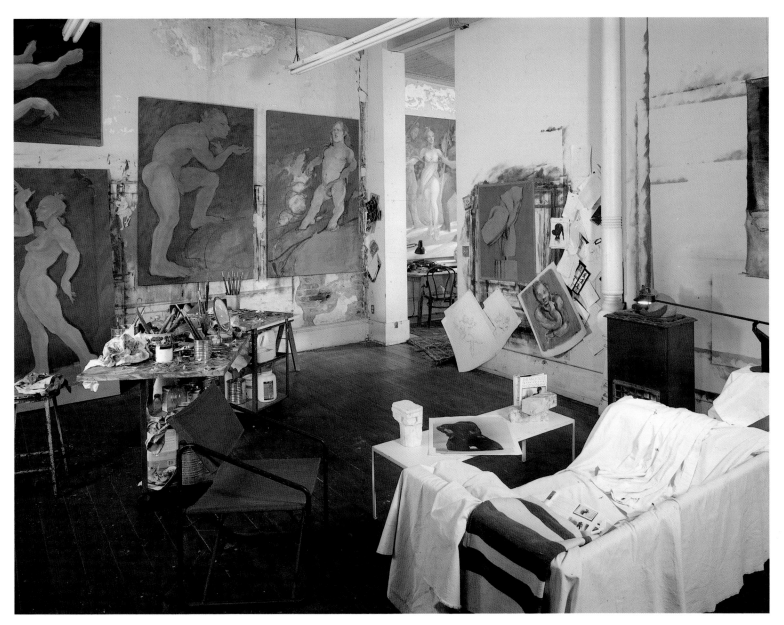

Dureau's paintings (some still in progress), sketches, and paintings fill the studio walls. "When I forgot about style, I knew I was an artist," Dureau says. He developed his own approach, which he calls "storytelling art." The artist always begins with a particular person, then turns to the universal. From left to right, the paintings are: *Fallen Figure* (1988), *Dance for Two* (1986), *Oedipus,* and *Mercury* (both works-in-progress). Through the doorway is a glimpse of *Center Ring* (1986). The large painting on the right wall is *The Javelin* (1989). The smaller work suspended by a corner is *Earl Leavell* (1982). On the table in the foreground is a photograph entitled *Torso of Glen Thompson* (1989). For Dureau, nakedness universalizes the figure and frees it from a specific time. Fusing the carnal and the imagined, his works express the forcefulness of human desire in classical romantic allegories.

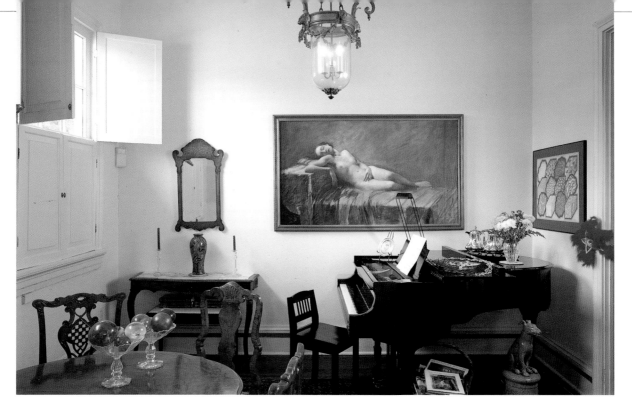

Creoles typically used the same room for everything from sleeping to entertaining. The front room of Dorian and Kell Bennett's small Creole cottage, built in 1833, still has many purposes: living room, music room, or dining room. Even when silent, it seems filled with music. The languorous nude was painted in Italy in the 1920s by Alessandro Pomi. The work to the right is *A Study for Rimbaud's Dream* by Robert Gordy, a New Orleans artist active in the 1970s. A red feather Mardi Gras Indian armband is pinned to the door jamb. The paneled shutters can be opened at the top to let in light and closed at the bottom to ensure privacy (the house abuts the sidewalk).

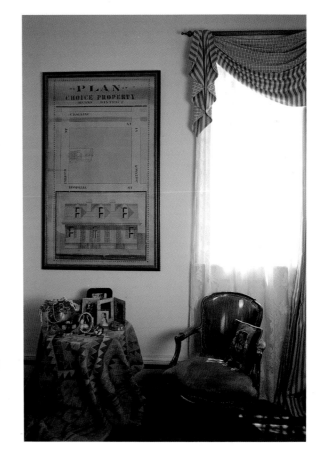

The second parlor displays a watercolor plan and elevation of a typical Creole cottage of the 1840s. These elaborate illustrations were made to help sell houses, and this one seems quite appropriate in realtor Dorian Bennett's house. On the rug-draped table are clustered family photos and a silver bowl overflowing with Mardi Gras beads. The classic window drapery is in the eighteenth-century style.

Two treasured photographs by Clarence John Laughlin hang in the back parlor, *Linger Not in Ruins* and *Elegy for the Old South (No. 6)*. Laughlin embodied the ethos of New Orleans and the Deep South. "The mystery of time, the magic of light, the enigma of reality—and their interrelationships—are my constant themes and preoccupations," he wrote.

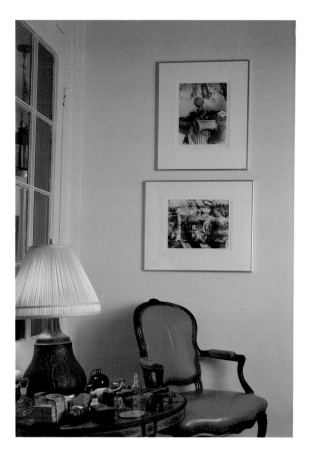

Atop an eighteenth-century Italian marquetry table is a crowd of miniature treasures, many related to the theme of music. The clutter keeps people from putting drinks down on the antique table.

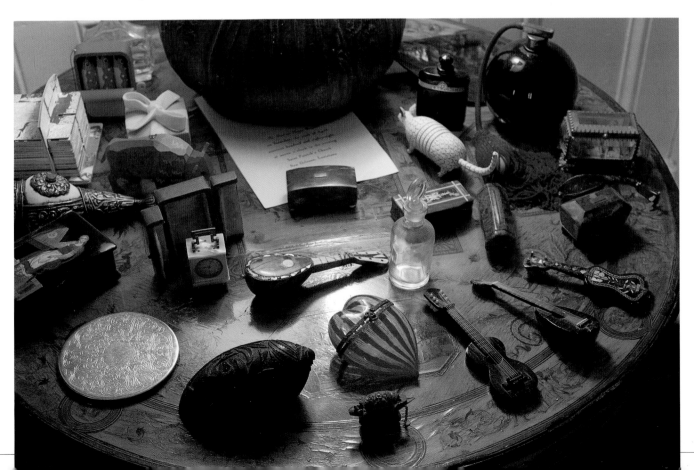

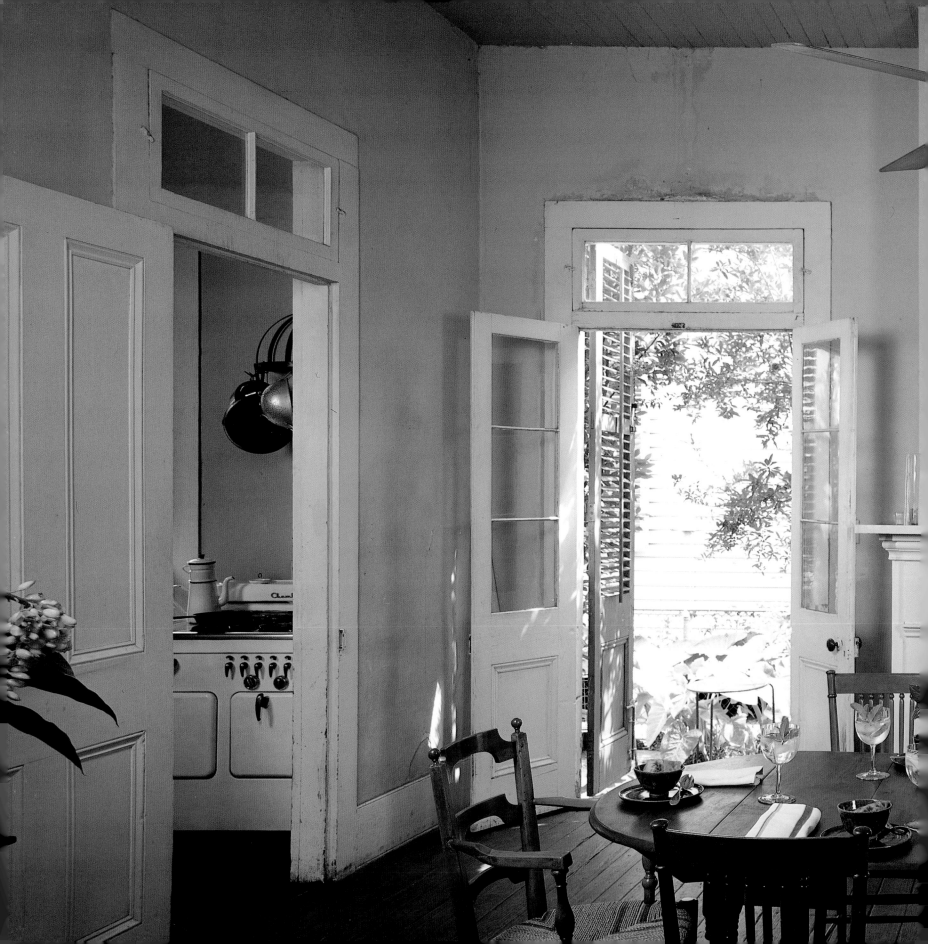

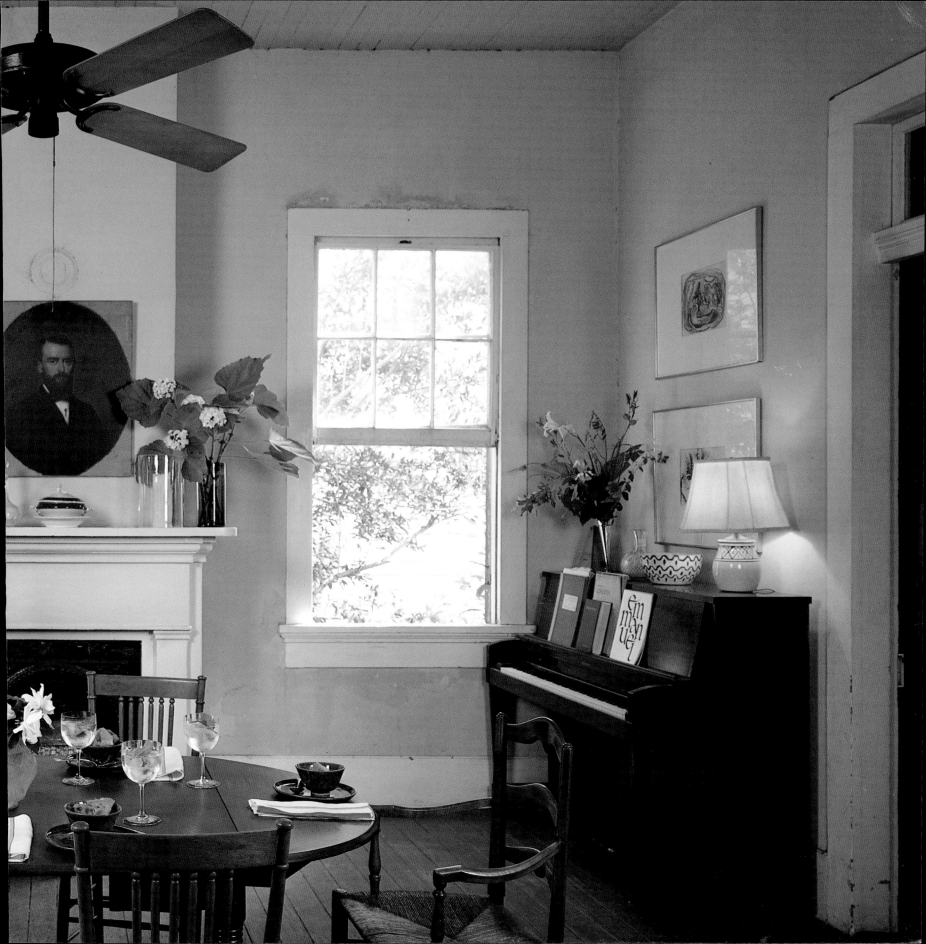

Preceding Pages:
Gardenias from the garden grace the dining room table in this mid-nineteenth-century Creole cottage in Bywater. The room is furnished with family heirlooms. Presiding over the room is a portrait painted by Francois Bernard in 1866. Its frame was lost many years ago and has not been replaced. Cuttings of cashmere bouquet decorate the mantel. The yellow walls show their age and lend the room a comfortable antique feeling.

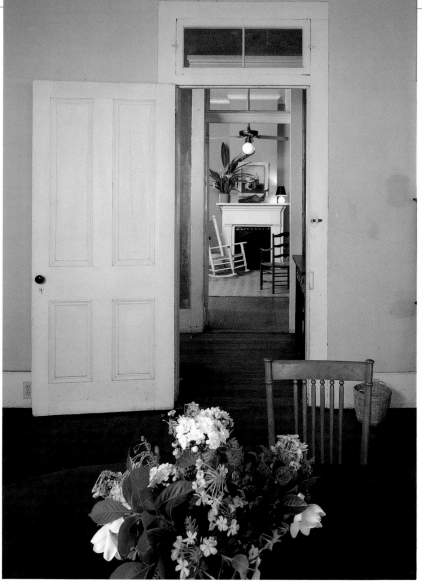

This view looks from the dining room, across the center hall, and into the sitting room/guest room with its rocking chair. Ceiling fans cool the downstairs rooms. The flower arrangement in the foreground mixes gardenias, cashmere bouquet, and plumbago, all from the garden.

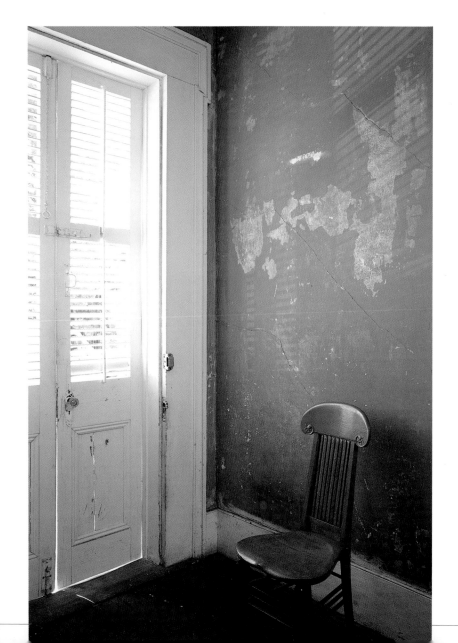

The plaster walls in the center hall were stripped of their wallpaper and rubbed with diluted green paint to create this mottled patina. The elegant late nineteenth-century oak chair belonged to the owner's grandmother. The louvers covering the French doors cast shifting shadows across the antiqued plaster wall.

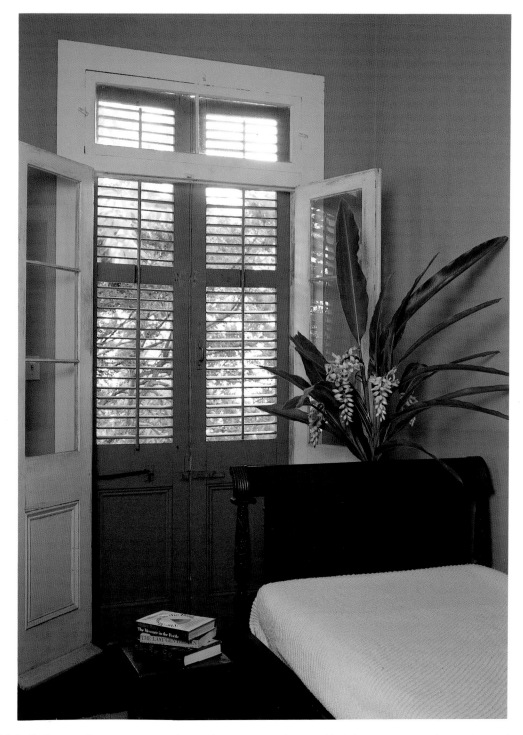

Splendid shell ginger welcomes guests in the combination sitting room/guest bedroom. The daybed, probably dating from the 1880s, has a grape-leaf design carved into its posts. When the current owners bought the house, they found that its shutters had been cobbled together into a shed at the back of the property. They disassembled the structure, and reconditioned and rehung the shutters on the house's French doors. They choose not to tamper too much with an old house. "Listen to it," they advise. "Make changes 'with' rather than 'to' the house."

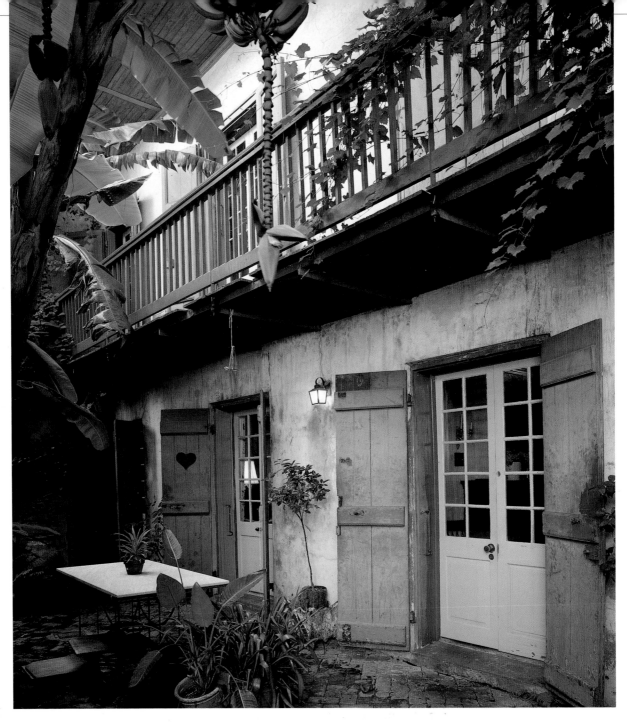

The secluded courtyard of Peter W. Patout's 1825 garçonnaire in the lower French Quarter is filled with plants typical of Creole gardens. Bananas shade the brick-paved court, and citrus trees in New Orleans–made cast-iron planters frame the French doors. A native muscadine grapevine clings to the gallery balustrade. Some of the plants in this urban garden are from historic Creole gardens such as Valcour Aime's *jardin Anglais* in Saint James Parish. The quiet, verdant court makes a fine place for contemplation and entertaining.

The two-story, originally four-room, masonry building lies hidden at the back of its lot behind a later Victorian shotgun cottage. Its stucco exterior has achieved a mellow patina, and traditional Creole colors highlight its woodwork. The gallery and stout shutters are painted verdigris, and the French doors are oka, an ivorylike shade of yellow. When the cooling rains come, the French doors are swung open to let the refreshing breeze sweep through the one-room-wide house.

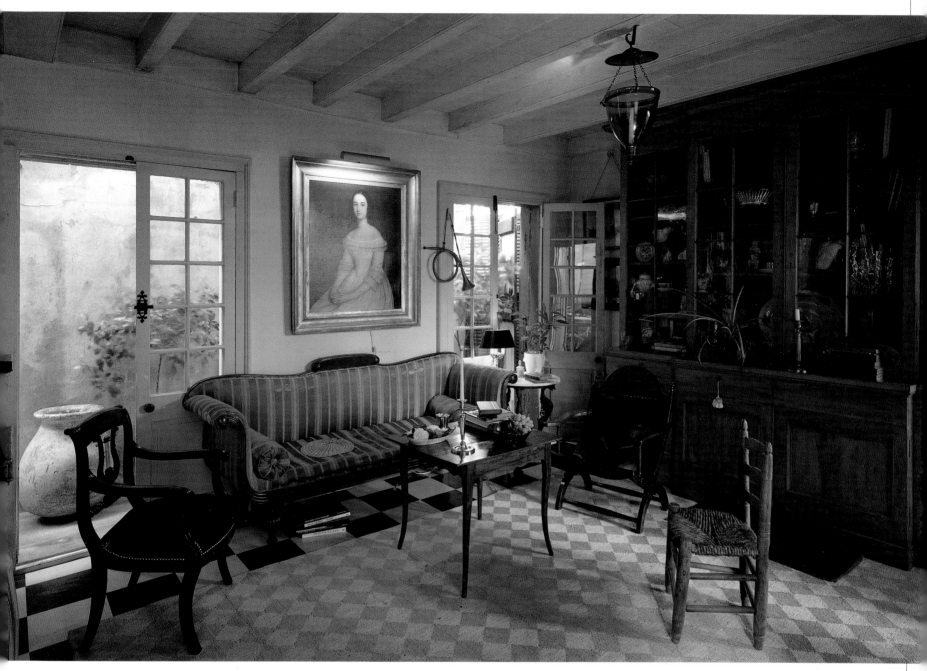

The ground-floor salon in antique dealer and Louisiana furniture connoisseur Peter W. Patout's home evokes the Creole era. The beam-and-board ceiling and casement doors are typical of French influence in Louisiana. Presiding over the room is a serene portrait of Felicité Emma Aime, Mr. Patout's great-great-great-grand-mother, painted by Jacques Amans in 1838. The Federal-style mahogany sofa was probably made in Massachusetts about 1815. The Louis XV-style table with cabriole legs came from the Godchaux house in the French Quarter. The Louisiana Federal chair with the lyre back and black horsehair seat, by master furniture maker Francois Seignouret, is one of a suite made for the priests at Saint Louis Cathedral. The cherry wood and black leather chair with melon headboard, called a *butac* by the Creoles, was made in Louisiana during the Spanish era. The circa 1835 white pine bookcase with *faux-bois* finish was found fifty years ago in Natchez, Mississippi. Hanging from the ceiling is a green glass lantern from about 1810. A sisal floor-cloth gives a practical and informal touch to the room.

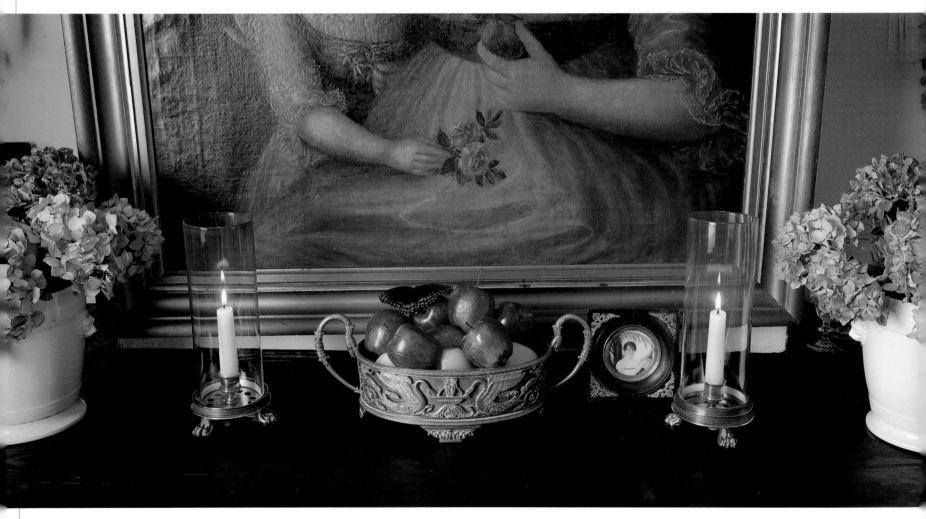

Flowers and fruit, in art and in life, commune atop the
black-painted mantel in the salon. Apples fill a brass
Empire compote with swan motif made about 1815.
Dried native oak-leaf hydrangeas fill old Paris porcelain
cachepots. Charles X brass candle cylinders flank the
compote. The round Empire miniature painted on ivory
depicts Madame Marie de Saint-Vrsin holding sheet
music and dates from about 1815.

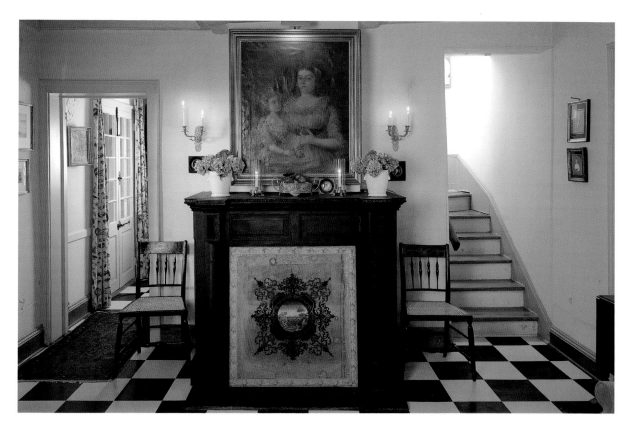

A portrait of Madame Michel Fortier II and her daughter, Marie Felicité Julie Fortier, painted about 1785, hangs over an 1820s Creole mantel with colonnettes and coffered capitals. The picture is by José Francisco Xavier de Salazar, a Yucatan-born artist active in New Orleans in the late eighteenth century and the first portrait painter in the city. The wood mantel, a fine example of Creole design, is painted a traditional black. A painted and papered summer screen made in the mid-nineteenth century covers the fireplace. To the right and left are New England fancy chairs with cane seats.

Originally the four-room building had a kitchen and workroom on the first floor and two equal-sized bedrooms, reached by exterior staircases, on the second floor. In the 1940s, architect Richard Koch removed the exterior stairs, inserted a small kitchen on the ground floor, constructed the internal staircase seen here, and made one of the bedrooms smaller to make room for a modern bath. One of the elegant upstairs mantels was moved to the downstairs salon. The modern black-and-white tile floor is strikingly effective in the compact space.

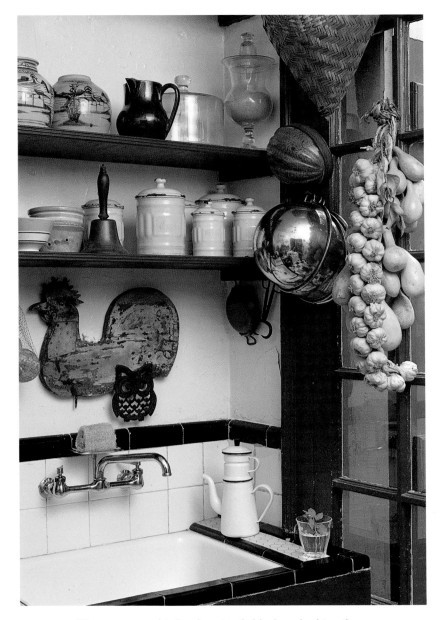

The cozy 1940s kitchen has simple black-and-white tile countertops. The door and cabinets are painted *gros rouge*, a favorite Creole color. Creole garlic hangs in a braid, along with a conical Louisiana Indian basket. To the left of the basket is a glass urn with brownish raw sugar from the family plantation in Patoutville, Louisiana. Pale pink French enamelware canisters hold coffee, chicory, and other staples. The rooster weather-vane was the gift of a cousin; the white, French drip coffeepot belonged to Mr. Patout's grandmother. Many New Orleanians begin each day with café au lait, just as their ancestors did.

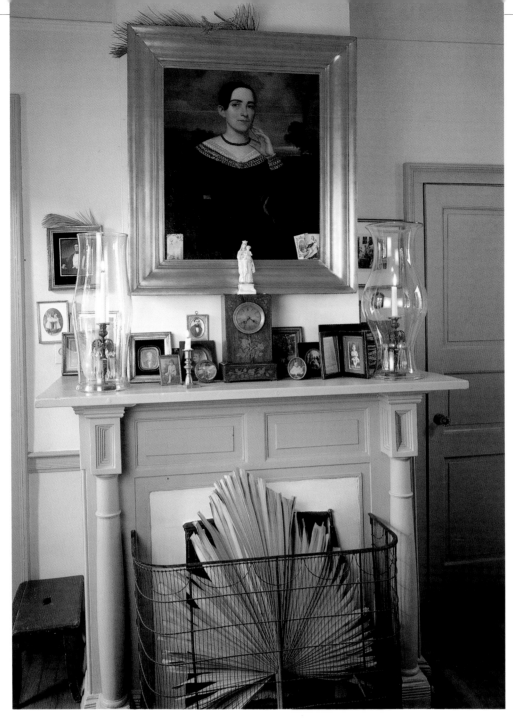

Mr. Patout has assembled portraits of his ancestors about his verdigris bedroom mantel, which he treats like an old Creole "family altar." Charlotte Mathilde Grevemberg du Martait, affectionately known as "Tante Mathilde," died at thirty-four. This posthumous mourning portrait was painted in 1843 by Adolph Rinck from a daguerreotype. Behind her is a red Louisiana sunset at Albania plantation on the Bayou Teche. Blessed sago palm fronds are tucked above the gilt frame. The small, white, old Paris porcelain statue atop the French

rosewood clock is of Notre Dame de Prompt Secours, patron saint of New Orleans. Portraits and photographs of family and friends, living and dead, crowd the mantel in a perpetual reunion. Tall early nineteenth-century hurricane shades shelter a pair of bronze French *girondoles* (candle holders with prisms) with a heron or crane motif, possibly made for the southern market. A clipped and dried palmetto frond serves as a summer screen behind an 1820s wire fire screen from New Iberia, Louisiana.

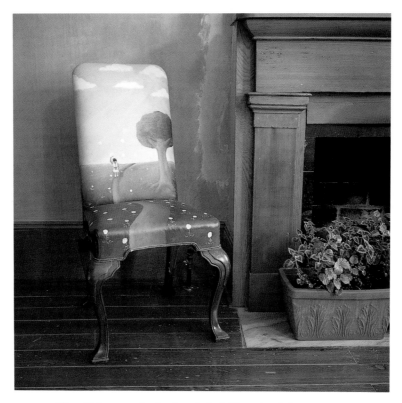

New Orleans artist Darlene Marie Francis, eighteen, painted this high-back Chippendale chair depicting Bonchee, a little girl blowing bubbles that become clouds in the sky. Francis says of her work, "When I started drawing Bonchee, my dreams began to express the way I think about life. Bonchee is a little black girl who believes in her heavenly father who takes her on many journeys. She befriends all types of mankind and beautiful animals and sees wonderful places." Francis is a member of Ya/Ya, Young Aspirations/Young Artists, a nonprofit arts and educational guild that provides fresh New Orleans talent with both artistic training and the business skills necessary to market their joyously New Orleanian work.

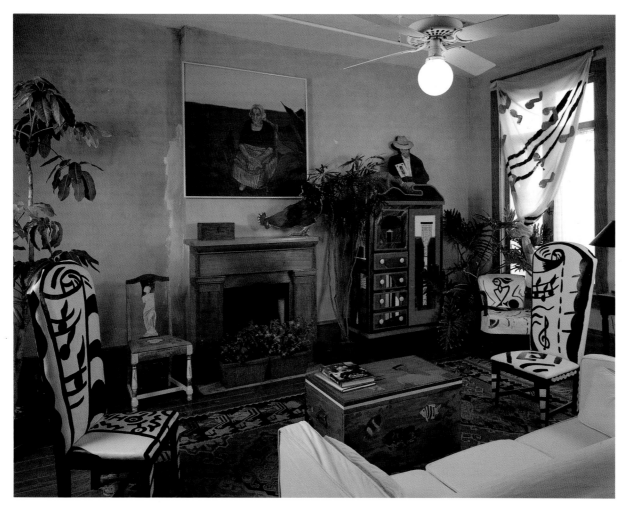

New Orleans–born painter and sculptor Jana Napoli founded Ya/Ya in 1988 with the proceeds of a small inheritance. "Ya Ya" is a Yoruba word meaning eldest daughter. Napoli started the arts and educational guild the year her beloved mammy, Adeline Edwards, died. She says of herself and her city, "I was raised in the arms of a black woman. Look at our colors! We are black and white mixed. All our children are raised to be gracious. New Orleans' art is the art of living. As an artist, I wanted to find a new format, a new way to communicate, a new way for art to talk. By chance I had two chifferobes in my house. That was the seed of Ya/Ya." Napoli opened an art gallery and bed-and-breakfast in an 1830 American townhouse on Baronne Street on the edge of the high-rise district, and she began to scout out young New Orleanians at the Robouin Vocational High School. She put paintbrushes in their hands, old furniture in front of them, and hope in their lives.

"These young people did not have access. But in New Orleans there is social mobility if you have style." Young Aspirations/Young Artists is using style to create access.

The walls of the upstairs parlor of the bed-and-breakfast over the Baronne Street gallery are coated with a mixture of water, salt, and red Mississippi clay. A painting by Napoli, *Lucita* (1988), hangs over the fireplace; her cut-out sculptures, *Gilded Rooster* and *Don Tomas,* sit atop the mantel and chifferobe. Ya/Ya artists created other pieces seen here including *Musical Chair* by Daymien Persley and *Venus de Milo Chair* by Frederick Dennis. The tall chifferobe, entitled *Downtown N.O.,* is by Ezel Bernard; the painted drape is by Daymien Persley; and the blue chest in the foreground, by Fred Dennis, is called *Fred's Aquarium.* Another of Persley's *Musical Chairs* stands to the far right.

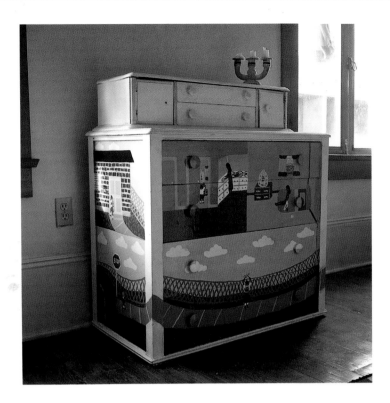

Darlene Marie Francis transformed an old chest of drawers into a piece she calls *A Storybook*, depicting the story of a little girl who brings home a bird only to find it stops singing. The girl's mother tells her that a caged bird will not sing, so, in the bottom panel, the young girl lets the bird go free.

"Real New Orleans; funk all the way," is how artist and educator Jana Napoli describes this corner of her combination art gallery and bed-and-breakfast. The painted table, by Lionel Milton, is called *Lionel's Table*. Darryl White, who made the painted child's chair, says of his work, "You look, then feel. Everything has a shape, personality, life, style, character. I help the chair express itself." Some painted Mexican gourds from Guerrero and a married woman's formal kimono from Kyoto complete the tableau.

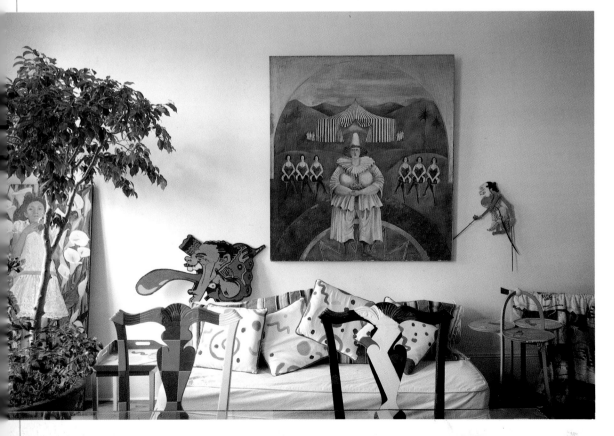

The light-flooded dayroom of J's B&B on Baronne Street is a characteristically narrative New Orleans room. It brings together works by, and memories of, Jana Napoli's friends. Behind the small tree is one of Napoli's paintings, *The Death of Childhood*. Ya/Ya artist Lionel Milton made *Lionelism*, the cut-out wall piece with the red tongue. The painted fabric pillows are by Daymien Persley. The two chairs in the foreground are by Carlos A. Neville (left) and Darlene Marie Francis (right). Francis calls her chair with the white lightning bolt *Enlightenment*. The orange side table to the right is also hers. Presiding over all this festivity is a painting by Northern Irish artist Elizabeth Taggart called *Circus Lady*, painted in London in 1973.

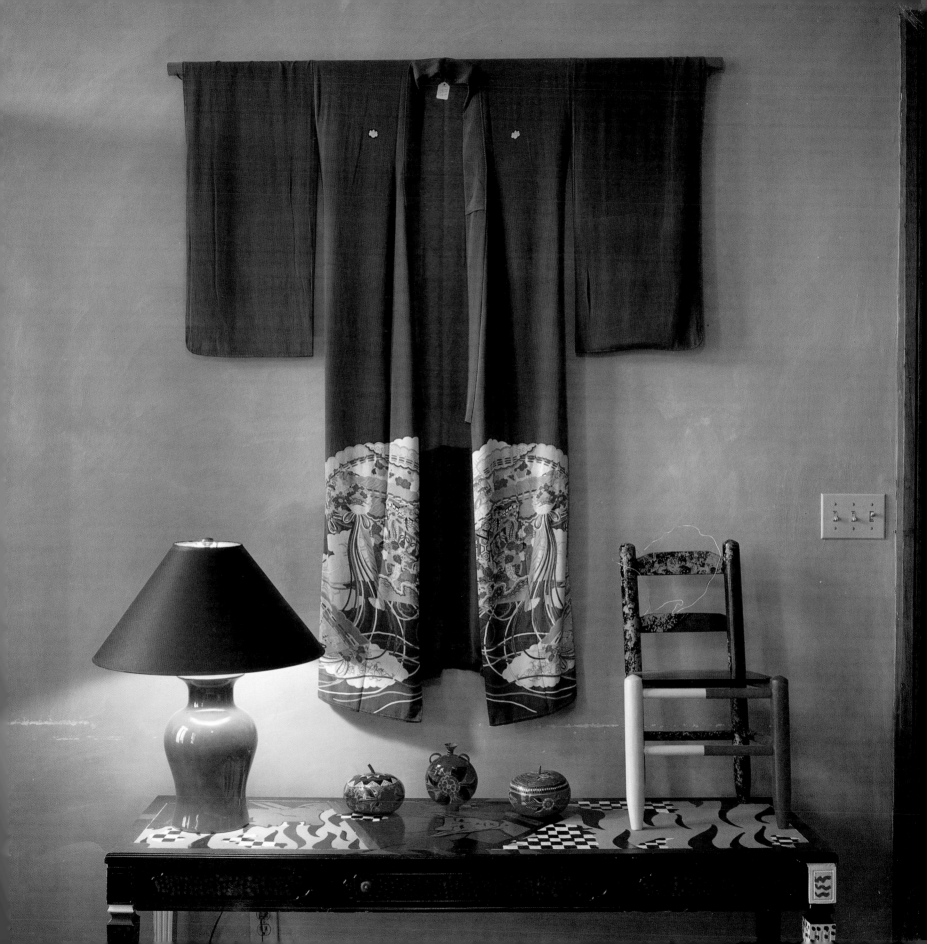

The Red Room has no windows, and, wishing to accentuate its nighttime feeling, Dyer painted a night sky of low clouds and scattered stars on the ceiling. In an unusual reversal, he took the electric lights out of the chandelier and returned it to candles; it looks as if it were ascending into the dramatic sky.

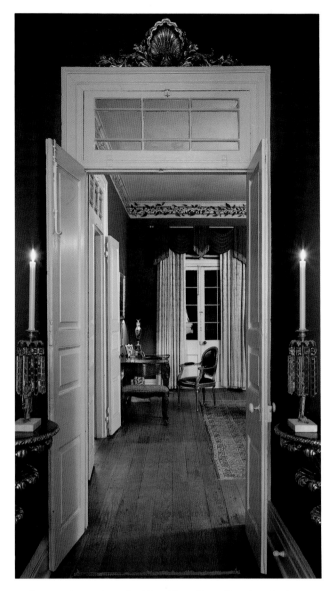

Decorative painter Joel Lockhart Dyer lives in a large French Quarter apartment near Jackson Square in a subdivided mid-1830s Creole townhouse. He likes to entertain and regards his house almost as a scenic set. This view through the entrance hall into the Green Room shows his refined sense of color. The walls are a soft, chalky green, and the woodwork is an antique ivory. He selected colors that would look old, as if they had "turned." The painted frieze of stylized Japanese magnolias along the top of the parlor wall is an example of his work, as is the maroon cornice over the French doors, a tromp l'oeil "drape" that looks three-dimensional.

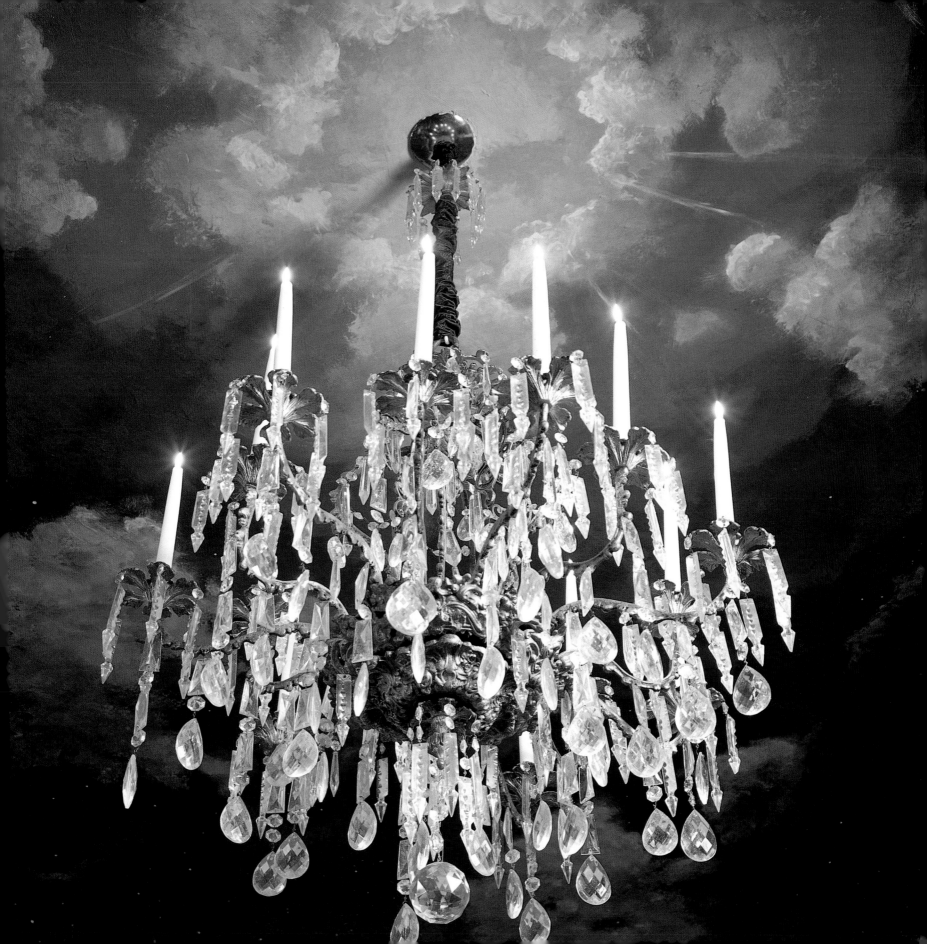

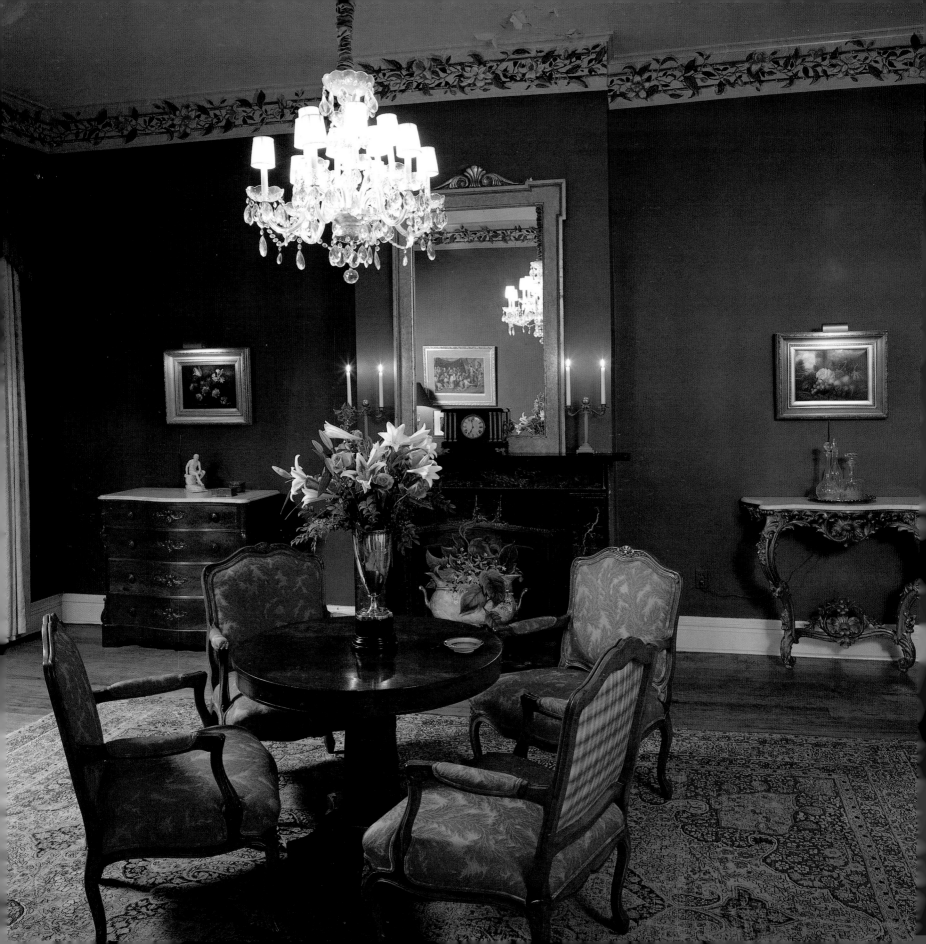

The spacious Green Room is sparsely but elegantly furnished. Its dark walls make it seem cool and cavelike. The peeling ceiling is deliberately preserved. Atop an American Empire table is a silver loving cup, a yachting trophy from Moss Point, Mississippi, awarded in 1929. The mirror frame is Dyer's design, as is the tromp l'oeil "marble" urn fireplace screen. Dyer has the New Orleanian taste for fantasy.

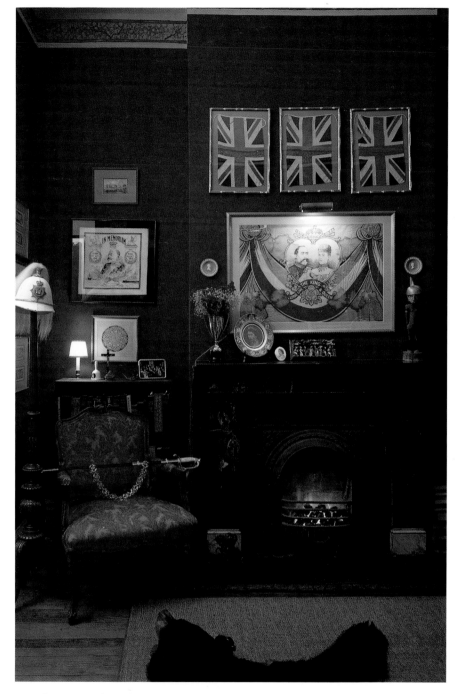

Texas-born Dyer is a fervent Anglophile in Francophile New Orleans. In this clubby city, he has lightheartedly formed his own club, the Society of Saint George, which celebrates the queen's birthday each June in grand style. Not just anyone can join, of course. Says Dyer, "A person must have the right pedigree, be recommended by a member, and meet the rigid requirements of the nominating committee. And since I'm a strong believer in monarchy, I *am* the nominating committee." He gave his bedroom the look of one belonging to a retired British

colonel. The framed bunting over the mantel, made for King Edward VII's coronation, was found in a car trunk in West Texas. The three Union Jacks are English street pennants. The mantel holds a porcelain souvenir plate of Queen Elizabeth II and an African figurine with a Venetian mask on its head. At the far left is a black-and-white mourning handkerchief from Edward VII's funeral. Dyer painted the bamboo-framed frieze along the top of the walls.

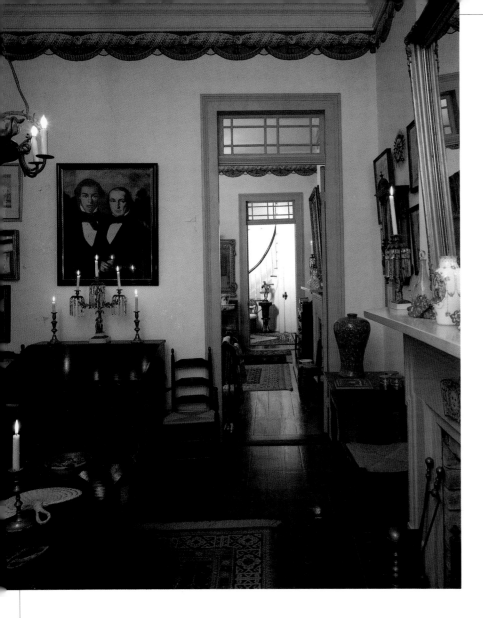

The Nathan-Lewis-Cizek house in Faubourg Marigny was built in 1836 in the Greek Revival style. Architect Eugene Cizek and artist Lloyd Sensat have restored the house and furnished it with old Louisiana pieces. This view looks from the front parlor through the master bedroom and into the pantry, with its curved stairs. Presiding over the parlor is a reproduction portrait of Asher Moses Nathan and his adopted mulatto son, Achiles Lion. At the far left is an 1830s lithograph of Bernard-Xavier-Phillippe de Marigny, the Creole plantation owner who subdivided Faubourg Marigny in 1808. The walls are trimmed with border paper, and the door frame and original mantel are painted a Creole putty. The 1780s walnut desk under the portrait was found in Aboyelles Parish, Louisiana, and the walnut ladderback chairs were made in Louisiana between 1790 and 1810. A graceful Korean vase stands on a corner table. The red-stained floors are southern pine.

A curved stairway in the pantry, or service room, leads to a second-floor bedroom. The newel and handrail are Honduran mahogany and the stair treads are cypress. Painted a Creole putty, the door of the broom closet under the stairs has its original hand-forged hardware. An American-made bronze harlequin from the 1870s stands atop an 1840s walnut stand. Ginger leaves bring a touch of the garden into the house.

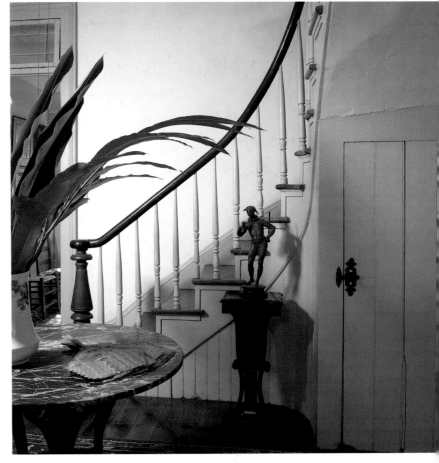

Like many New Orleanian homes, the Nathan-Lewis-Cizek house has gone through several changes. It was broken up into three units in the 1890s, and for about fifty years a Chinese-Creole family operated a laundry there. When the house was restored in the late 1970s, the walls of the dining room and parlor were scraped to reveal their many layers of paint. Eugene Cizek designed the Greek key door surround between the two rooms, and artist Lloyd Sensat painted the school chair (right corner) about 1970 and titled it *The Perfect Student*. The chandeliers came from an old movie theater. The two rooms are sometimes used to stage art exhibits.

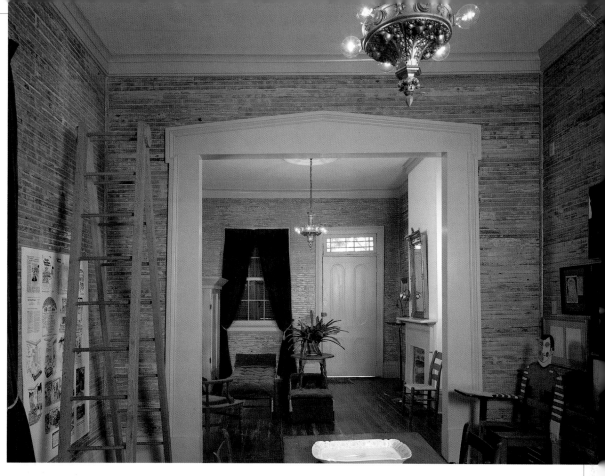

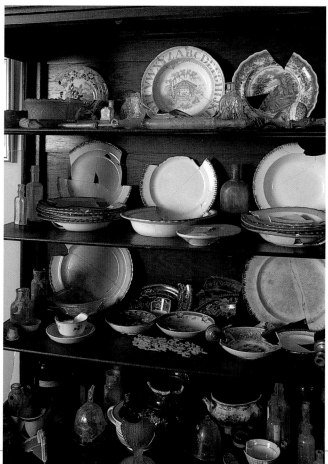

A breakfront in the foyer displays some of the thousands of artifacts that have been excavated on the property by the Delta Chapter of the Louisiana Archaeological Society. Eugene Cizek wrote his dissertation on Faubourg Marigny, and he was a founder of the Marigny Improvement Association. Today he teaches in the Tulane University School of Architecture and is active in efforts to preserve the threatened plantation houses that line the River Road between New Orleans and Baton Rouge.

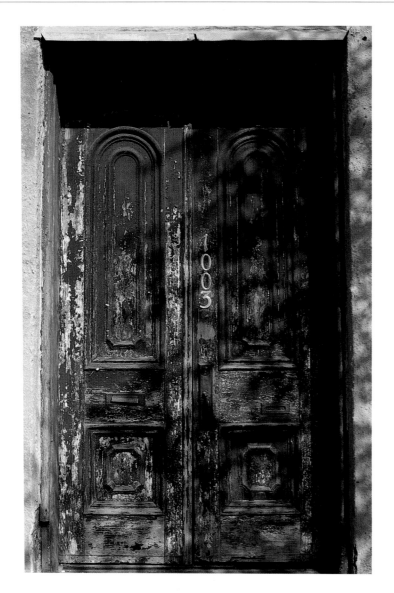

The peeling wooden doors of the old Franklin Temperance Hall in Marigny keep a low profile. The 1857 Italianate-style hall is home to two contemporary New Orleans sculptors: Elizabeth Shannon lives upstairs and Clifton G. Webb downstairs. While the city's economic decline has been hard on its working-class neighborhoods, it does provide affordable live-work spaces for artists.

Sculptor and alligator trapper Elizabeth Shannon was raised in the bayou and swamp country of Morgan City, Louisiana. She caught this eight-and-a-half-foot 'gator near Houma, mounted it on a ladder, trained a strong light on it, and entitled it *Caught*.

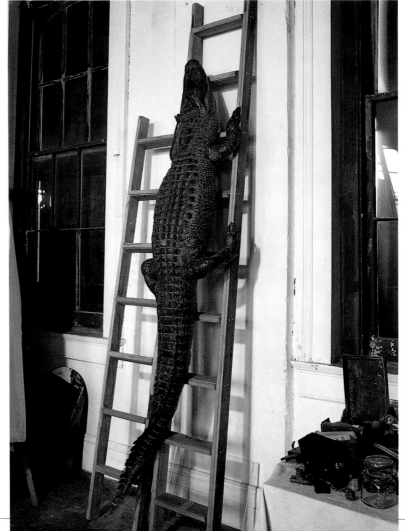

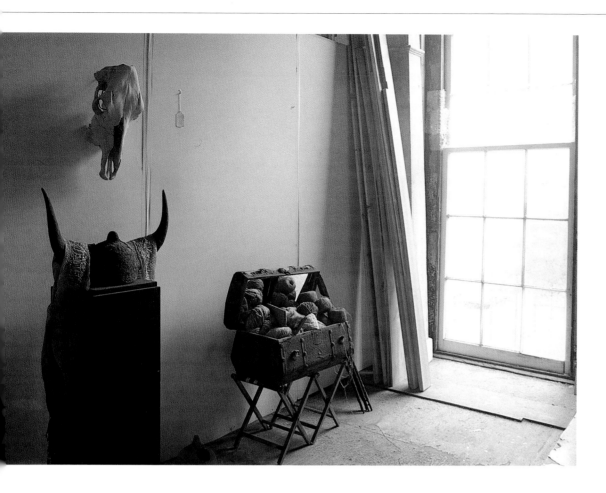

Shannon creates narrative installations. In this corner of her studio is a vignette for a 1992 show at the New Orleans Contemporary Arts Center entitled *Pondering the Question*. Under the cow skull is an African Mossi helmet draped with snakeskin. The trunk is filled with Louisiana cotton from which Acadian women once made blankets.

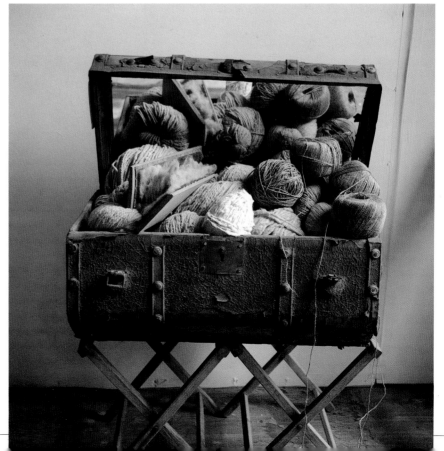

An old trunk filled with Louisiana *cotton jaune* gathered at Melrose plantation becomes art in Elizabeth Shannon's studio.

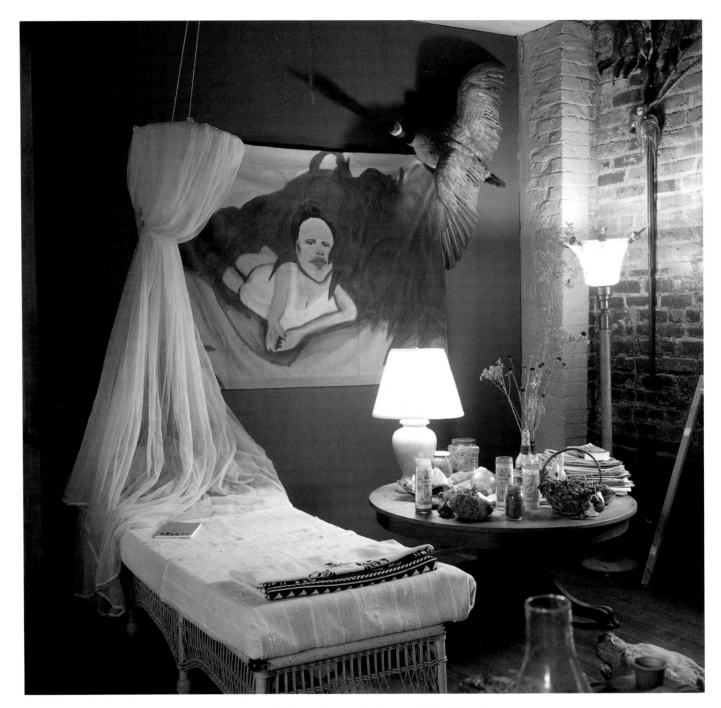

A corner of Shannon's space harbors a wicker Victorian daybed draped in mosquito netting. The painting is by Dub Brock, a Mississippi artist, and is part of his Cane Field series (ca. 1980). Mounted on the brick wall is a standard Shannon made for her witch doctor costume for her Mardi Gras krewe, the Society of Saint Anne.

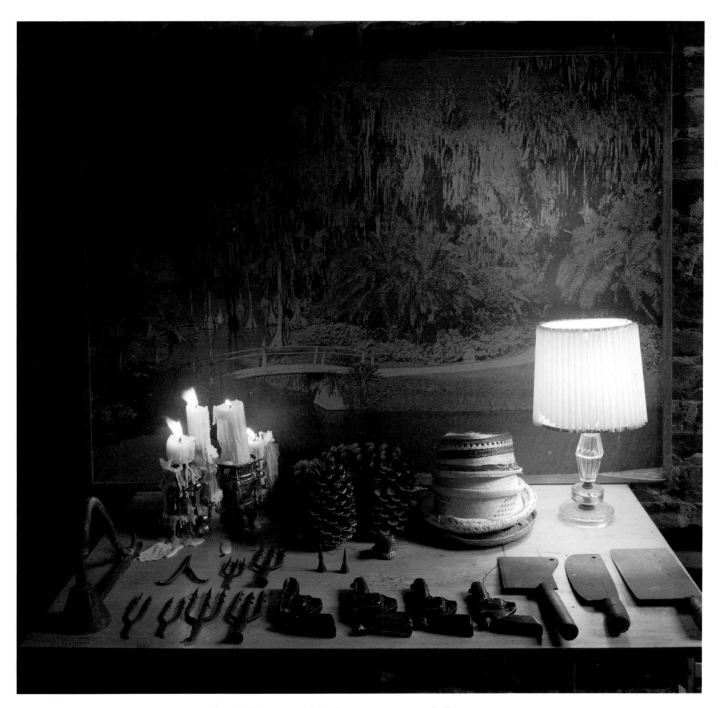

In the living area of the former temperance hall
Elizabeth Shannon has created an assemblage of power
objects. A 1950s dime-store lithograph of Florida's
Cypress Gardens is the backdrop to an array of weap-
ons, real and simulated. The metal barbs to the left are
Amazonian fish-spearheads; in the center are soapstone
revolvers made in Brazil; to the right are three rusty
cleavers. Haitian straw hats are piled next to the lamp.
The candles "pray that the violence won't happen."

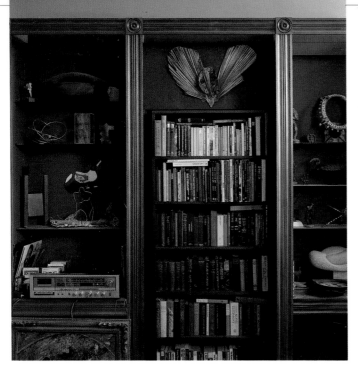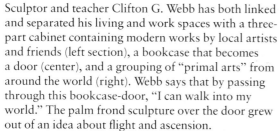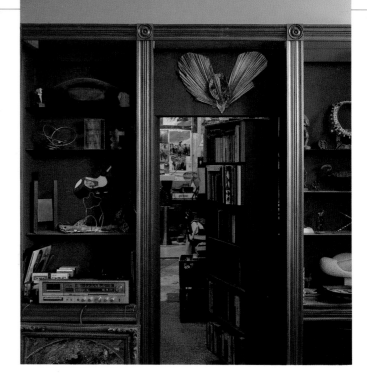

Sculptor and teacher Clifton G. Webb has both linked and separated his living and work spaces with a three-part cabinet containing modern works by local artists and friends (left section), a bookcase that becomes a door (center), and a grouping of "primal arts" from around the world (right). Webb says that by passing through this bookcase-door, "I can walk into my world." The palm frond sculpture over the door grew out of an idea about flight and ascension.

The wall on the studio side of the bookcase-door is a collage of posters of Afro-American musicians. The signboard came from an exhibit at the annual Jazz and Heritage Festival in New Orleans.

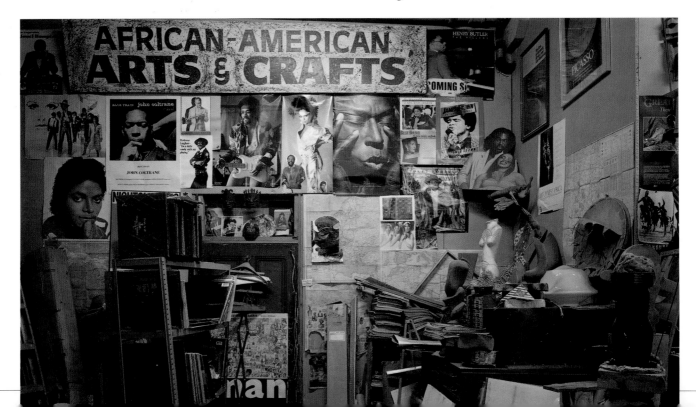

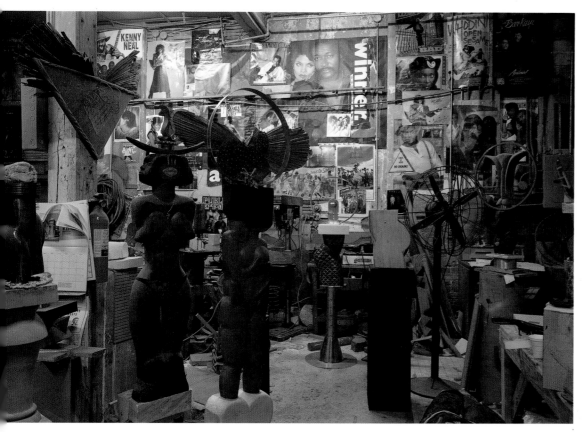

Peering into Clifton Webb's studio is a look into the swirling chaos from which art emerges. "Extreme chaos," he says. "I draw from it. I see a piece of wire on the floor and it becomes part of my work." Richly colored mahogany, fine marble, dark iron, and bright brass—along with sand, pebbles, leaves, and small stones—are selectively fused in his works. Basic forms like the circle, rectangle, and triangle are joined with the human torso to create pieces that speak of human union. The dark torso with a boulder (far left) is an unnamed work-in-progress. The mahogany figure with red lips is *The Great Mother*. The embracing couple to its right is entitled *Patience and Endurance* and represents "the idea of human love. What it takes to be together." In the center distance is a mahogany, copper, white marble, and brass piece called *Forever on the Path*. On the black pedestal is another work-in-progress. "One day I will make the connection," Webb says, "and the work will find its completion."

Webb uses power and hand tools in his work. Emerging from the wood is a piece called *The Prodigal Child*. "Every day is new," say Webb. "We see as long as we have our minds open. Sculpture takes mass or matter and gives it new life as a result of human will. It stimulates us to think and to know ourselves as human beings; to know our environment in depth as well as surface. Permanence is a transitory notion. New life will make new things."

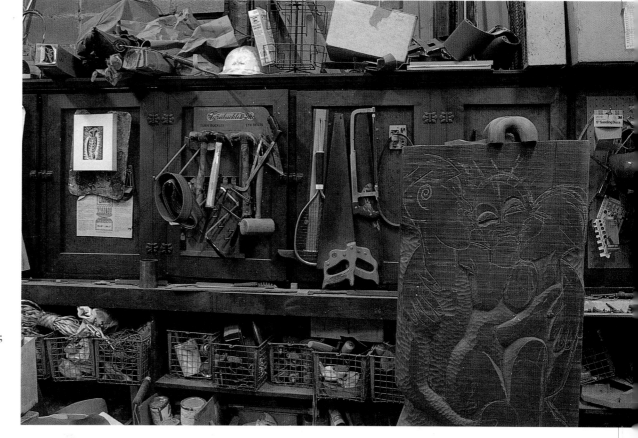

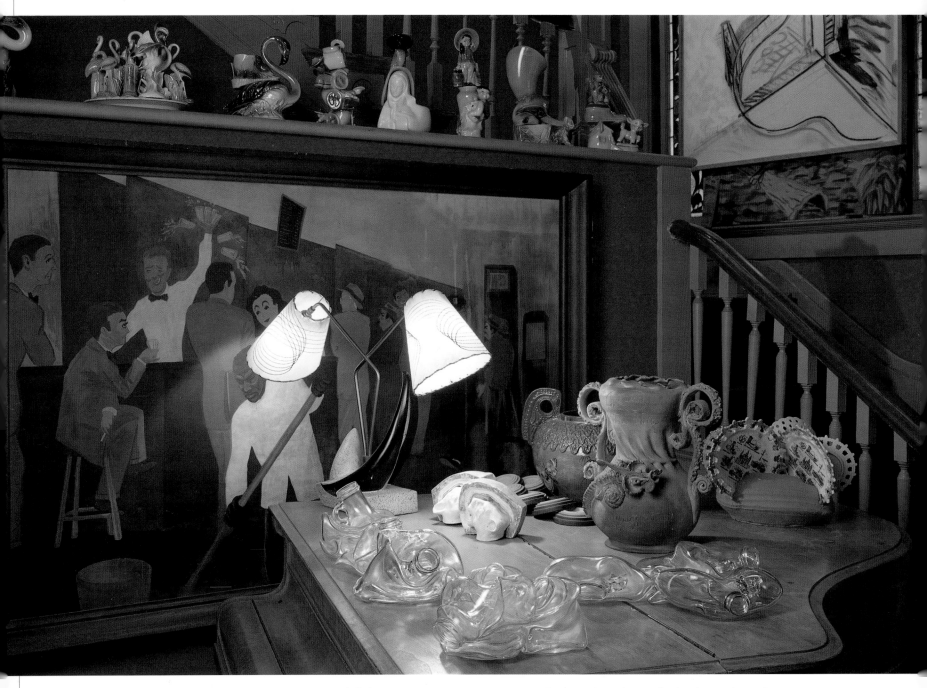

Robert Tannen cannot be pigeonholed. He is a conceptual artist, sculptor, architect, urban planner, ecologist, educator, community activist, and even a humorist. His work sharply criticizes our contemporary throwaway consumer culture. This might be his strongest connection with his adopted city, a place that has never been quite at home in mainstream America. With Jeanne Nathan, he has turned their large Georgian Colonial Revival house on Esplanade Ridge into a live-in installa-

tion piece, both inside and out. The foyer introduces the visitor to the juxtapositions they are about to experience. A 1950s lamp lights Tannen's *Glass Bottle Pieces* atop a piano. The terracotta pot with loopy handles is the work of George E. Ohr, the "mad potter of Biloxi." The painting in the background, by Brother Gregory, was discarded by a Canal Street bar. In the upper right is a partial view of a study for Tannen's *Odalisque*, a 1988 installation of a grand piano lying on its side.

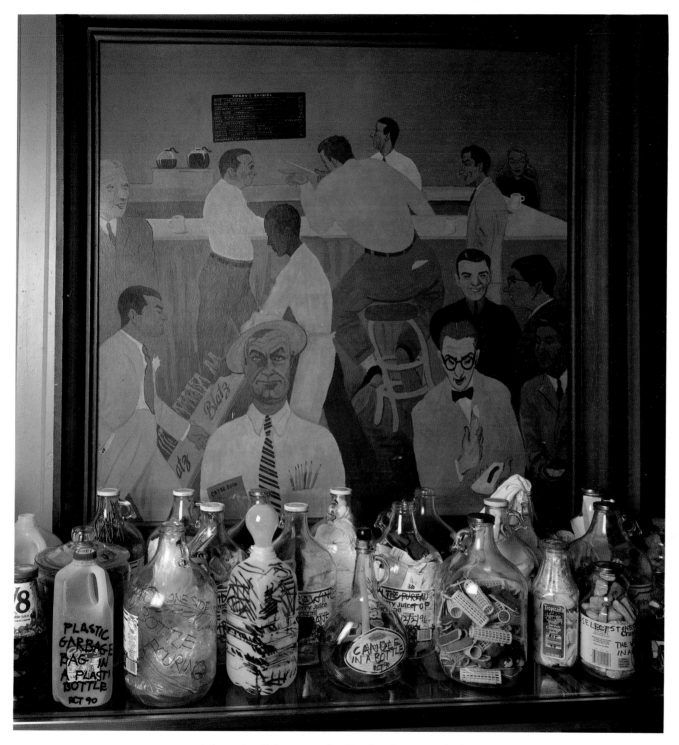

A foyer detail shows another Brother Gregory painting
from a defunct Canal Street bar. Tannen saves the
detritus of everyday consumer culture and repackages,
labels, and displays it. From useless objects, he creates
thought-provoking art.

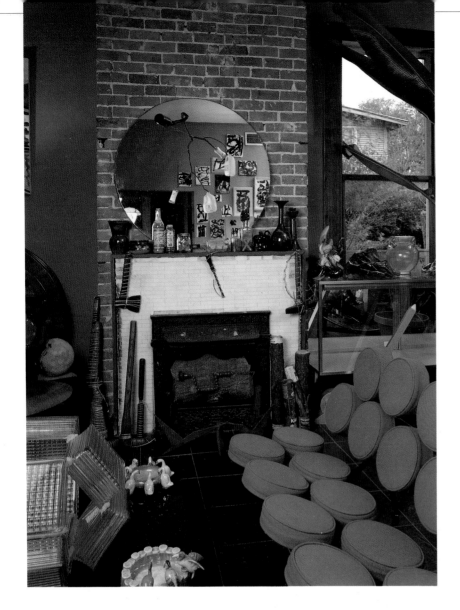

Tannen likes to work with objects found in New Orleans. The orange George Nelson Marshmallow Sofa, made in the 1950s, was discarded by a local bank. A previous owner of the house had stripped one parlor wall down to the brick and removed the mantelpiece; Tannen left the wall the way he found it. Ranged along the mantel are late nineteenth-century American art pottery and Tannen's refilled bottles. Reflected in the mirror is his *White Trash* mobile. In and along the fireplace are several of his *Wired Tools* (1980s).

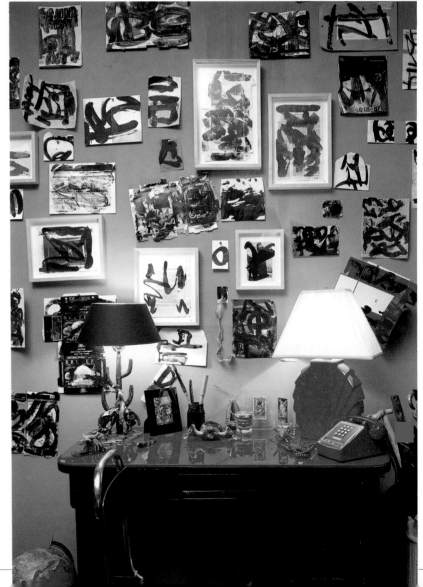

Robert Tannen recycles even his junk mail. Once he bought the finest rag paper for his sumi-ink art; now he uses everything from throwaway advertisements to bank statements. It is one more instance of the New Orleanian fascination with the transformation of the everyday into art, a kind of Mardi Gras of debris. Jeanne Nathan made the red desk.

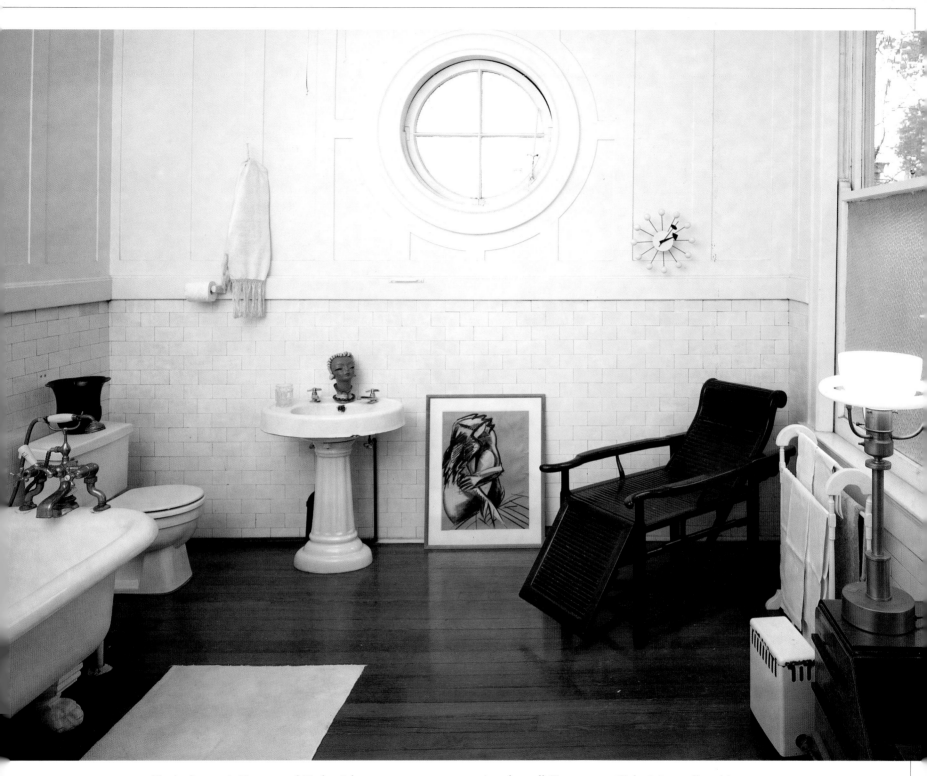

The bathroom in Tannen and Nathan's house was perhaps originally a bedroom. They left the fixtures as they found them and furnished the room with an eclectic collection of objects. On the wall is a 1950s George Nelson clock. The chair beneath it is late nineteenth-century Chinese. Gail Nathan did the drawing propped against the wall. Tannen says, "I don't just collect things of value, I collect things of interest. New Orleans is a very real place to live. As the economy and the environment have gone downhill, I like it even more." Who but a New Orleanian could look at things that way?

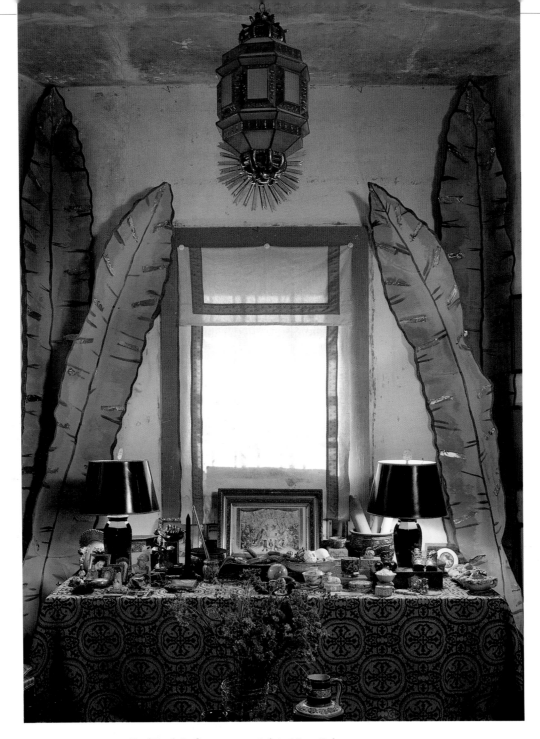

Paul Poché's first summer job in New Orleans was
making Carnival masks, and ever since he has been
fascinated by Mardi Gras. Today he builds fanciful floats
for city krewes. His Bywater home is alive with Mardi
Gras mementos. Giant, bright green, paper "banana
leaves" from a Carnival float frame the dining room
window. Personal treasures crowd the altarlike table,
like offerings, before an old engraving of a Mardi Gras
king.

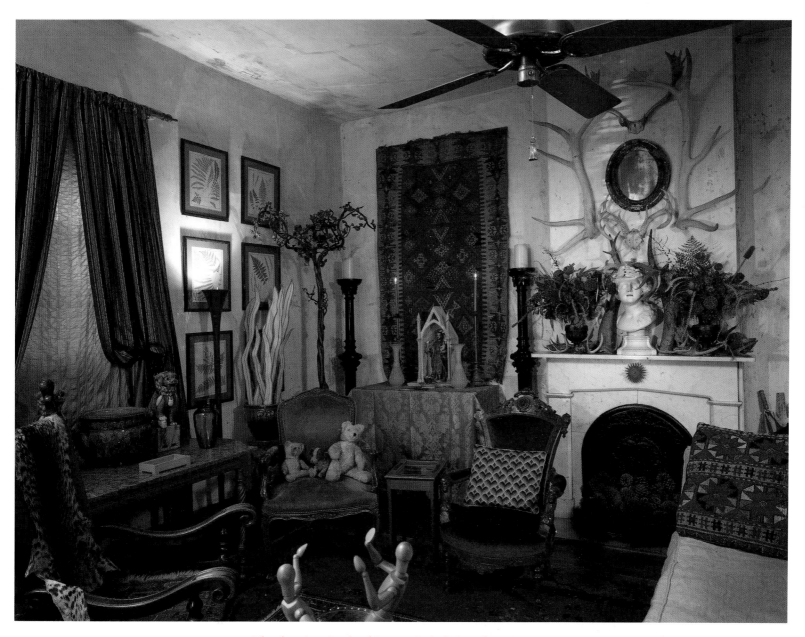

The elevating rituals of Roman Catholicism, the extravagance of grand opera, and Paul Poché's own sense of mystery and transformation pervade his Creole-plan house. He remembers a childhood fantasy of wanting the statues in church to come alive and fly out of their niches. His sitting room seems to embody that sense of the inanimate coming to life. A Carrara marble bust of Orpheus, the poet-musician with magical powers, presides over the room from the mantel. The elk horns over it were won by Poché's grandfather in a steamboat race on Bayou Lafourche. The gold papier-mâché mother-in-law-tongue plant that ripples like flames was made for the Heron float in the 1988 Comus Mardi Gras parade.

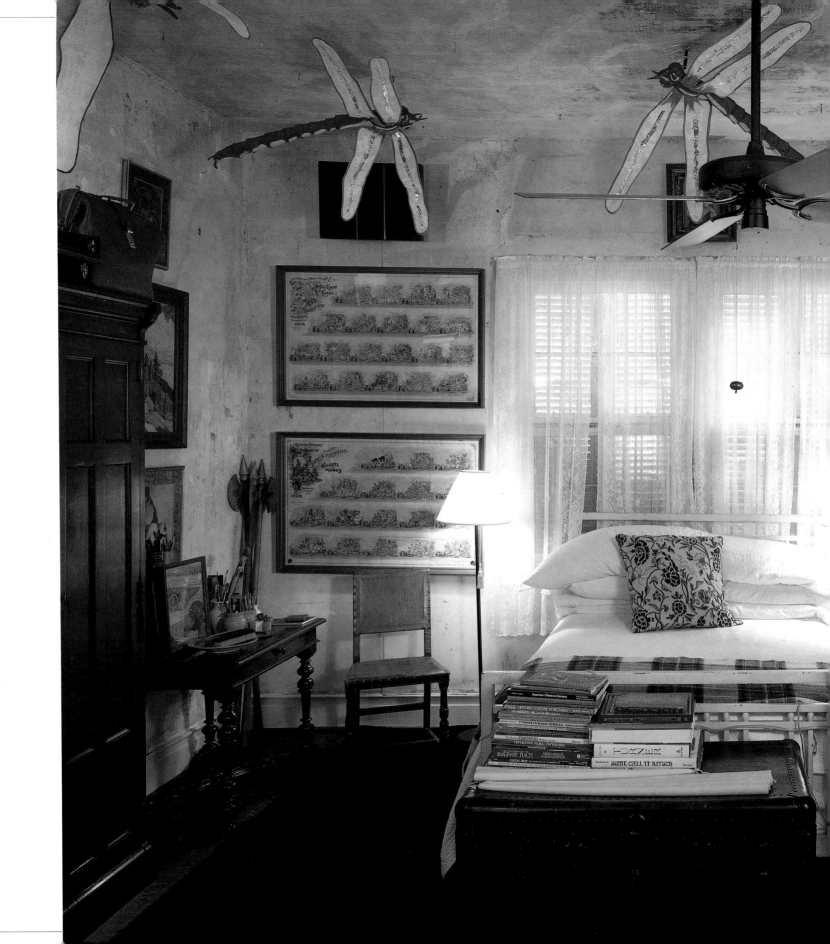

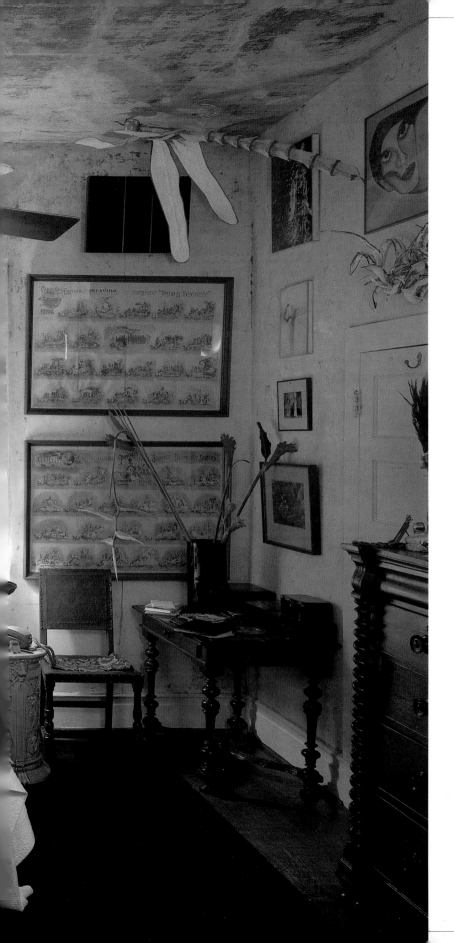

The stripped plaster walls of Poché's house are the timeworn backdrop to a remarkable collection of Carnival memorabilia. The ceiling-fan-cooled bedroom is alive with vivid papier-mâché dragonflies made for the 1990 Comus Entomological Empire Mardi Gras parade. The antique oak cabinet to the far left came from the Custom House on Canal Street. Flanking the windows are four old Mardi Gras "bulletins" depicting parades and floats from the past. At the upper left are the floats of the 1909 Comus parade on the theme Flights of Fancy, beneath it the Momus Signs and Superstitions parade of the same year is depicted. At the upper right is the 1896 Proteus parade on the theme Dumb Society, under it is the Rex parade of that year on Heavenly Bodies. Old-line krewes still secretly construct new floats on wooden-wheeled "cars" that have but one day (or night) of glory.

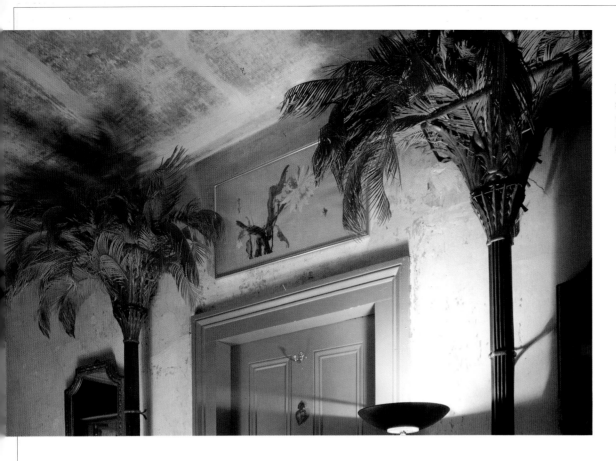

Dried sago palm fronds erupt from fanciful ballroom sconces that Poché calls "Italian downspouts." The Chinese watercolor over the door is of the night-blooming cereus; Poché remembers being allowed to stay up late as a child to smell its sweetness.

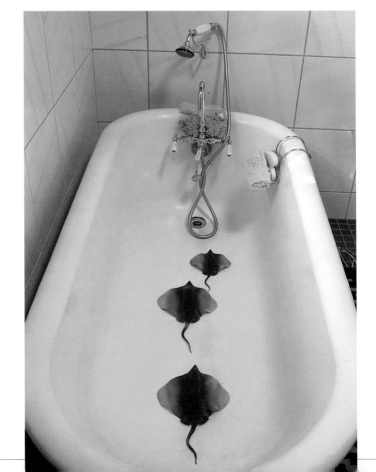

A claw-foot bathtub is home to three plastic manta rays from a tourist shop in Pass Christian. "I bought these just for fun," says Poché.

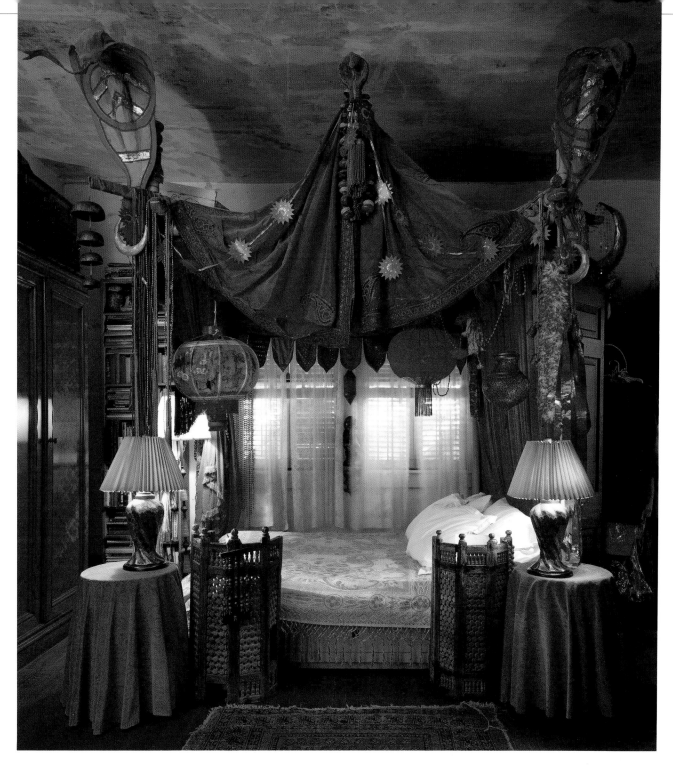

The gorgeously canopied bed in the Tent Room is an assemblage of many elements. The papier-mâché cobras are from a Mardi Gras float and the cloth Indian drape came from New York City. The gold stars once decorated a Twelfth Night party. "If this bed could talk," says Poché, "we'd have to shoot it!" The fine curly maple veneer armoire to the left is filled with fancy costumes.

The entrance hall of antique dealer Marcus Fraser's Bywater Victorian cottage looks through the white-painted, bay-windowed side room, down the side gallery, and into the backyard. A statue of the Virgin stands on an old chest; a tassel from a theater curtain hangs from the gingerbread arch. The entrance hall serves as a bar when Fraser throws parties.

The white walls of the sitting room are a foil to an eclectic array of treasures. The 1920s escritoire painted with scenes of Venice, rescued from the curbside of a defunct Magazine Street used-furniture store, now houses stereo equipment. The orange ceramic jar is probably from the 1940s. Used in Catholic mass, the three-tiered bell to the far left was struck during the elevation of the host. The watercolor of a window opening onto blue sky (center) is by Newcomb Art School artist Anne Francis Simpson and dates from the early part of this century.

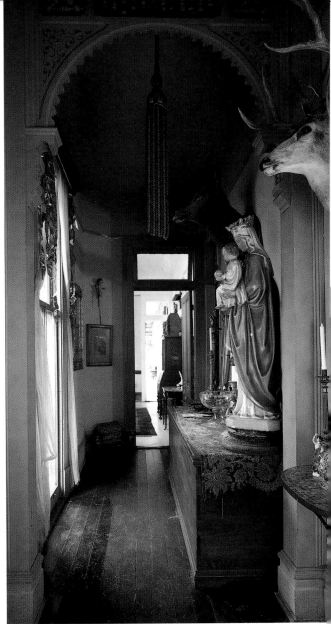

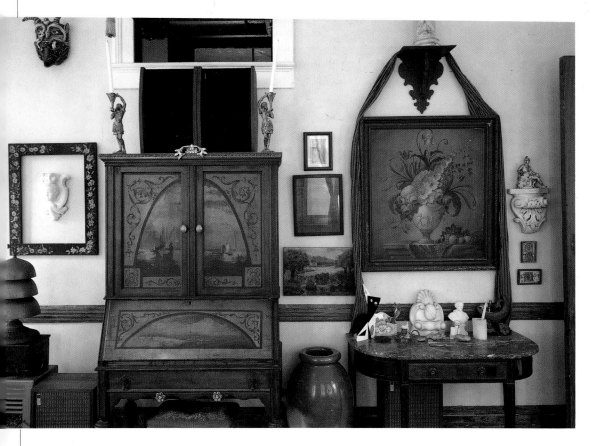

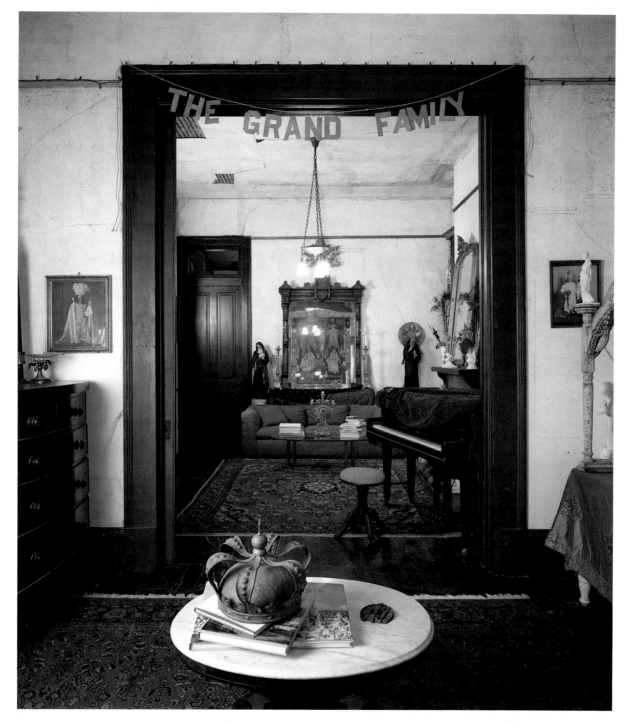

When Fraser bought this old cottage, he stripped the wallpaper to reveal the patinated plaster underneath. Like many Orleanians, he believes in living with things the way they are. Religious, Masonic, and Mardi Gras mementos enliven the front and back parlors. The large crown probably once topped a daybed. The tinted photograph to the left of the archway, by Wood "Pops" Whitesell, shows Comus in his regalia. The partly obscured photo to the right shows the king and queen of a children's ball, a distinctive New Orleanian tradition. "The Grand Family" banner is an old Masonic decoration. In the second parlor, carved wood polychrome statues of Saint Scholastica (left) and Saint Benedict (right) flank an Eastlake mirror. Fraser found the statues of the brother and sister saints separately and reunited them.

The bay-windowed side sitting room opens onto the side gallery with an aloe plant and leads into the kitchen. An Art Deco lamp hangs over a red, white, and silver 1950s dinette table. Around the table are wooden Victorian pressed-back chairs painted in a spiderweb design by Nita and Zita, two Gypsy sisters from Hungary who lived on Dauphine Street. These exotic dancers made their own costumes and painted their furniture, rooms, and the front of their house in red and silver designs. New Orleanians have always appreciated expressive people with a sense of individual style.

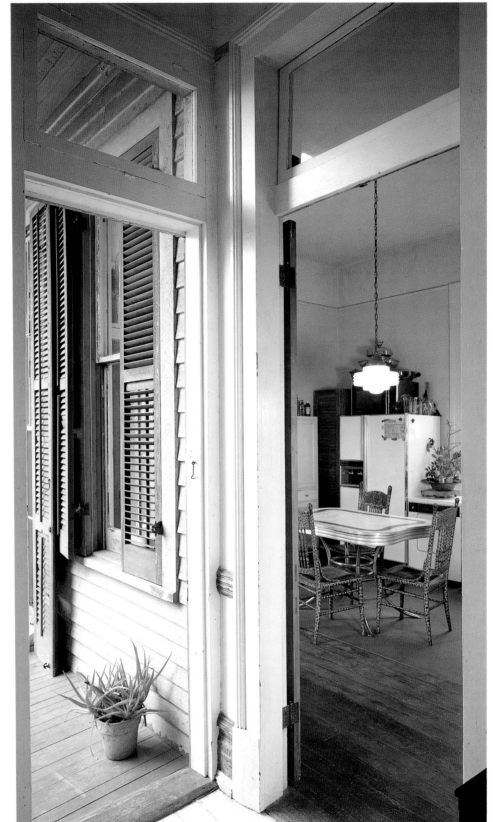

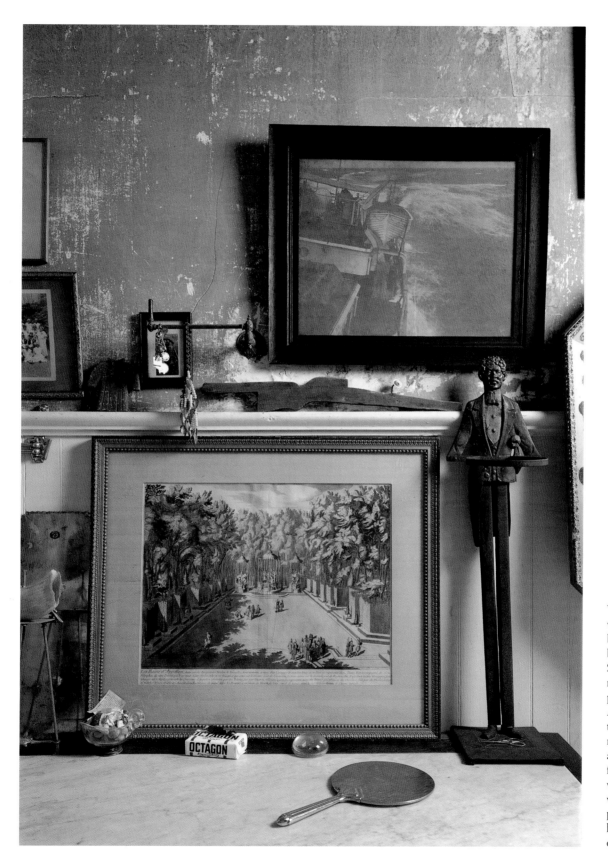

When the wallpaper was stripped from the bathroom walls, a rich blue color was revealed. Standing on the white marble bureau is an old print of the Baths of Apollo at Versailles. The tall cast-iron figure to the right was originally an ashtray holder. An old gas fixture protrudes from the wall, partially obscuring a vintage photo of a football player. The black frame holds an old photograph of a ship at sea.

CHAPTER THREE
Verdant Enclaves

I alight at Esplanade in a smell of roasting coffee and creosote and walk up Royal Street. The lower Quarter is the best part. The ironwork on the balconies sags like rotten lace. Little French cottages hide behind high walls. Through deep sweating carriageways one catches glimpses of courtyards gone to jungle.

WALKER PERCY, *The Moviegoer,* 1961

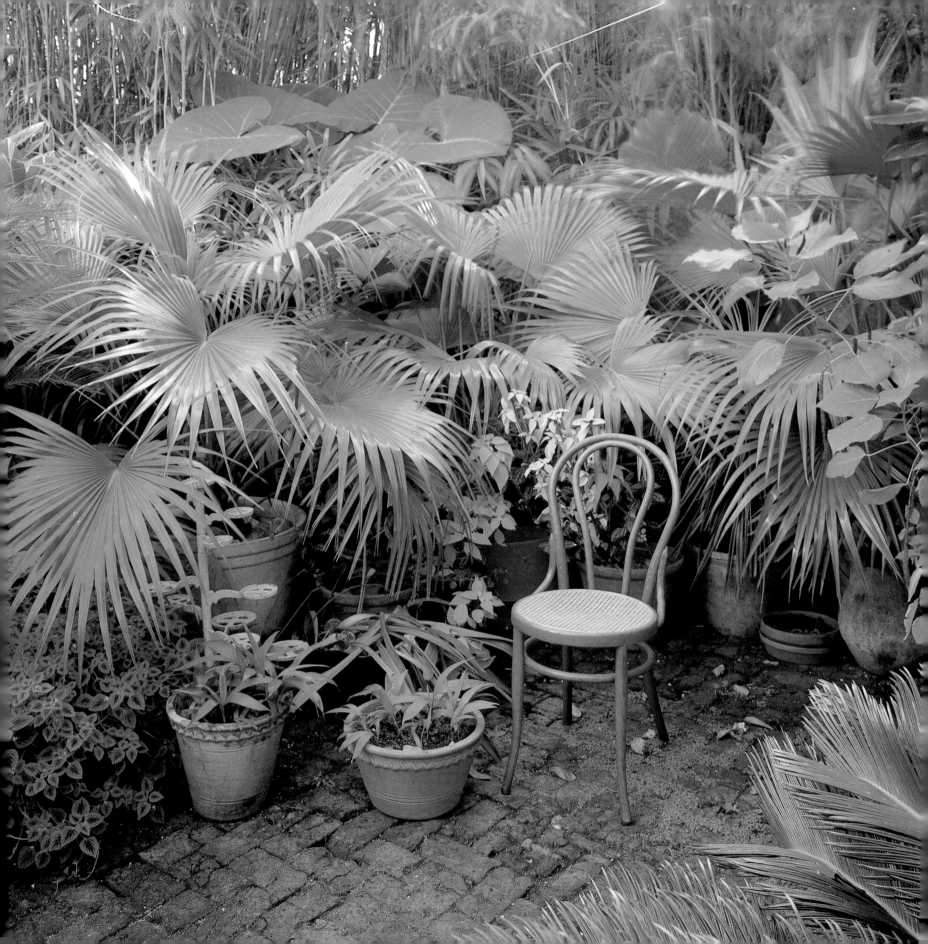

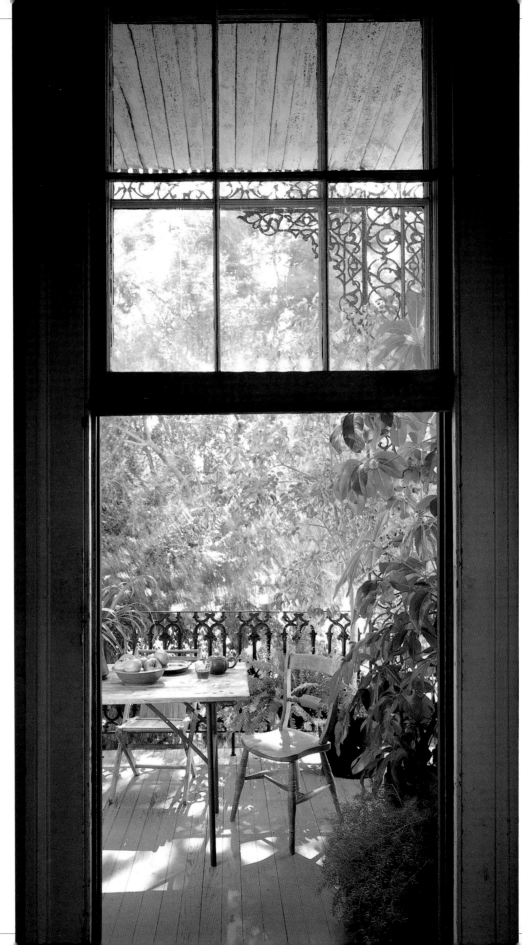

Preceding Page:
"The garden is the reason I live here," says Paul Poché of his junglelike Bywater backyard. Here he grows exotic palms from seed in clay pots. Fan palms rustle behind a Thonet bentwood chair from the Ursuline convent on State Street. Bamboo, grown from cuttings from the family chicken yard, screens out the neighbors. Roosters crow, hens cluck, and jeweled spiders weave intricate webs in this lush, brick-paved oasis.

Old New Orleans houses, designed before air conditioning sealed people inside their homes, open out to hidden courtyards, elevated galleries, and private yards. Here guillotine windows open onto a lower French Quarter gallery set for afternoon tea. Some call these gallery gardens, or hanging gardens. This private enclave seems to merge with the trees in the park across the street. A piece of fine old cast iron brackets the view.

The conservatory of this Greek Revival house in the Garden District was a later addition. It makes a lush setting for informal parties spiced with Zydeco, blues, and even African drummers. This junglelike garden room inspired the setting for Tennessee Williams's play "Suddenly, Last Summer."

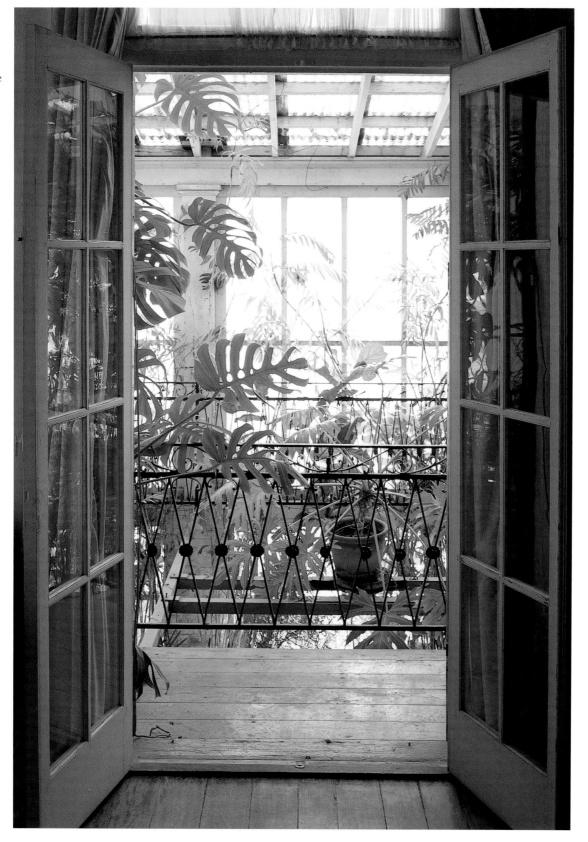

Following Pages:
Light filters through rustling banana leaves in a hidden French Quarter courtyard. Early each morning the owner of this house spends a contented hour before going to work tending his plants and clipping greenery and flowers for the house. The cuttings for these flourishing banana plants came from nearby Tremé.

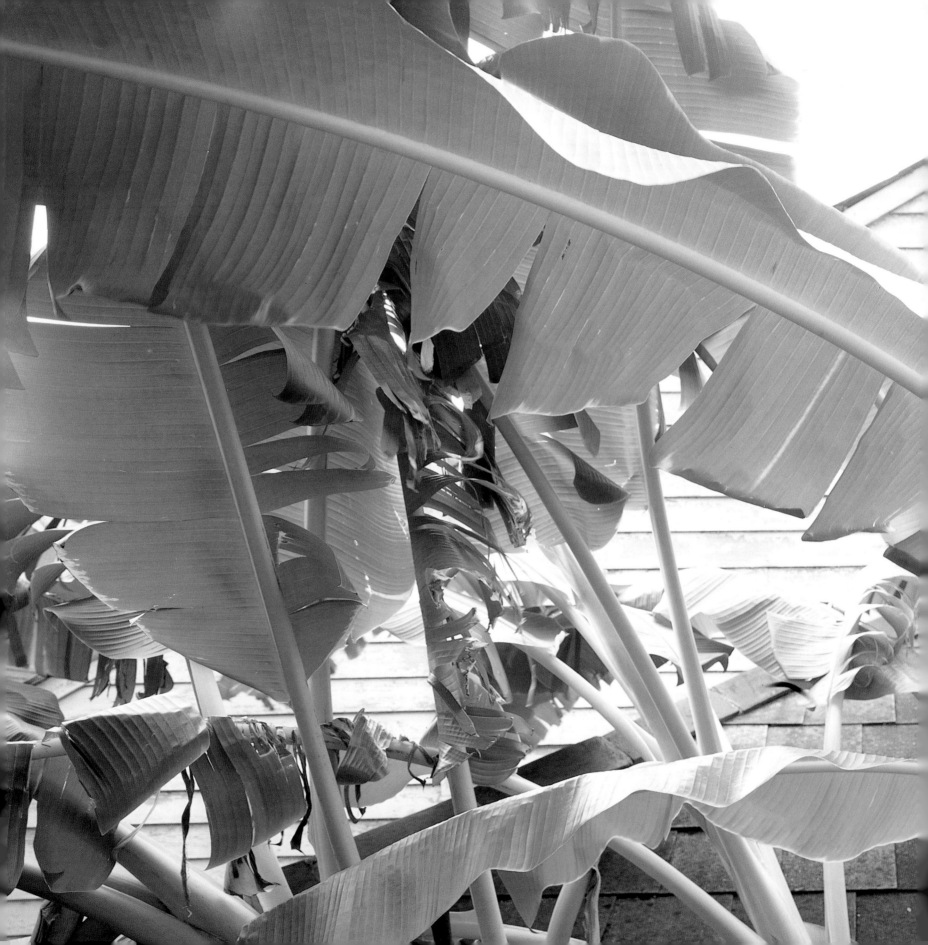

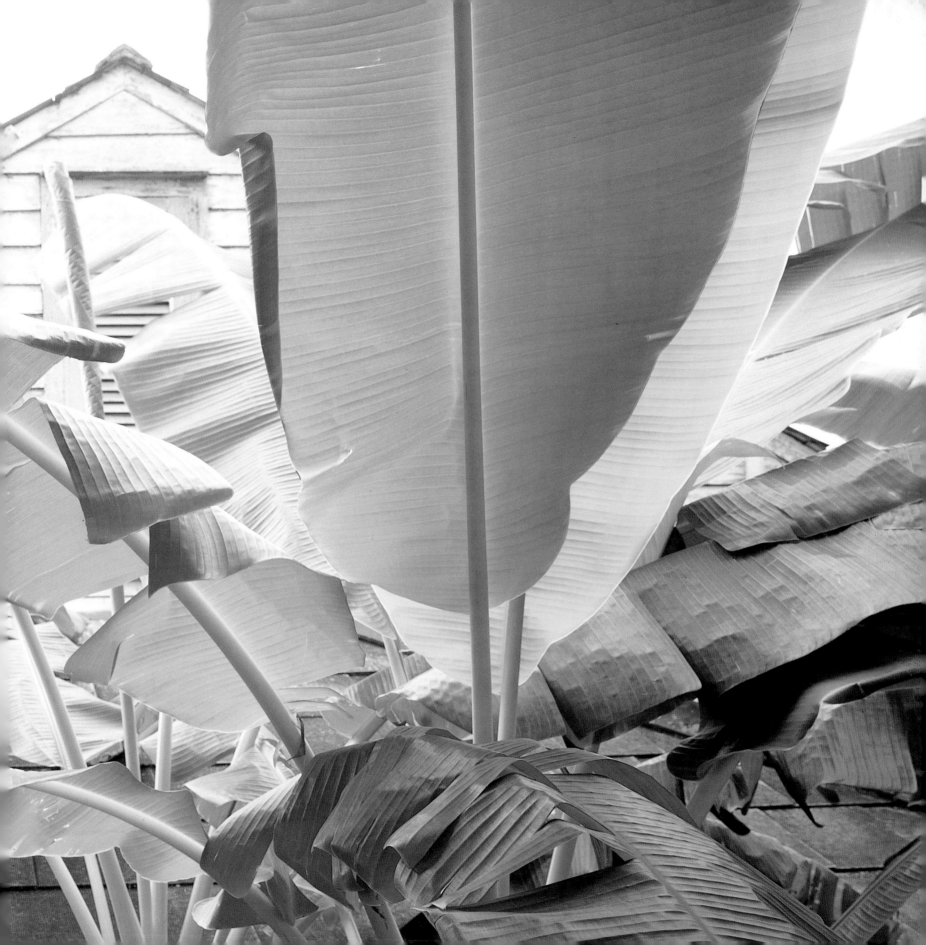

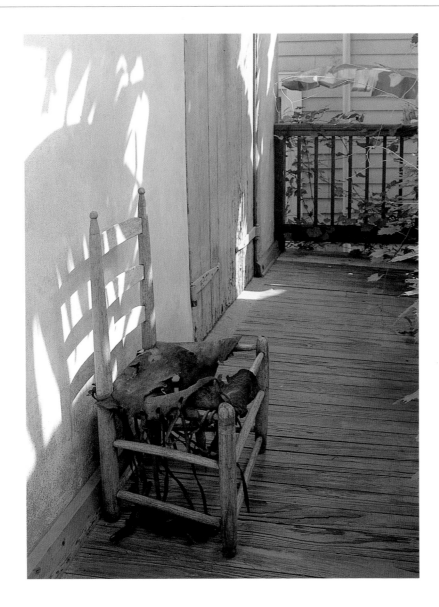

Banana leaves cast changing shadows over a second-floor gallery where an old ladderback Louisiana chair with a cowhide seat weathers away.

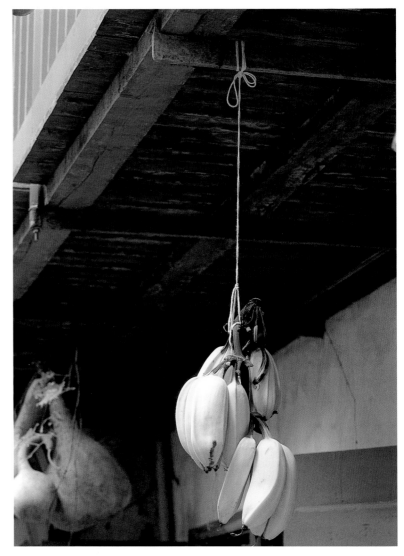

Hands of bananas hanging from the gallery's underside ripen in the peaceful sun of a quiet courtyard.

A banana stalk with its maroon bloom thrives in the lower French Quarter.

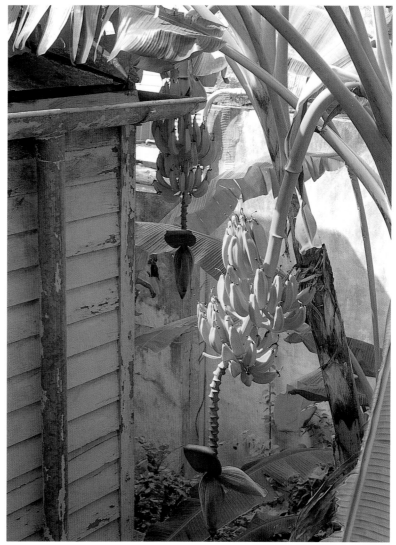

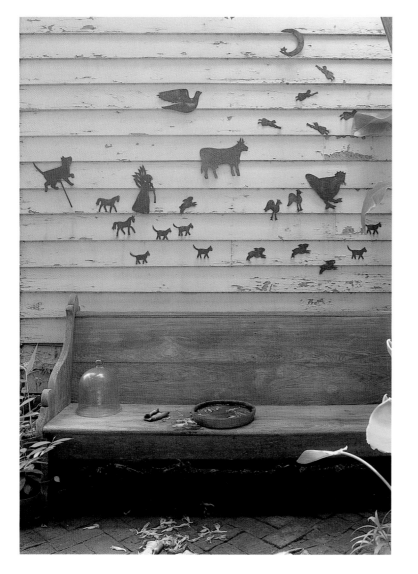

Iron Haitian cut-outs are sprinkled across a clapboard wall on one side of a courtyard garden. The cypress pew with fleur-de-lis finials came from an old black country church. The antique glass cloche, a miniature greenhouse, was used to protect young plants. Petals from a banana bloom lie sprinkled on the ground.

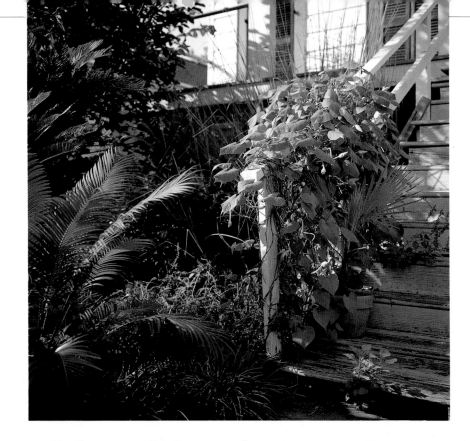

The front steps leading to the Cooper house gallery are draped with a moon-flower vine, whose large white blossoms open and release their sweet scent only at night. Vetiver grass sprouts behind it. A queen sago palm appears in the lower left.

New Orleans houses were built for Louisiana's sub-tropical climate. The side galleries of traditional houses allow ventilation and offer shelter from heat and frequent downpours. This Victorian side gallery in the Bywater neighbor-hood opens the house to the garden. The white, painted cast-iron crane in the lower left, a rescued discard, decorates the brick-paved patio-garden.

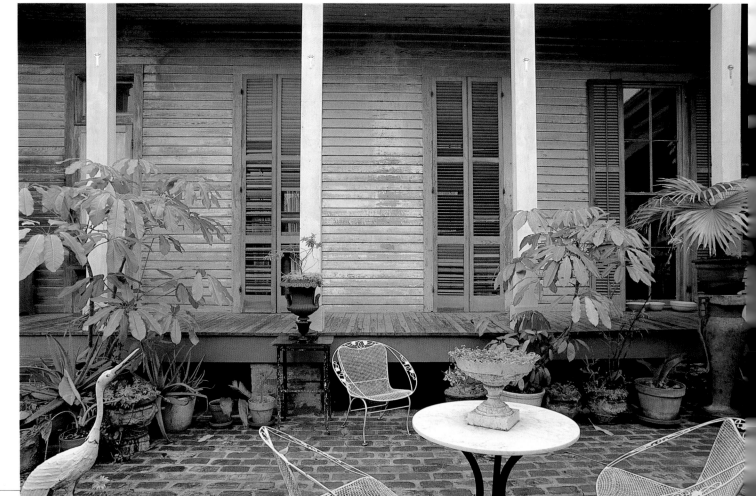

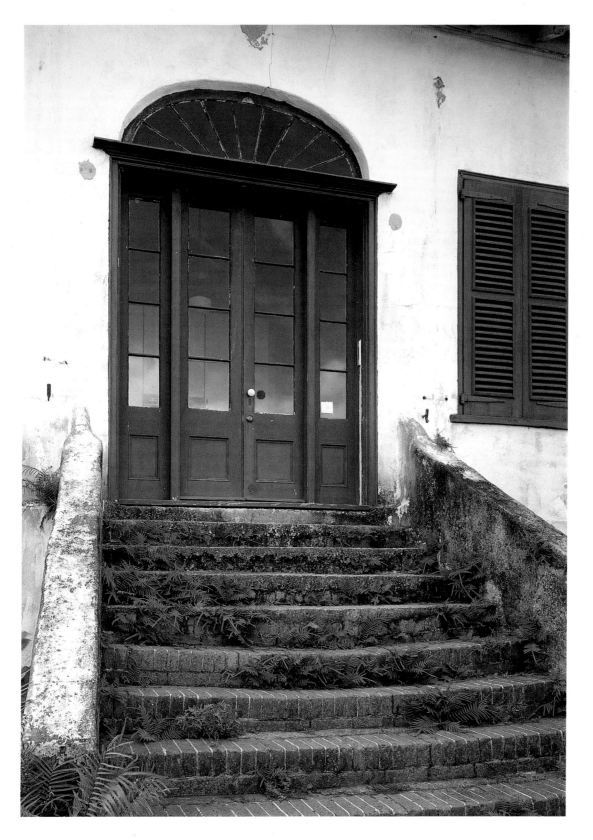

It is hard not to garden in New Orleans! As garden historian Charlotte Seidenberg notes, "If you do nothing, nature will eventually provide her own garden." Resurrection ferns, whose nickname alludes to their habit of flourishing after every rain, sprout all over New Orleans—from gutters, rooftops, chinks in walls, and the bark of old oaks. These ferns have lodged themselves in the crevices of the back steps of the Lombard house in Bywater.

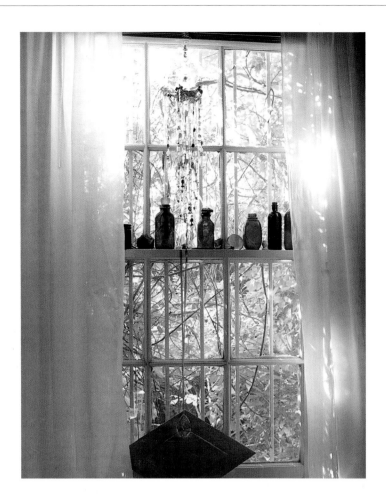

A living curtain of green screens this bedroom window and filters the light in an old house. Blue bottles in a window are supposed to keep the "haints" (ghosts) away. The mobile suspended in the window is fashioned from Mardi Gras beads.

Green is the basic color of evergreen southern Louisiana. Here potted plants are mounted on a board fence, which itself is covered by microscopic lichens that have turned the wall a soft green. An African mask peers from the lower left corner.

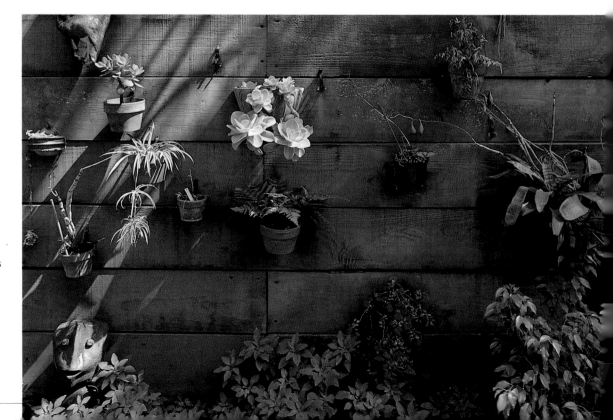

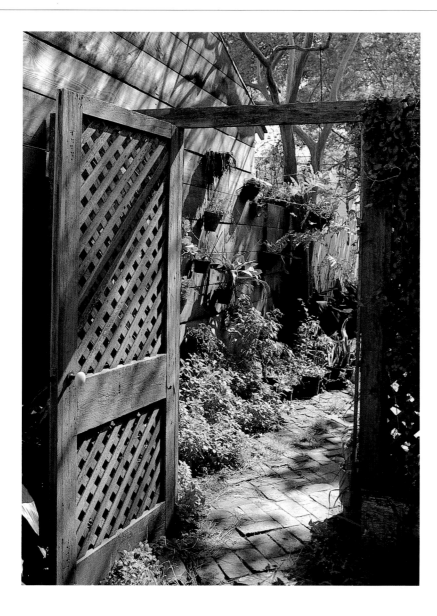

A latticed door opens into a luxuriant side garden in the Bayou Saint John neighborhood.

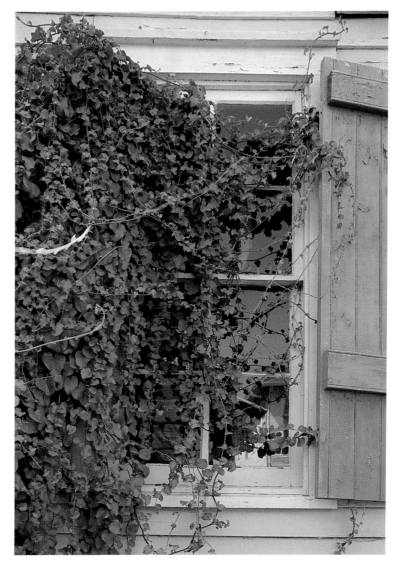

Most of New Orleans was originally a swamp, and the city gets almost six feet of rain a year! Left to itself, the environment would revert to wetlands. Here a vine engulfs the shuttered window of a house on Bayou Saint John.

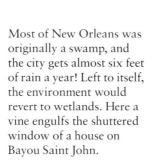

The alabaster-like beauty of a backlit elephant-ear leaf shows the dramatic effect of strong sunlight on the city's thriving vegetation. A native of Asia and the East Indies, the elephant's ear can attain giant proportions in well-watered New Orleans.

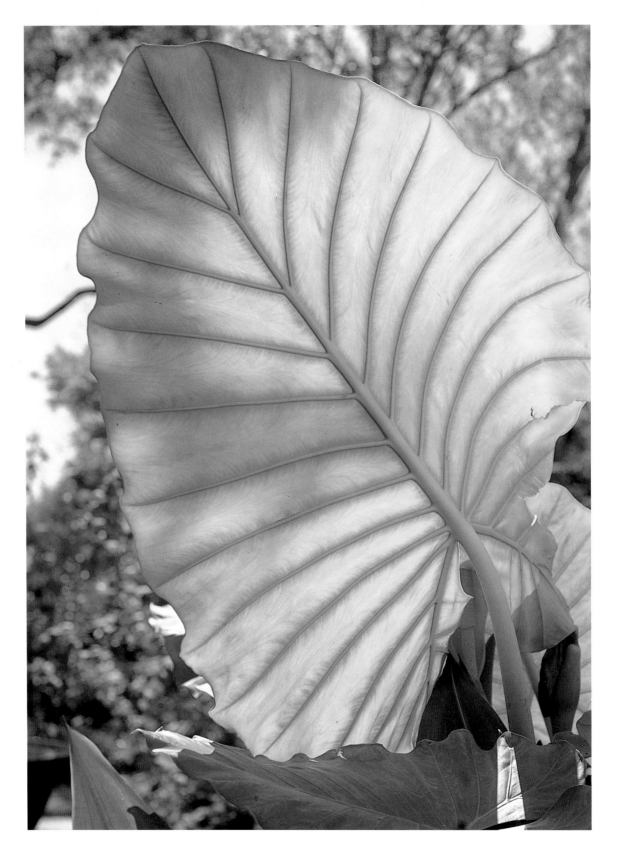

Sun-dappled elephant-ear plants flourish in Henri Schindler's downtown garden.

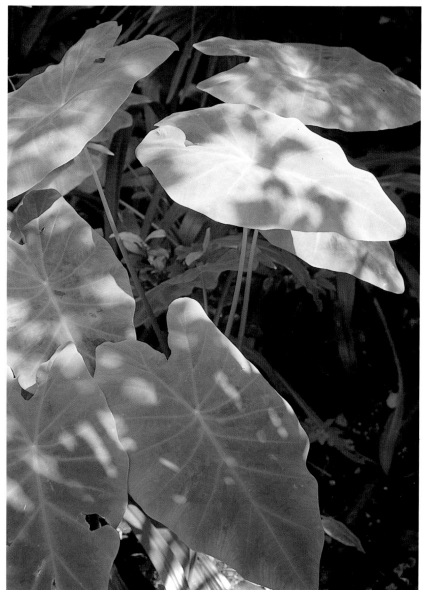

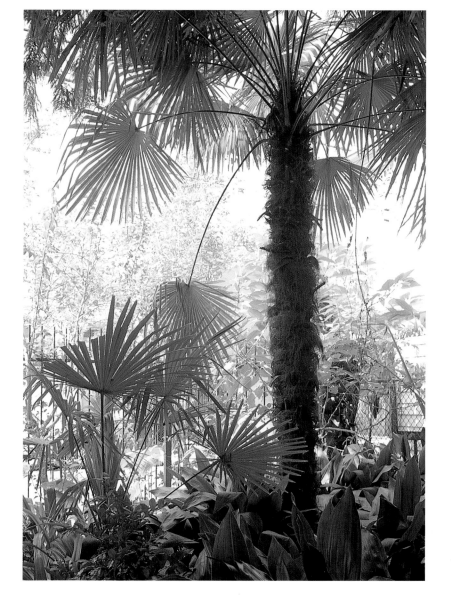

Tall windmill palms and a dense ground cover of shade-loving aspidistra screen out the street from the front garden of this Bywater cottage.

An arbor of cashmere bouquet forms an archway into a side garden. As early as 1914, George Washington Cable wrote that New Orleanian gardens were moving away from formality and toward "informal, freehand, ungeometrical gardening."

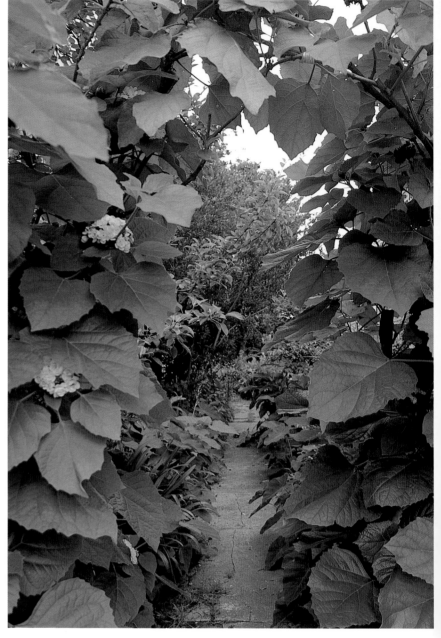

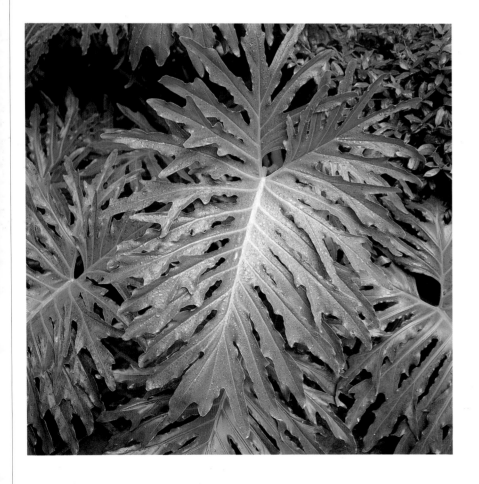

Raindrops bejewel a freshly drenched split-leaf philodendron in an Uptown garden.

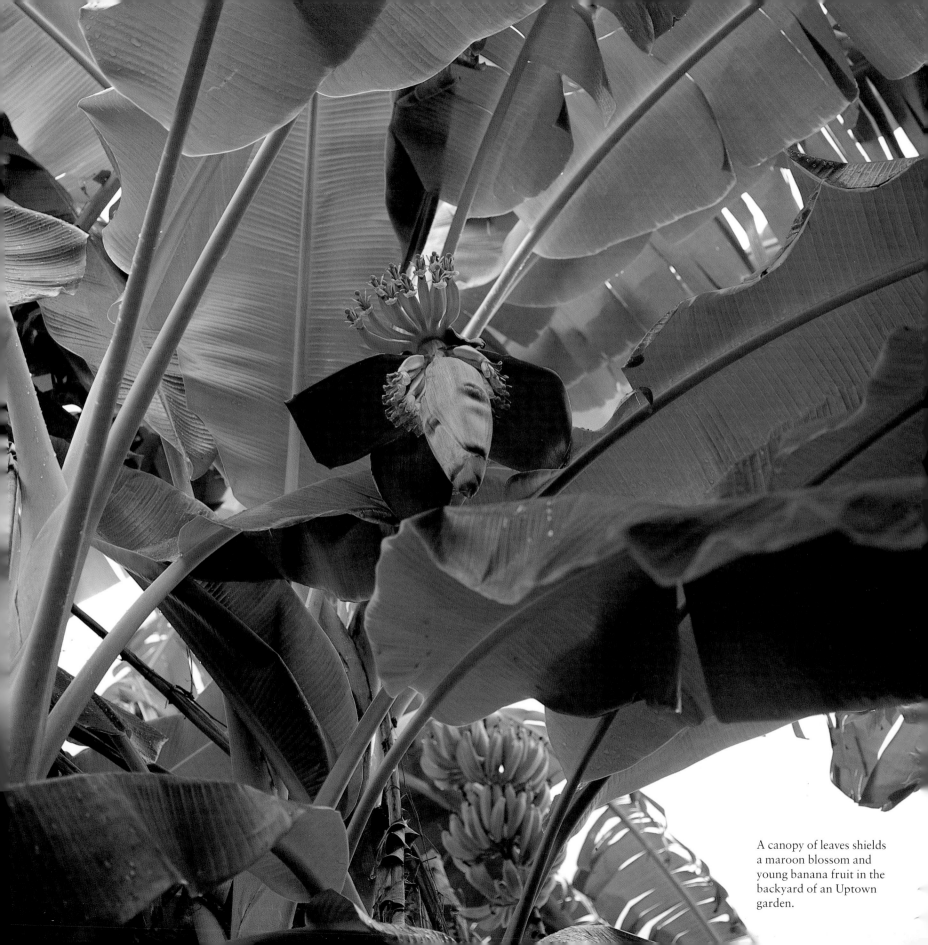

A canopy of leaves shields
a maroon blossom and
young banana fruit in the
backyard of an Uptown
garden.

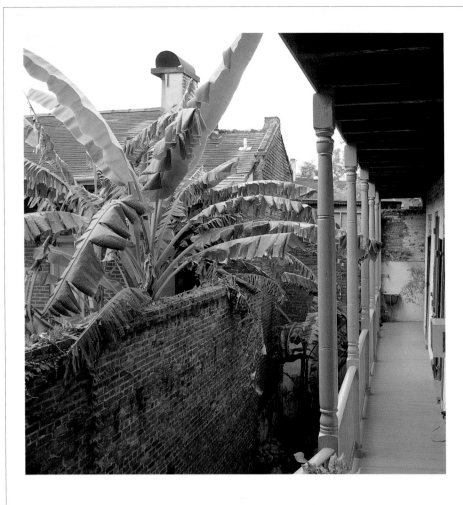

The Lala-Norris house in the French Quarter is unusual in that it was never subdivided. The second-floor gallery of the slave quarters, or dependency, gives access to several small rooms set at right angles to the main house.

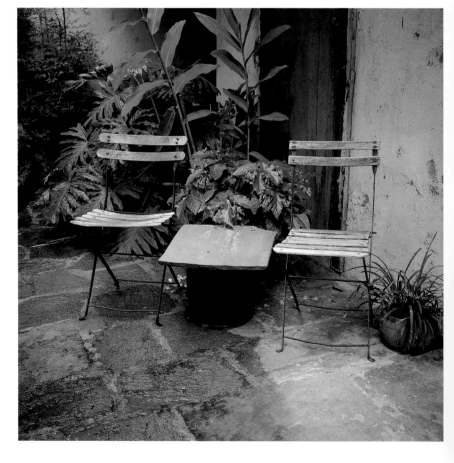

The Norrises have furnished their courtyard with iron furniture, which lasts much longer than wood in the humid climate. French garden chairs flank a small table improvised from a piece of slate set atop an upside-down English crock. A red begonia blooms behind the table. Some prized ginger grows in the far corner; its sweet white flowers attract fluttering butterflies.

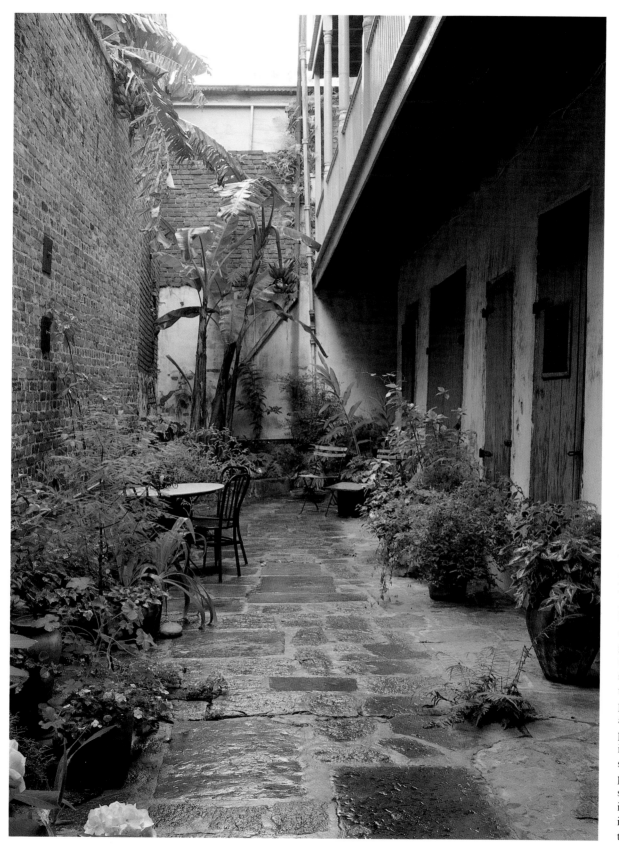

The flagstone-paved courtyard of the Lala-Norris house, designed by Alexander T. Wood and built in 1832, leads to the dependency and its ground-floor kitchen (right) and to the former stables. Betty Norris kept the bananas and ivy planted by the Lala family and added some potted plants. "I can relandscape in twenty minutes," she says, "just by moving the pots around." It takes some sophistication to live in a place without changing what made it so attractive in the first place.

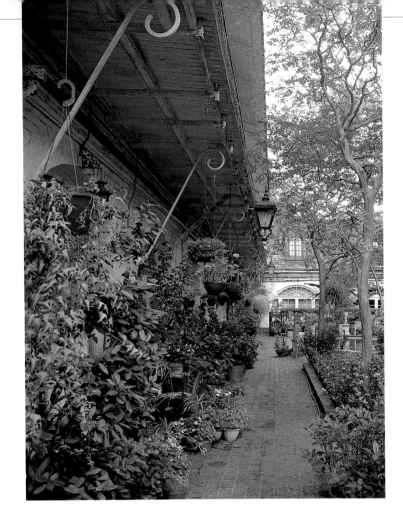

Former utilitarian spaces have been transformed into green enclaves, especially in the French Quarter. Preval's Livery Stable was built in 1834 to serve the nearby row houses of the well-to-do around the corner on Royal Street.

Blooming shell ginger from the garden fills a room with its presence and fragrance. The dark, arching foliage is a perfect counterpoint to the delicately colored, drooping blossoms. On the wall is *Sweet Afton* by Robert Gordy.

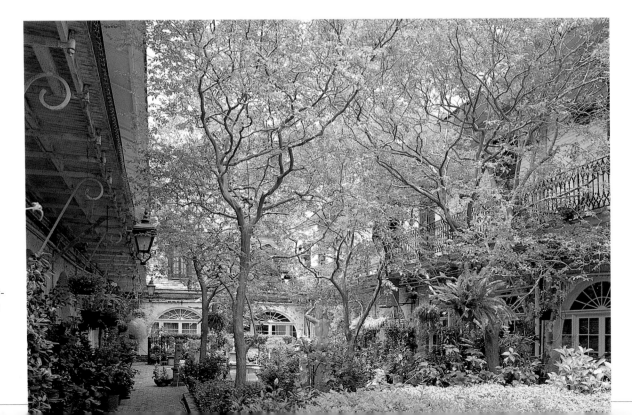

The converted Spanish Stables surround a plant-filled outdoor room that almost hides a small swimming pool.

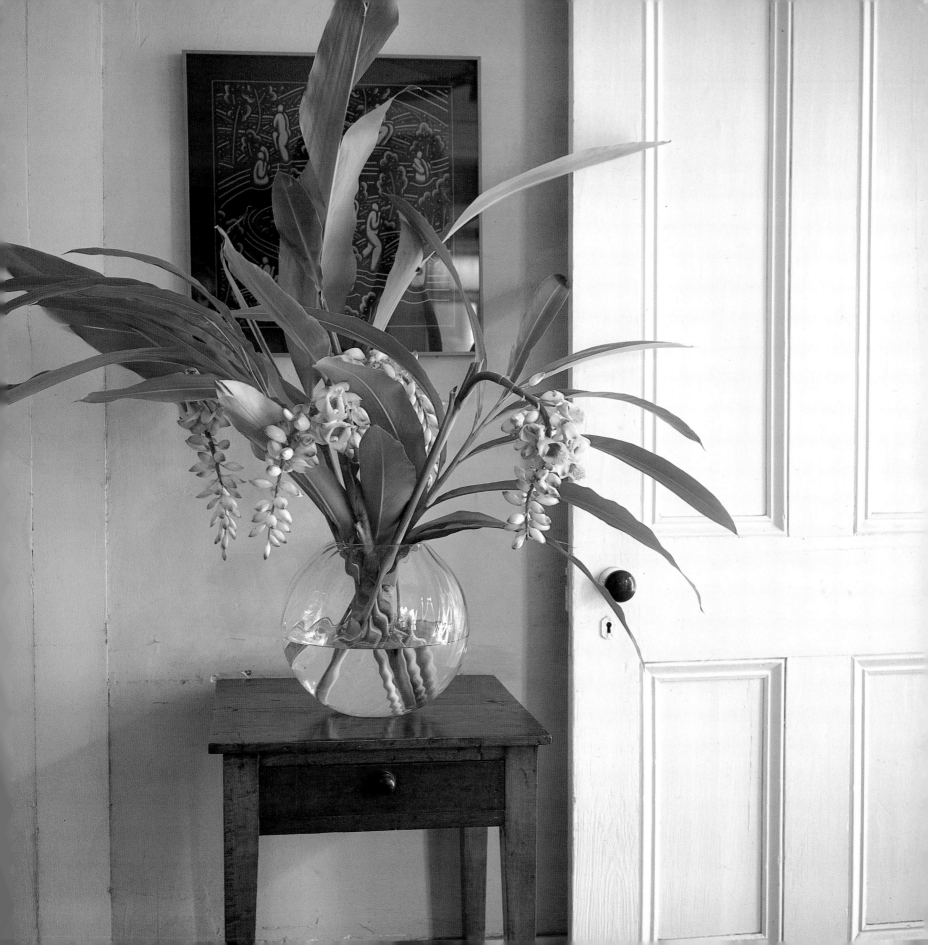

A living lattice of vines lends privacy and shade to a rear gallery in the French Quarter. A spiky aloe plant grows in the flowerpot.

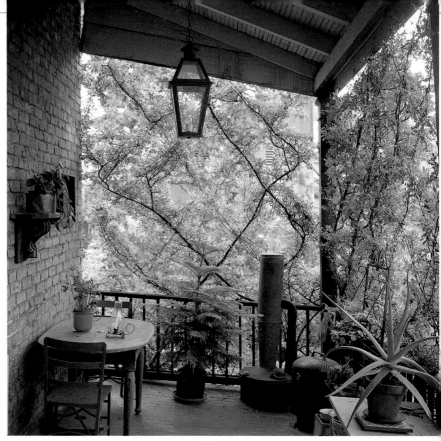

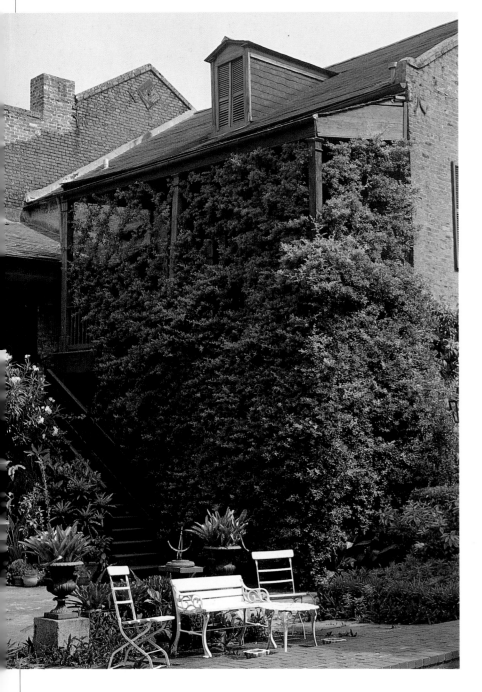

Nature and architecture fuse in this French Quarter townhouse, where a lattice of vines completely obscures the rear gallery of the Scalia-Melton house. Flamelike red and gold plants sprout from cast-iron Victorian garden urns.

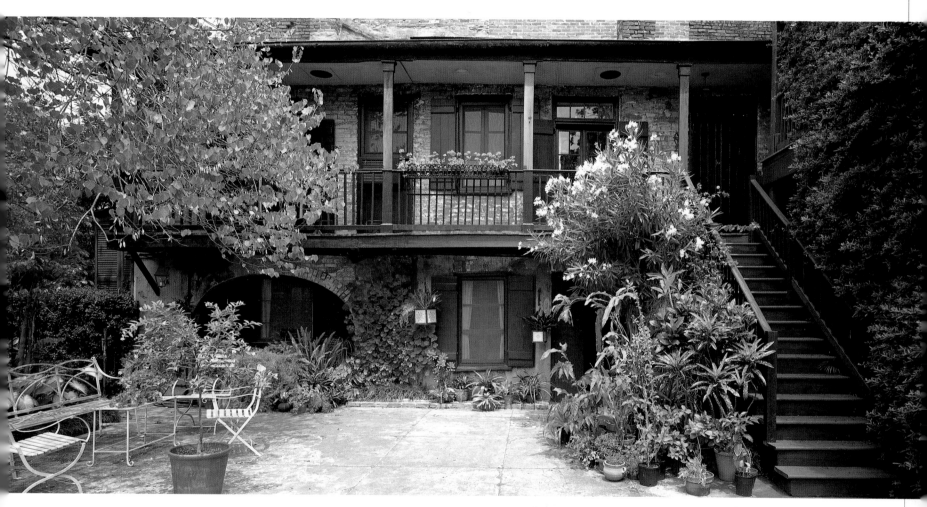

Clusters of potted plants enliven the rear court between
the Scalia-Melton house (far right) and its dependency,
or service wing, seen here in full view. The tall plant with
white blossoms is an oleander, a Mediterranean native
introduced by the Spanish via Havana in the eighteenth
century. The oleander is the city's official flower.

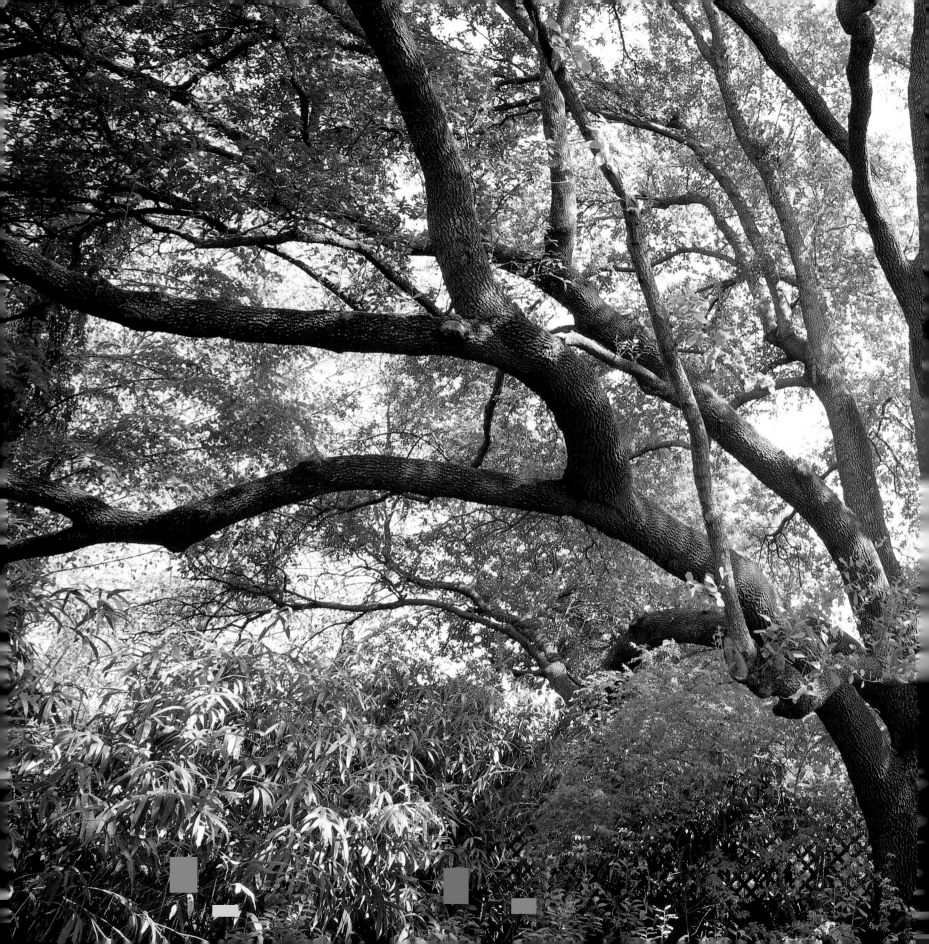

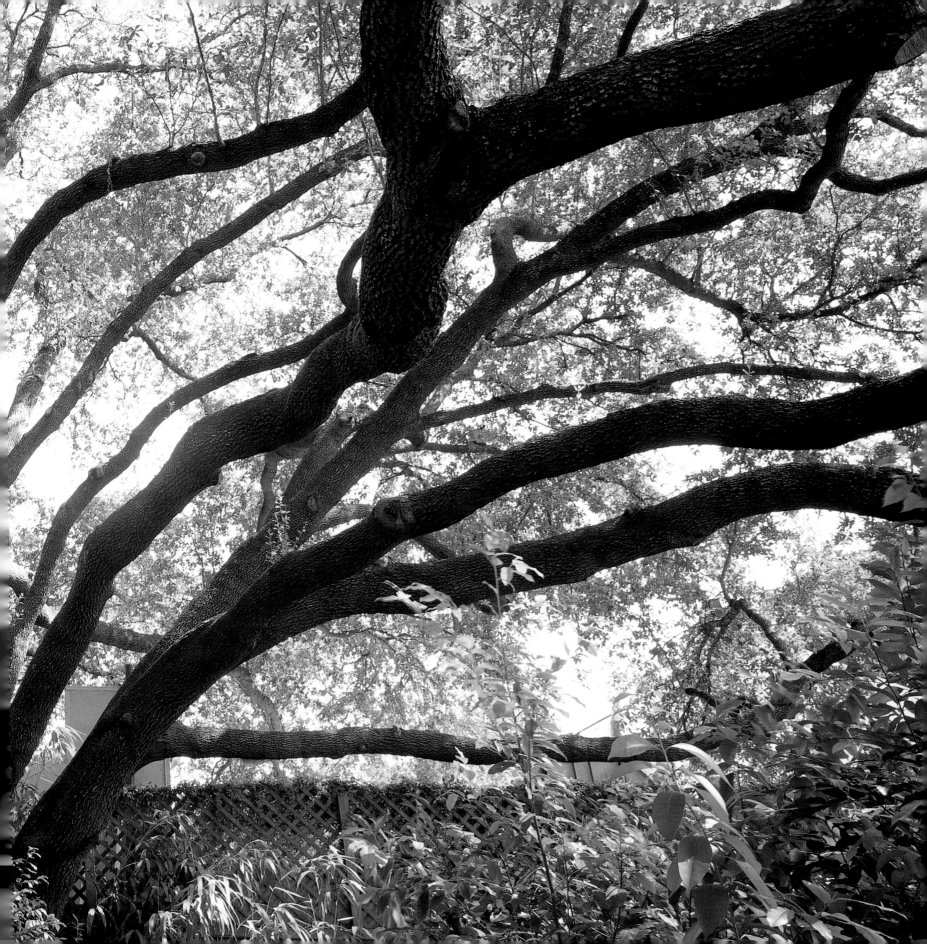

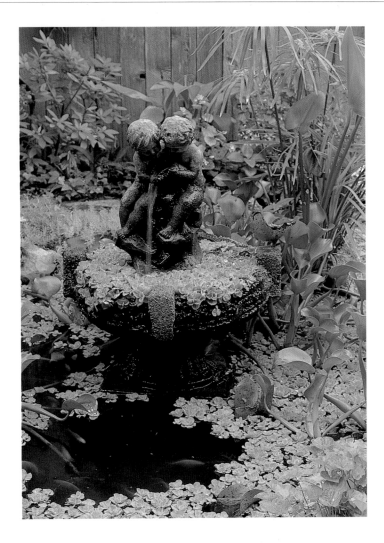

A garden sculpture of two boys holding a fish pours water into a small pond in a Bywater back garden. Vivid fish sparkle in the dark water beneath floating water hyacinths.

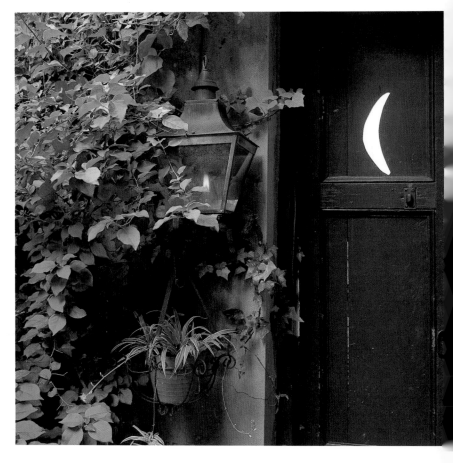

Preceding Pages:
The Southern live oak is the great tree of New Orleans. Its native range is the coastal plain from Virginia to Florida and along the Gulf Coast into Mexico. The trees' strong, thick trunks and broad-spreading canopies are memorable elements of the Louisiana landscape. This fine specimen reaches up to the sunny sky in a backyard in Faubourg Marigny.

Intense magenta bougainvillea drapes an old wall in this lush garden. A native of South America, this showy evergreen vine is one more living link with the tropics. Gas lamps are something of a New Orleanian signature; the crescent cut-out in the door is a more literal symbol of the Crescent City.

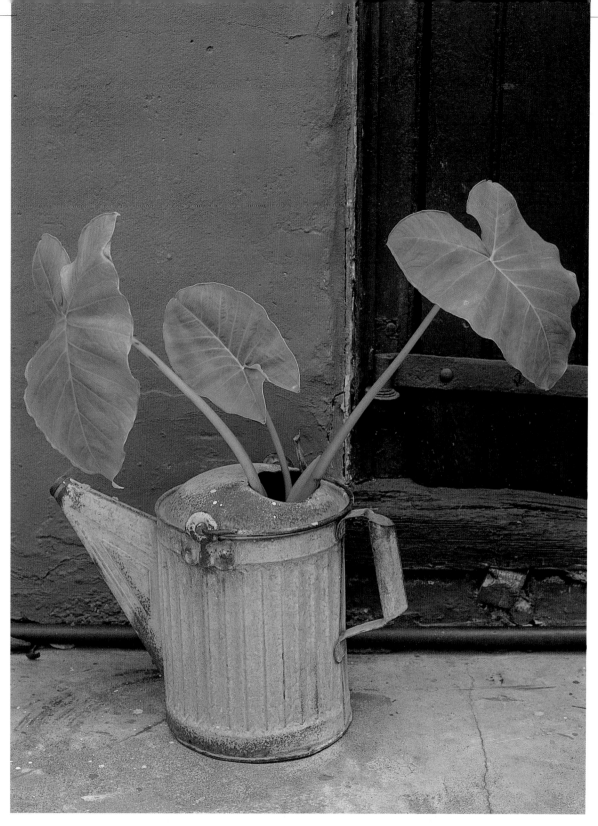

New Orleanians have a knack for effortlessly harmo-
nizing the simplest things. Here a few elephant ear leaves
in an old watering can create an elegant effect.

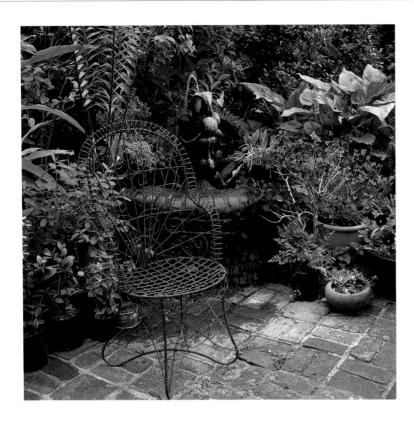

Horticulturalist and landscape contractor R. J. Dykes III believes that gardens should not only be looked at but used. In the back garden of his French Quarter cottage, plants from Central America join old New Orleanian plants, some taken as cuttings from an abandoned Louisiana plantation garden. A fountain sits atop an old well.

Gardens have become looser and less formal in contemporary New Orleans. The flagstone path in R. J. Dykes III's back garden penetrates what seems like a tropical jungle only barely under control. "My garden just happened," he says. Just a few years ago this was a barren space with an old board shanty. When carting debris to the city dump, Dykes spotted old discarded flagstones that once paved city streets and sidewalks. They now pave his *jardin sauvage*, which began as a vegetable garden with tomatoes, peppers, bananas, and herbs. The addition of subtropical plants created the lush oasis that flourishes today.

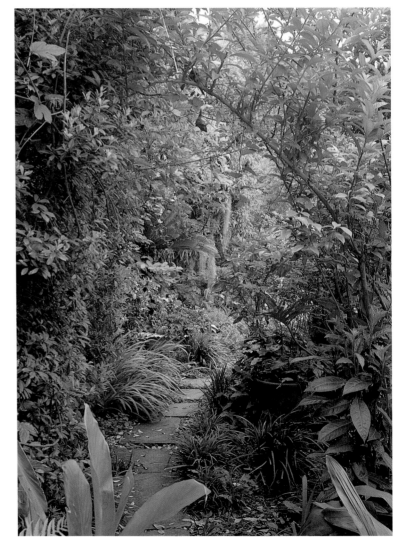

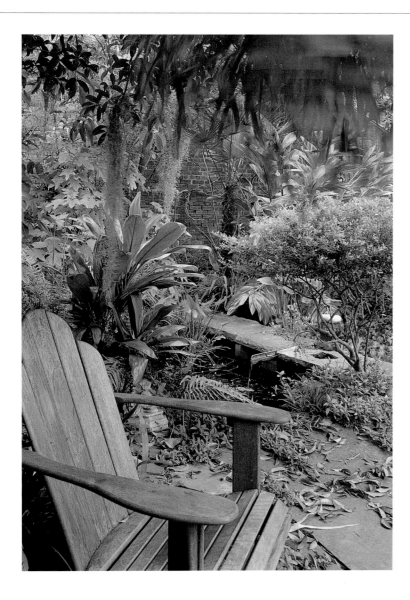

A teak Adirondack chair mellows to gray in the humid climate of New Orleans, and gray Spanish moss hangs from a tea olive. Dykes experiments with new plants at home before introducing them into his clients' gardens.

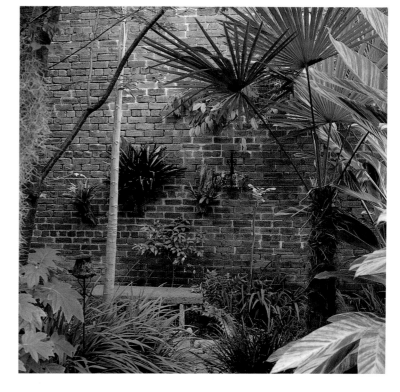

The brick wall of the neighboring house is hung with bromeliads. A windmill palm stands to the right; the yellow and green leaves are variegated ginger. Despite occasional freezes, subtropical vegetation is increasingly popular in New Orleans. Gardens have gone from the traditional evergreen plants and obligatory azaleas of a generation ago to more exotic Caribbean material.

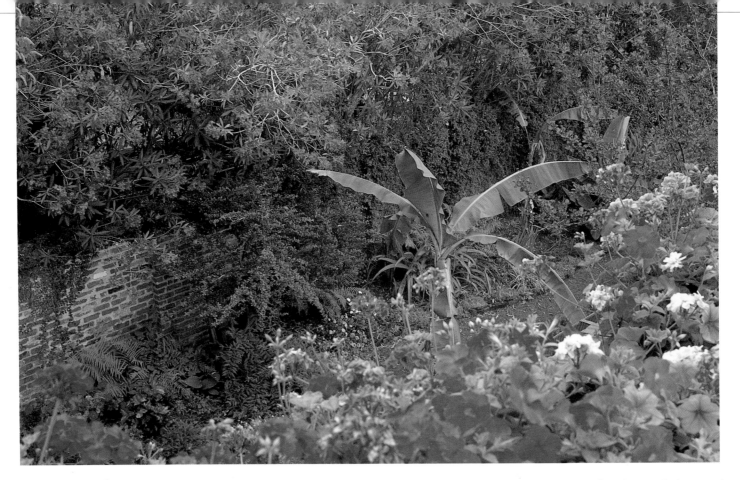

Petunias, ivy geraniums, oleanders, and, draping the wall, fragrant jasmine all flourish in the color-splashed world of this University District garden. Zen master Robert Livingston works almost daily in this labor-intensive, organic garden. "I make it up as I go along," he says. "I pay attention to details and re-use elements. I concentrate on the garden."

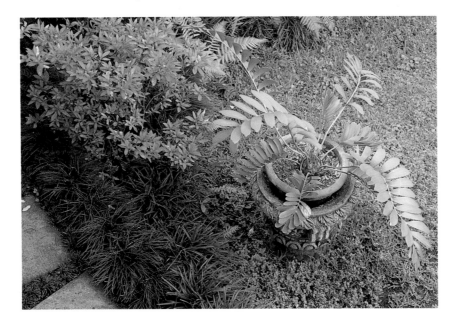

A cardboard palm reaches out from a Mexican stone urn in the Livingston garden. Monkey grass carpets the ground. Artist Elizabeth Polchow Livingston uses plants from this garden, and her Zen practice, as inspiration for her paintings.

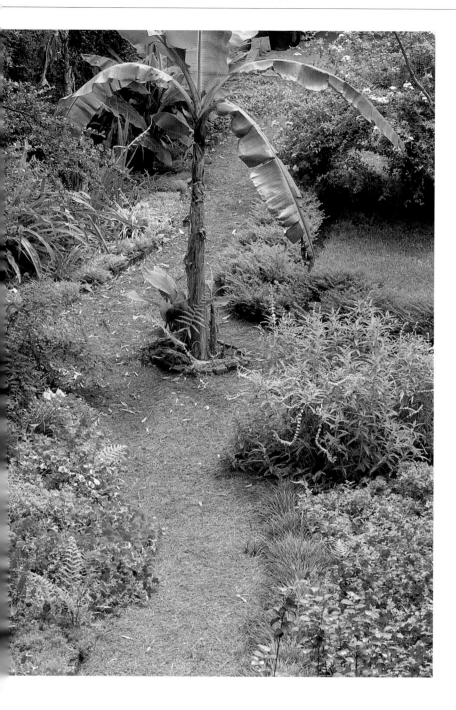

The Livingstons' Uptown garden seems far from the city and has a tropical flair. What was once a driveway is now a pine-needle-strewn path lined with Mexican heather. A Hawaiian banana tree, pink petunias, pansies, purple Mexican salvia, and stella d'oro day lilies flourish here.

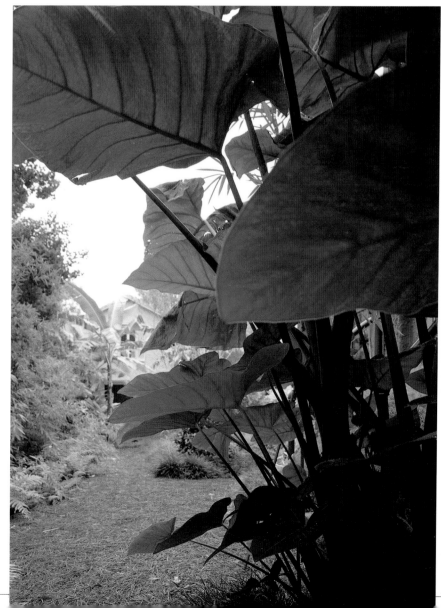

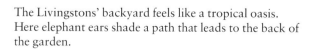

The Livingstons' backyard feels like a tropical oasis. Here elephant ears shade a path that leads to the back of the garden.

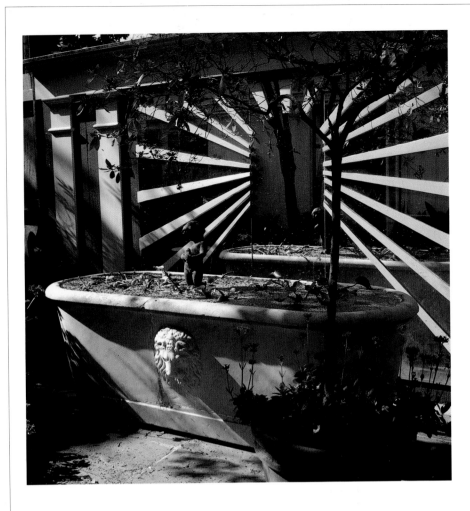

Mirrors mounted on the wall and converging boards that seem to recede into the distance create an illusion of depth in this narrow side "patio" in the Garden District. A Florentine marble watering trough that once graced the Harvey plantation is filled with water hyacinths and is alive with goldfish. The traditional plantings include palmettos, cane, and aspidistra.

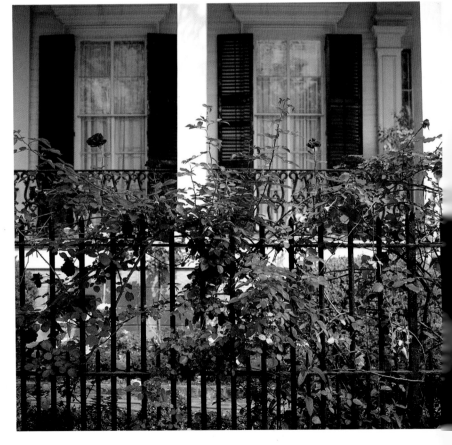

The blood red roses, black iron, and white columns of this house on elegant Prytania Street epitomize the Old South. The Garden District was formed in the 1820s when the Livaudais plantation was subdivided into large plots. When wealthy American and English businessmen moved upriver away from the dense Creole city, they built large houses here set in spacious gardens. The elite Garden District is a treasury of fine 1840s and 1850s antebellum architecture.

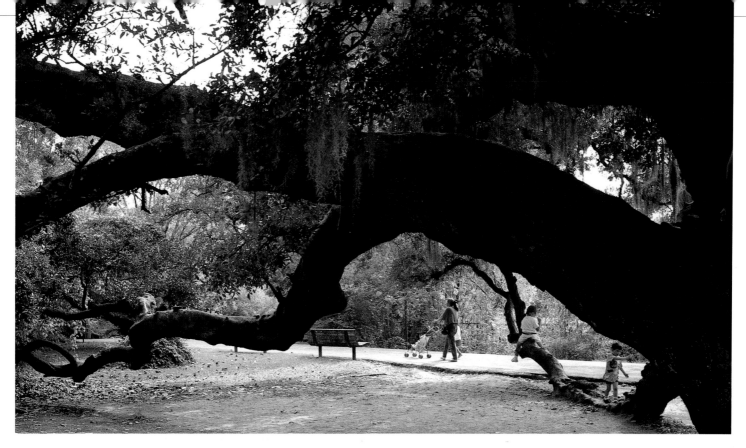

The great, heavy limb of an ancient southern live oak frames a young family enjoying Audubon Park. The city purchased the old Foucher plantation in 1871, and the park's wedge shape preserves the way the French crown originally subdivided the land. When the World's Industrial and Cotton Centennial Exposition was held in the park in 1884–85, it was embellished with a "profusion of tropical plants, flowers, shrubbery, and trees." The plants introduced for the fair influenced the way New Orleanians landscaped their gardens.

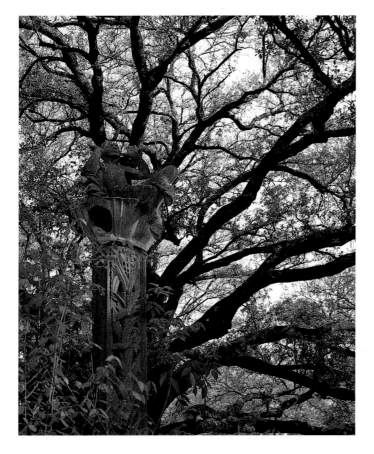

The sprawling branches of an ancient live oak in City Park forms a backdrop for sculptor Enrique Alfarez's *Satyr* (1930s). Lakeside City Park on Bayou Saint John was once part of the Allard plantation. New Orleans' parks are her most democratic verdant enclaves, and a satyr under an oak seems happily appropriate to the city.

CHAPTER FOUR

Cultural Revelry

Carnival is a butterfly of winter, whose last mad flight of Mardi Gras forever ends his glory. Another season is the glory of another butterfly, and the tattered, scattered fragments of rainbow wings are in turn the record of his day.

PERRY YOUNG, *The Mistick Krewe: Chronicles of Comus and his Kin,* 1931

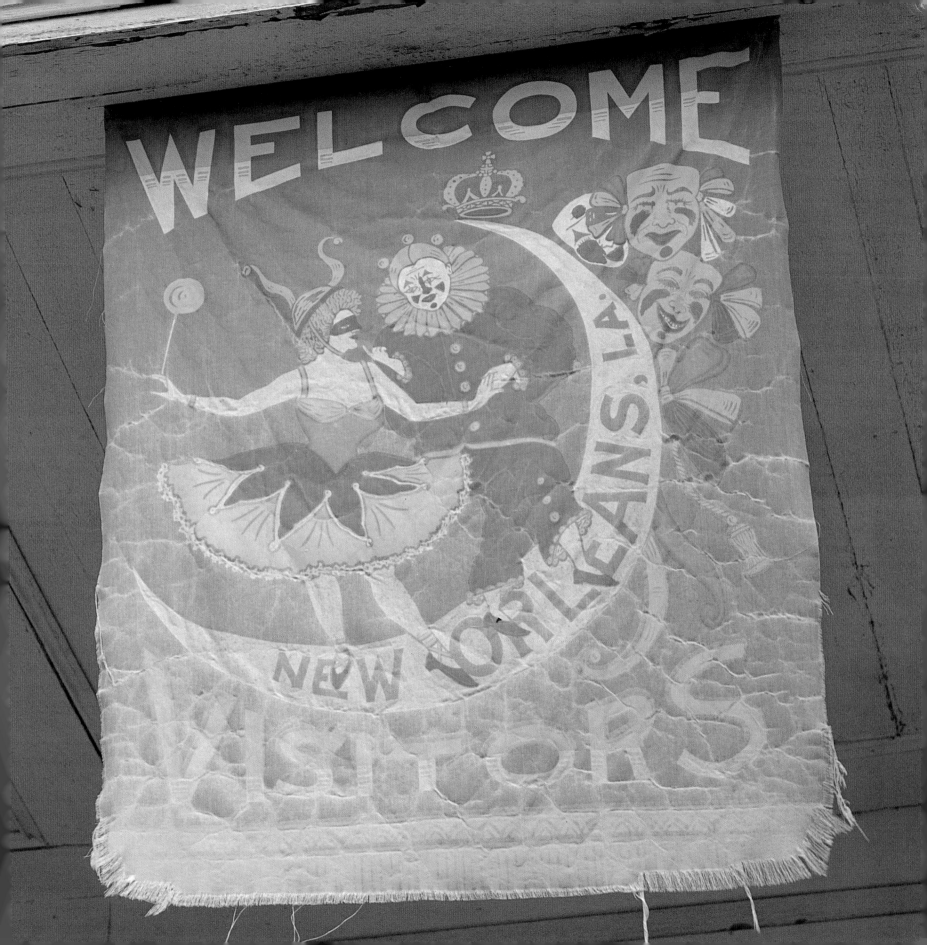

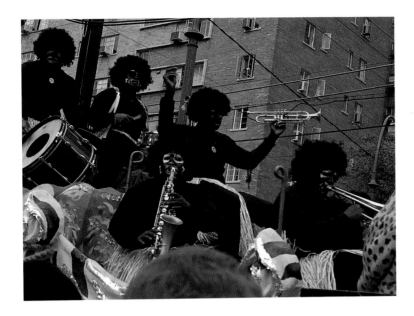

The Zulu Social Aid and Pleasure Club reverses even the Mardi Gras ritual of reversal. If the regal figure of Rex governs Carnival, so King Zulu in blackface mimics and mocks him. The first King Zulu, William Story, appeared on Mardi Gras in 1909 wearing a lard-can crown and carrying a banana-stalk scepter. Here a Zulu float of Afro-American musicians in blackface parades on Mardi Gras in 1992.

Preceding Page:
"Welcome Visitors! New Orleans, La." A civic culture with an enduring strain of revelry makes New Orleans a most distinctive American city. This gay banner of a masked ballerina and a clown in whiteface dancing atop the blue crescent of the Mississippi River was designed by Duvalle Decorators. Marc Cooper salvaged it when a Magazine Street flag and pennant shop went out of business, and he silk-screened more copies for friends. Citywide public street masking and private masquerade balls are old New Orleans customs. Make-believe is a cult in the Crescent City, and it is happily appropriate that a tattered yet festive banner depicting the fantasy of masking should greet guests at this New Orleans home.

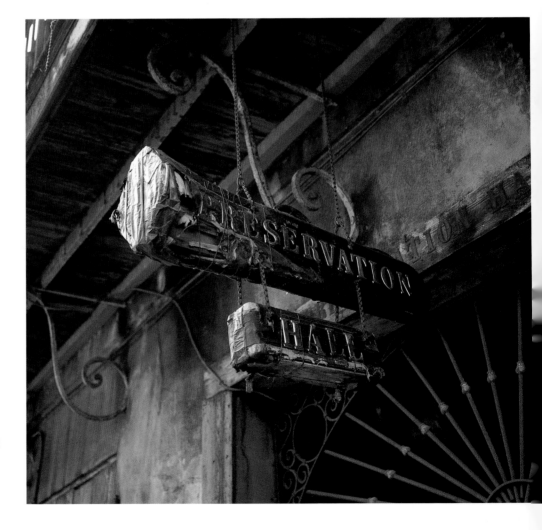

New Orleans is justifiably proud of her living tradition of musical invention. In this place West African, Caribbean, French, Spanish, Italian, German, and Anglo-American influences have mixed and swirled to create joyous and sorrowful music, both sacred and profane. The Society for the Preservation of Traditional New Orleans Jazz was formed in 1961 and presents jazzmen of the old school at its Preservation Hall on St. Peter Street in the French Quarter. Battered old instrument cases make its evocative sign.

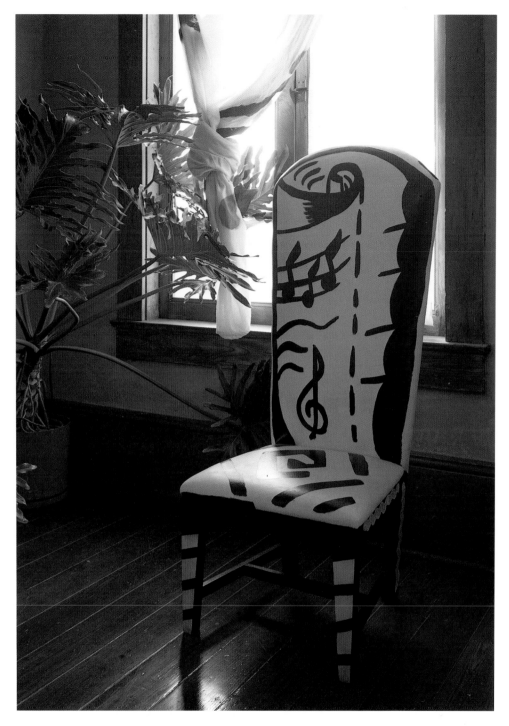

Music is an especially fertile influence on the visual arts in New Orleans today. This piece is one of Daymien Persley's *Musical Chairs*. Persley is a member of Young Aspirations/Young Artists, an artistic and educational guild that encourages the creative spirit of New Orleans. "In all my pieces I mix the mind with matter," says Persley. "For me, Peace, Love, and Happiness, and freedom of expression to everyone. Let it be a way of life."

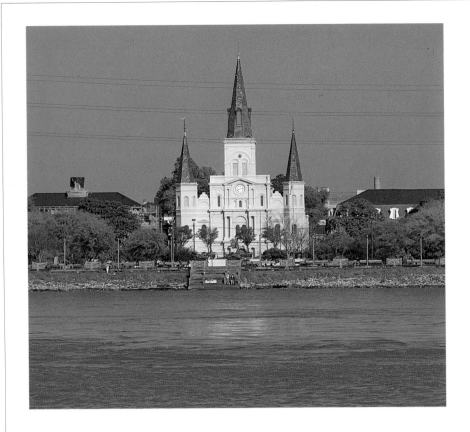

Both the spirit and the flesh find strong expression in New Orleans. After almost three centuries, pride of place still belongs to the Roman Catholic Saint Louis Cathedral, which looks across the old *place d'armes* (Jackson Square) toward the Mississippi River and the rising sun. The first church on this site, a rude structure of wood and adobe, was erected about 1720. It was replaced with a brick church that was engulfed, along with most of the city, in the great fire of Good Friday, 1788. The foundation of the present church was laid in 1789 with funds advanced by Don Andres Almonester y Roxas, and the building was dedicated as a cathedral in 1794. After its central tower fell in 1850, the present facade was designed by J. N. B. de Pouilly. Almonester is buried before the high altar, and every Saturday mass is offered for his soul and the church bells toll at sunset in his memory. The principal side altar of the cathedral is dedicated to Notre Dame de Prompt Secours, the patron saint of New Orleans. Every Wednesday evening, the congregation offers this prayer to her: "Hasten then to our help, as you once saved our beloved city from destruction by fire and from invasion by an alien foe," a weekly recollection of the 1815 Battle of New Orleans.

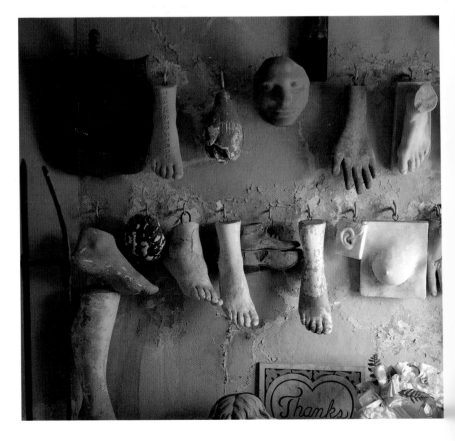

Religion seems earthier, more emotional, almost animist, in New Orleans. A side room of the chapel at Saint Roch Cemetery is filled with ex-votos, representations of various parts of the body, left by grateful believers whose prayers have been answered. Saint Roch chapel and cemetery were erected by Father Peter Leonard Thevis, a German-American priest, after the yellow fever epidemic of 1868 spared his parish. Saint Roch the pilgrim, with his staff, sores, and faithful dog, is remembered for his selfless nursing of plague sufferers in medieval Europe. Some New Orleanians still come to this place seeking cures.

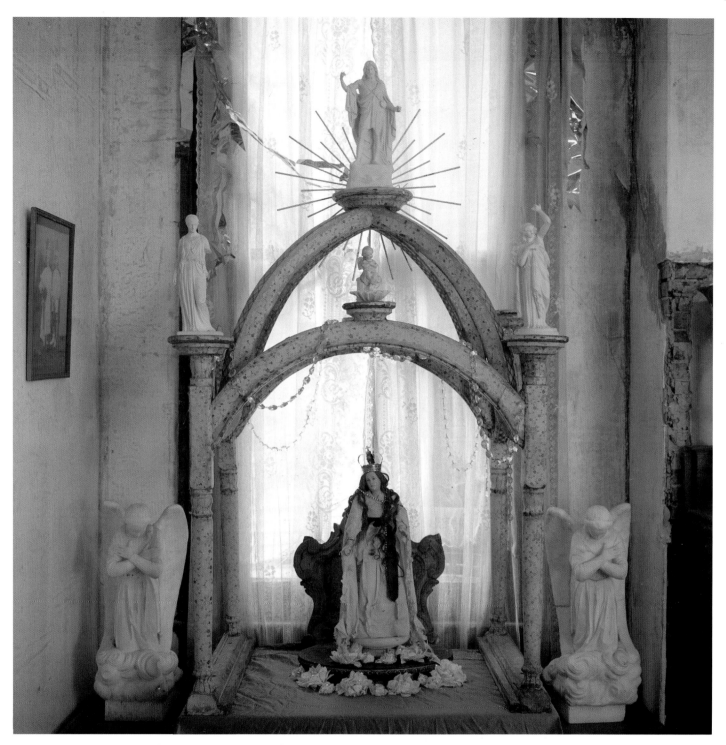

The Catholic tradition of home altars continues in contemporary New Orleans. The Gothic framework of this home altar in Bywater came from Biaccio Montalbano's Saint Joseph's Day altar in the Roma Room of his St. Philip Street delicatessen in the French Quarter. With it Marcus Fraser created this symmetrical and eclectic assemblage. The central statue with human hair is the Virgin Mary, who stands on a cloud of rhinestone lotuses. Flanking her are two marble angels in attitudes of supplication. At the apex is Saint John the Baptist. Two white figures standing like finials are neo-Grec bisque figurines representing Beauty. The painted wood canopy once supported an inscription that read "This is the only key to the fountain of grace today."

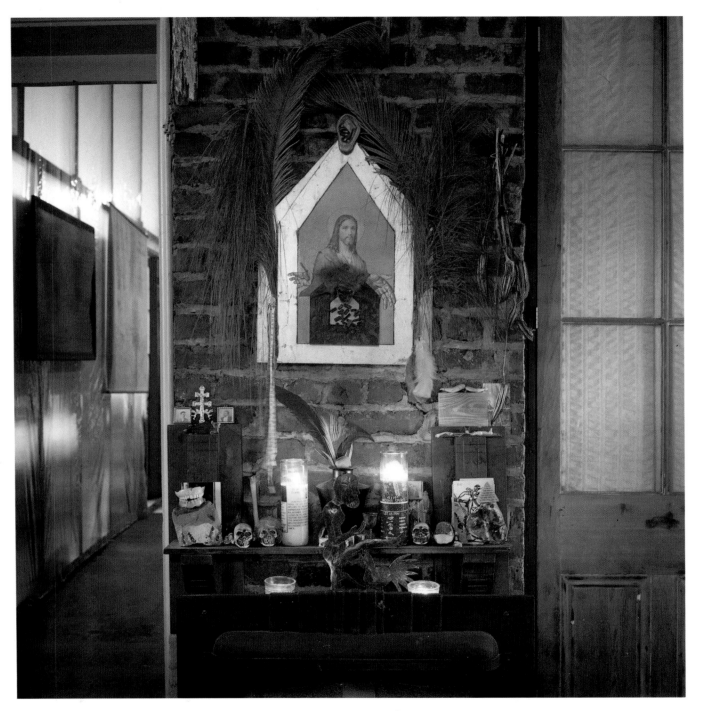

Sculptor Elizabeth Shannon has built an altar in her live-work space to which she brings various given, made, and found objects. Fascinated by the role of sacrifice in various communities, she attends the Black Hawk rituals at a New Orleans Spiritualist church each September.

Black Hawk represents the watchman, or guardian, and links Afro-Caribbean spirituality with Native American images. The ear attached to the frame of a lithograph of Jesus seems to ask that prayers at this altar be heard by all gods.

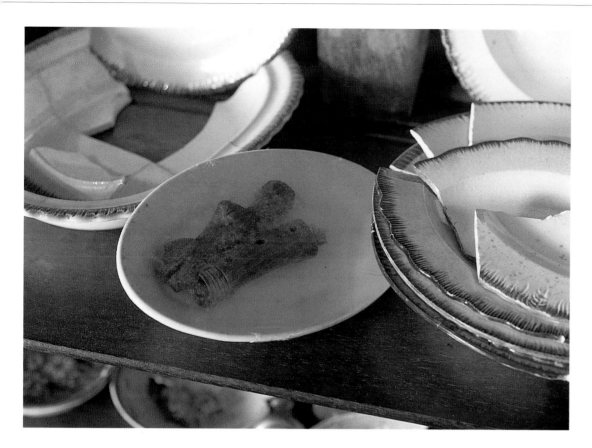

West African slaves brought the snake oracle and other beliefs to the Caribbean and colonial Louisiana. The Mande word for charm, "gris-gris," took root in Louisiana, and the religious practices of the Fon and Yoruba were also important. The name "voodoo" was given to their belief in sorcery and in the power of charms and fetishes. The object on this plate, excavated in the Faubourg Marigny, is thought to be a voodoo charm.

Louisiana voodoo, unlike that in Haiti, was dominated by women. Its most famous practitioner was Marie Laveau, a mulatto hairdresser who was born in 1783 and died in 1881. Some say she is buried in Saint Louis Cemetery No. 2, but popular legend claims she is buried here, in the Glapion family tomb in Saint Louis Cemetery No. 1. Known as the "wishing tomb," visitors etch red X's on its whitewashed surface with bits of brick. Marie Laveau herself always claimed to be a good Catholic. Lest death be too solemn, someone has decorated the tomb with plastic Mardi Gras beads.

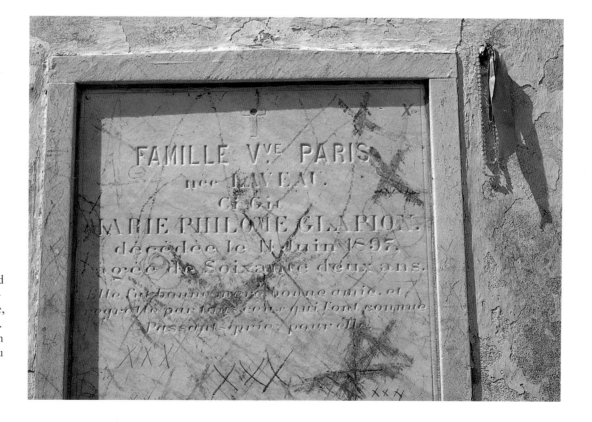

Boo at the Zoo is a present-day Halloween happening in Audubon Park. Here a young girl in a white evening gown confronts a giant spider web. Practice for Uptown society?

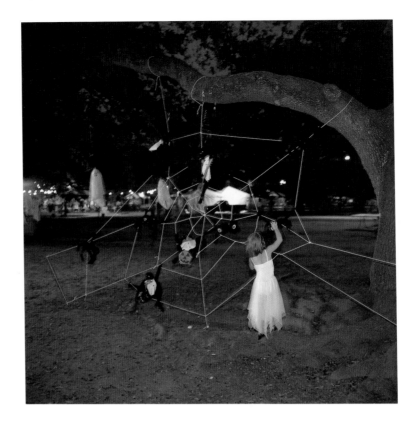

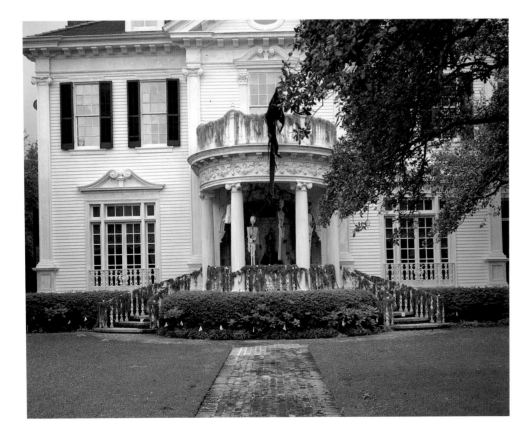

Even mansions sometimes "dress up" in New Orleans. This stately early twentieth-century Georgian Colonial Revival home on St. Charles Avenue Uptown is decked with spooky Spanish moss, small white skulls, and several hanging skeletons. It's hard to imagine grand houses in other American cities "masking" with such enthusiasm.

Halloween in New Orleans is another occasion to mask. Here two girls haunt Audubon Park as Death and the Senorita, although most New Orleanian girls seem to prefer the costumes of divas, princesses, and queens. Many adult residents will tell you proudly that more ballgowns and tails are sold in New Orleans than in New York City.

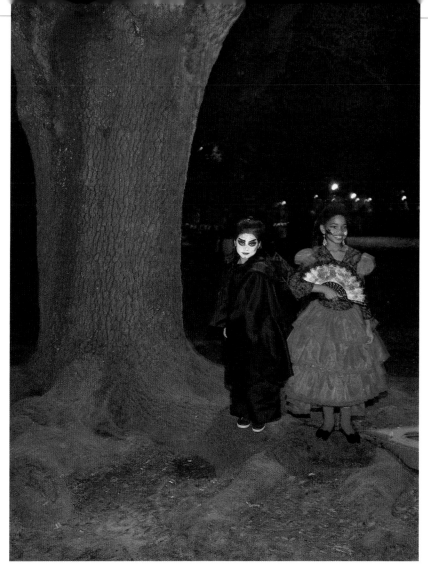

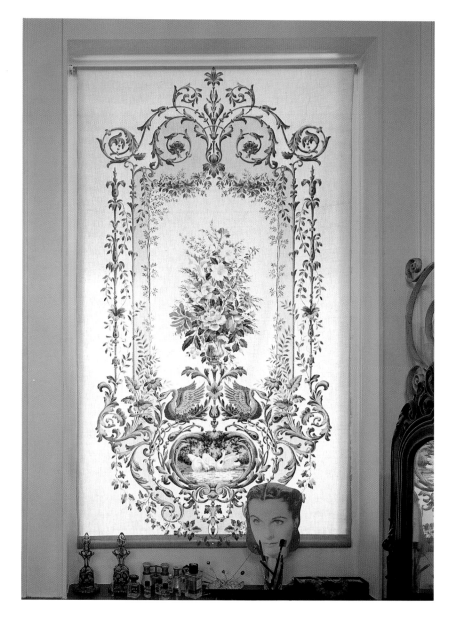

Masks and fanciful decoration seem to pop up everywhere in New Orleans. Propped up in front of this hand-painted Victorian shade in the Garden District is a Scarlett O'Hara paper fan. Now a bathroom, this room was built as a private family chapel.

New Orleanians love art and continually embellish their homes. This mural of Saint Francis of Assisi preaching to the birds was painted in 1989 by Scott de Montluzin in the hallway of an Uptown 1860s Greek Revival house. To make the mural look old, some plaster was left unpainted.

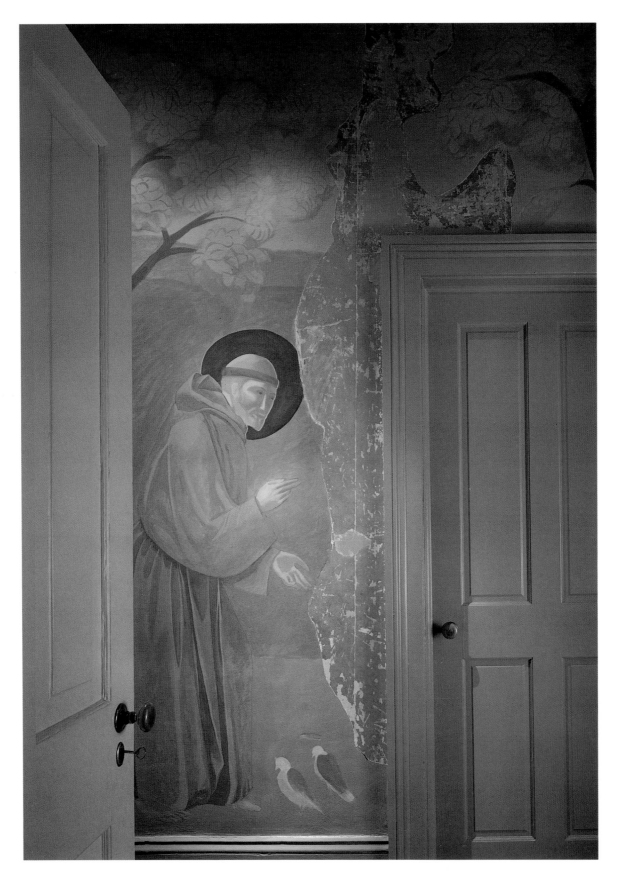

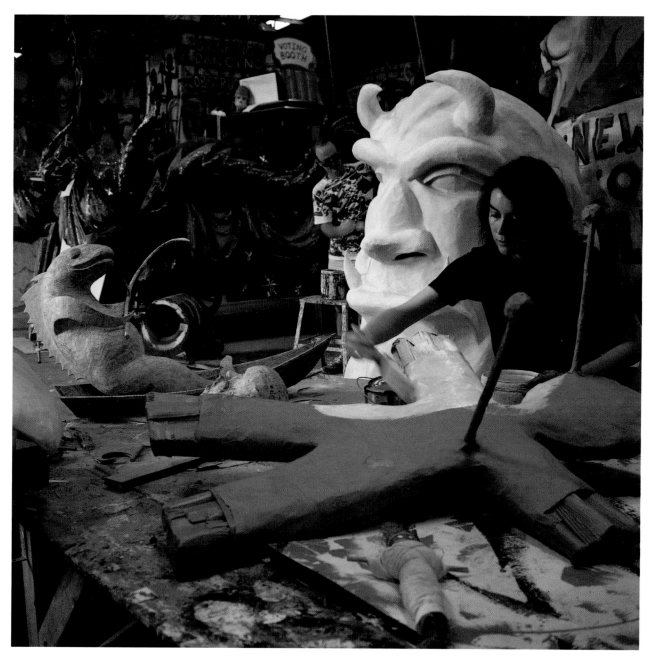

Art serves both the sacred and the profane in New
Orleans. Here Lisa Browning paints a giant voodoo doll
for a Mardi Gras krewe (Carnival organization) in the
Royal Artists studio. Behind her Mike Smith paints the
head of a horned beast for another krewe.

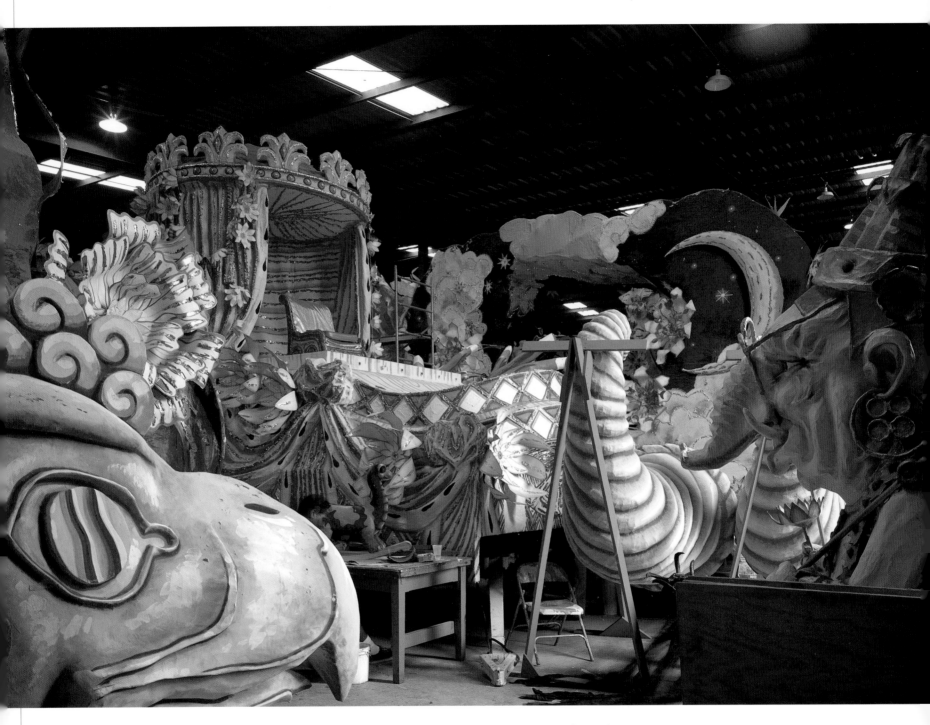

Waiting in the wings. It takes almost a year to plan and prepare for Mardi Gras. Here a solitary worker (can you spot him?) toils in a krewe den where extravagant, highly colored floats are built on wooden-wheeled carriages a hundred years old. The empty throne awaits its king-for-a-day.

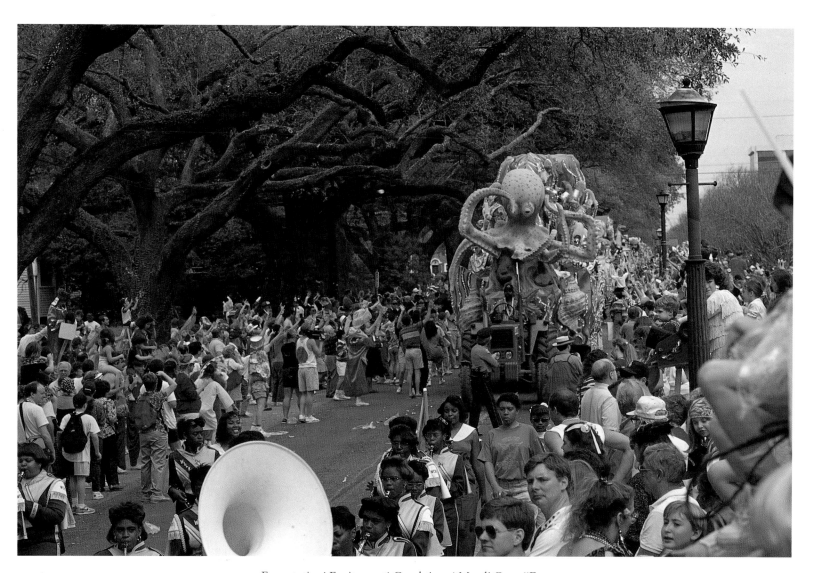

Expectation! Excitement! Good times! Mardi Gras, "Fat Tuesday," the last day before the forty days of Lenten fasting, is the high point of Carnival—and the entire year—in New Orleans. During the Carnival season a great number of different krewes take to the streets to mask and celebrate. Here the Jacques Costeau float from the Voyages of Discovery parade of the Rex Krewe dances its way down Napoleon Avenue in 1992.

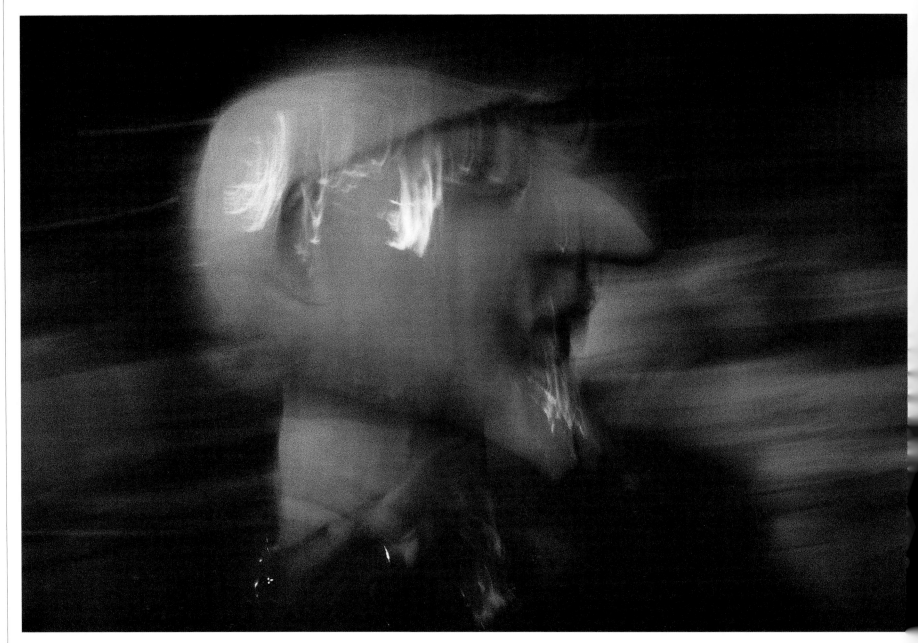

Carnival is motion; it is transient, almost hallucinatory movement. Here a giant bespectacled head flashes by as part of the passing parade.

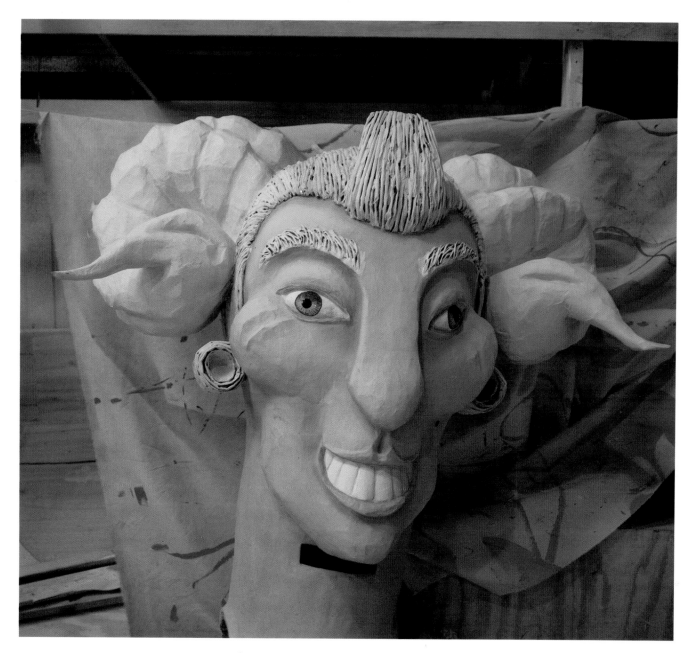

Carnival is about metamorphosis, temporary change,
and transformation. This giant grinning ram's head is a
faithful papier-mâché recreation of a "walking head,"
an elaborate mask worn by a parader, from the famous
1873 Mistick Krewe of Comus parade.

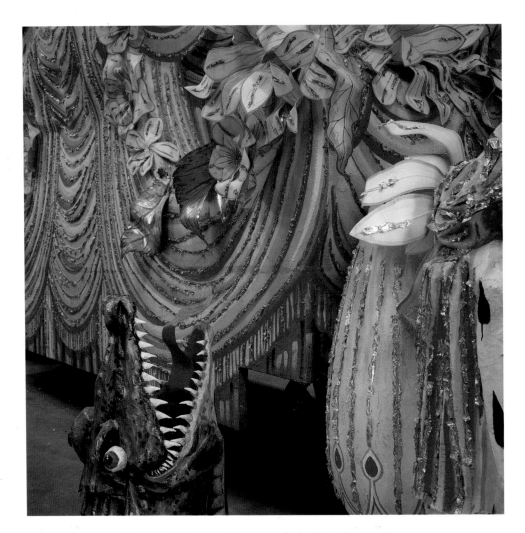

The Mistick Krewe of Comus was organized in 1857 by
six young Anglo-American men from Mobile, Alabama,
whose parade and ball on the theme of Milton's *Paradise
Lost* featured Comus, the son of Bacchus and the
sorceress Circe. With the organization of the Mistick
Krewe, Mardi Gras passed from the Creole to the Anglo-
American community. This detail of the Comus title car,
the unmanned float that announces each year's parade
theme, shows its gorgeous golden-painted stage curtain.
(The alligator is a "walking head.")

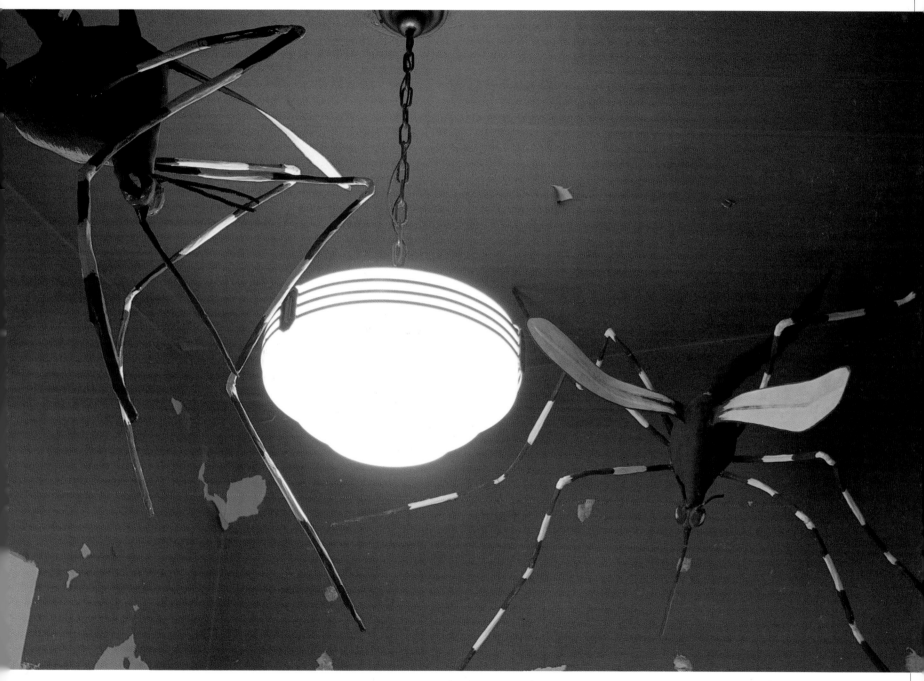

These giant mosquitos are souvenirs from the 1991
Comus parade, whose theme was the Entomological
Empire. (Southern Louisiana's gaudy insects need no art
directors; they are extravagantly colorful the way they
are!)

A few of the old-line krewes continue the tradition of torchlight parades with *flambeaux* carriers lighting the way for the floats. The Afro-American men who brandish these torches are often the sons or grandsons of those who carried them years ago. Here the *flambeaux* carriers light their kerosene torches on Napoleon Avenue for the Krewe of Babylon parade a week before Mardi Gras.

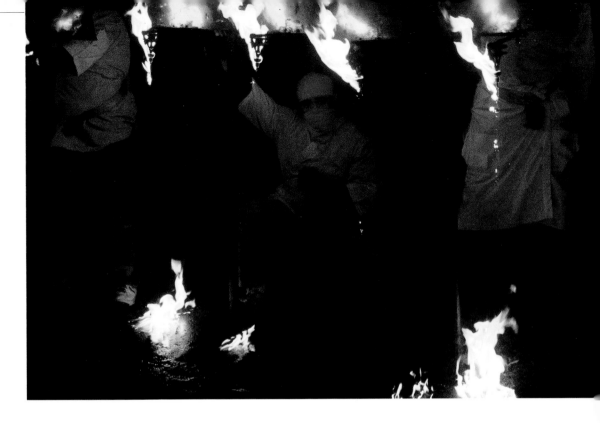

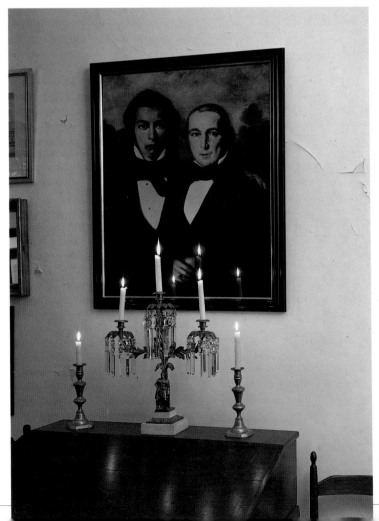

Candlelight remains a favorite kind of lighting in New Orleans. Here, in a house in Faubourg Marigny, five candles illuminate a copy-portrait of an Anglo-American father and his mulatto son. Under a custom known as *placage*, some wealthy Creole and American men kept women of color as mistresses before marriage into proper white society. A few men continued their relationships with two households, but most gave their former lovers houses in Tremé or Marigny once they married.

New Orleans has a special feel for the night. Dim lighting softens the effects of time and flatters old rooms, as in Mario Villa's house.

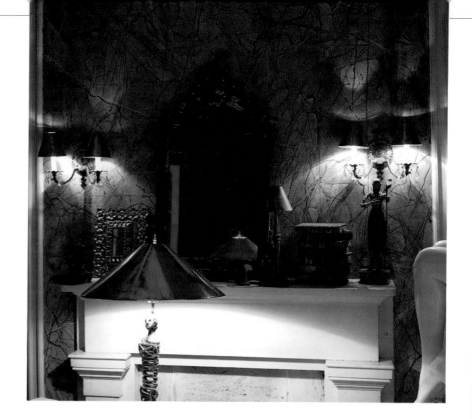

The Mardi Gras parade *flambeaux* carriers perform a special dance as they light the way for the parades. Some say it has its roots in the cakewalk of the 1890s.

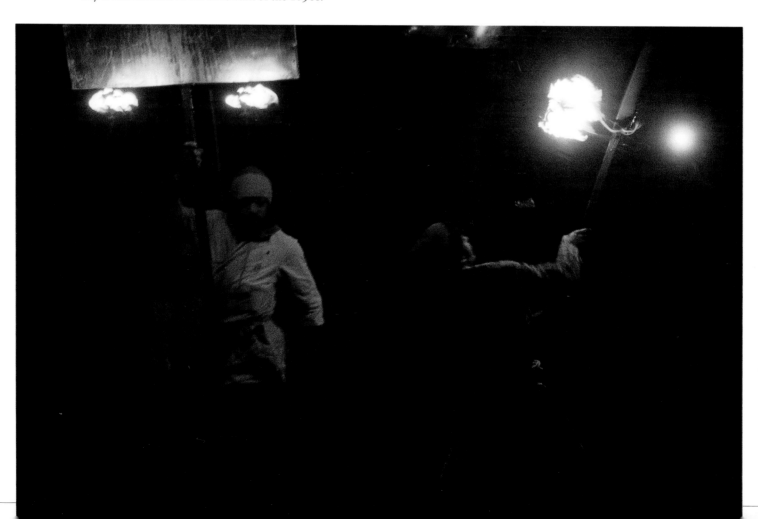

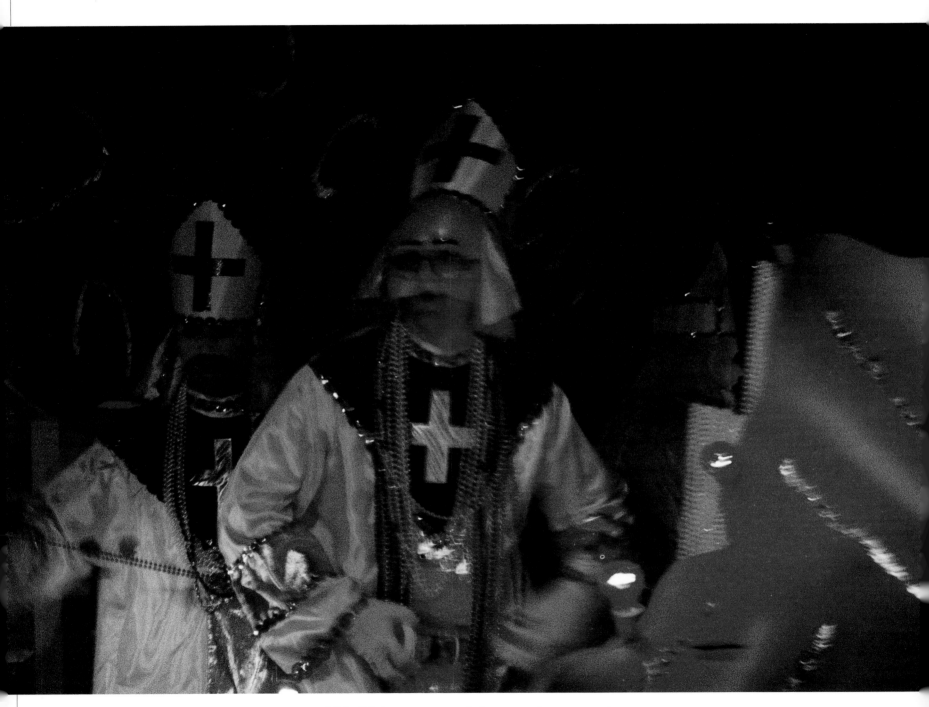

Night lighting casts a surreal glow on maskers costumed
like bishops in the Krewe of Babylon 1992 Mardi Gras
parade on the theme of *Carmen*.

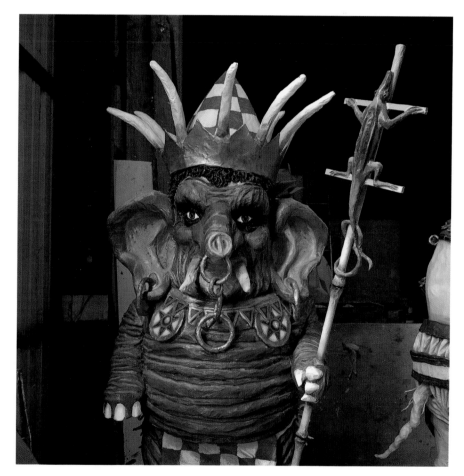

Strange amalgams of the sacred and profane appear at Carnival. This giant papier-mâché walking figure of an African elephant wearing a crown and carrying a crucified lizard was designed by Henri Schindler, the art director and float builder for the Mistick Krewe of Comus. It recreates a piece of the famous Missing Links of Darwin parade of 1873, the earliest year for which parade designs survive.

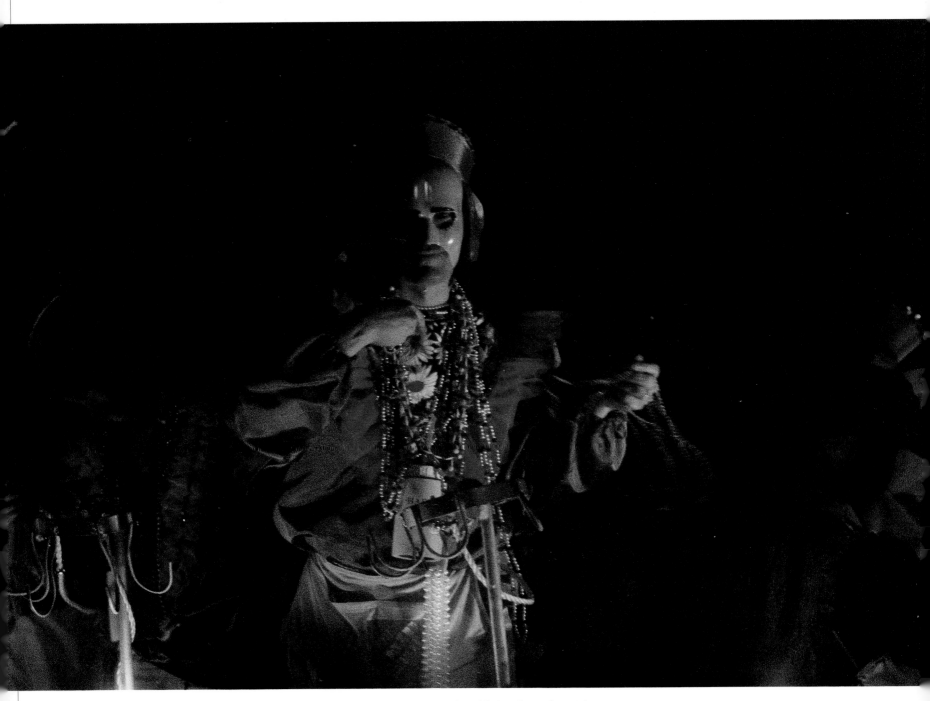

A brush with fantasy. With wild abandon a float rider tosses "throws" to the crowd in this nighttime Carnival parade.

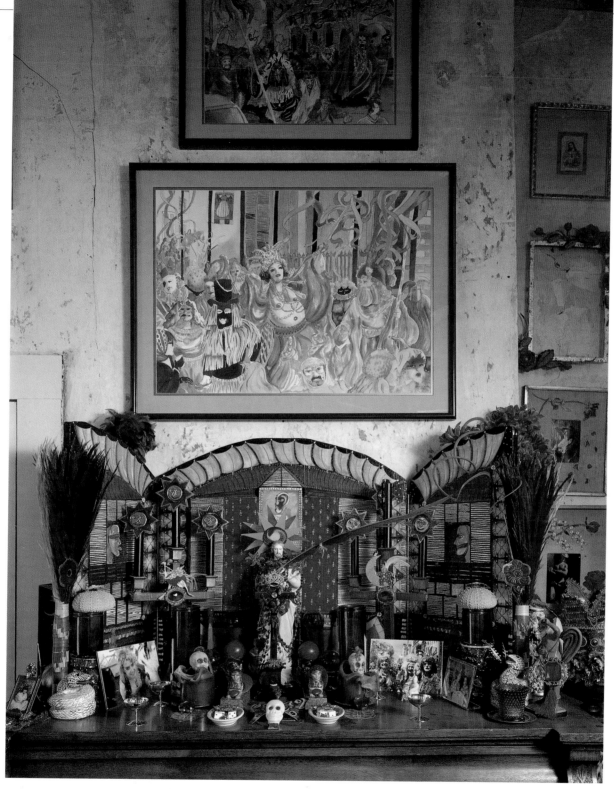

The dresser top in Paul Poché's bedroom is a tableau of Mardi Gras and memories. The watercolor at the top is by float designer Henri Schindler, and, below it, a watercolor by Stuart Auldt shows Poché in his Carnival costume. Juan Rodriguez made the triptych altar. The objects assembled here, like Carnival itself, are a festive concatenation of the sacred and the profane. Hidden at the center of these showy treasures is a tiny Mardi Gras bead with a star and crescent, the symbol of New Orleans.

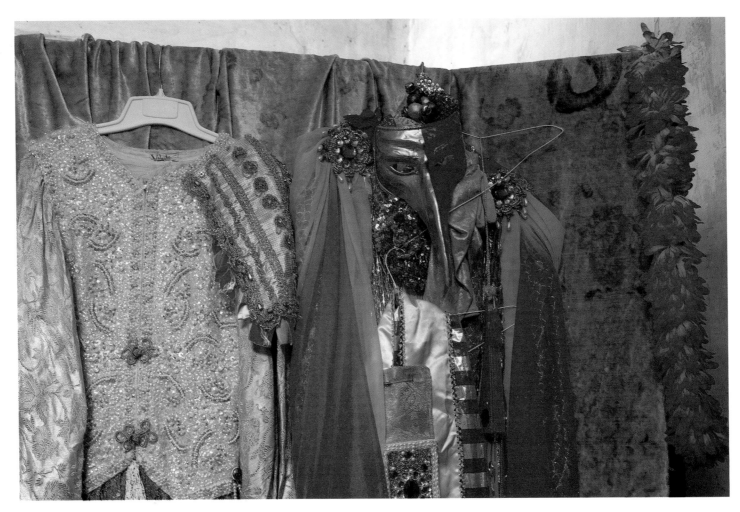

"Carnival is the glue that holds New Orleanian society together," says Paul Poché. And masquerade balls are the grandest New Orleanian functions. Draped in a corner of Paul Poché's bedroom are Carnival costumes, and a red and gold Venetian-style mask. Poché fashioned the white and silver costume out of one of his Aunt Florence's 1950s dresses.

In 1728 Ursuline Sister Madeleine Hachard wrote, "The women of New Orleans are careless of their salvation, but not of their vanity. The greater part of them live on hominy but are dressed in velvet or damask trimmed with ribbons. The Devil has a vast empire here."

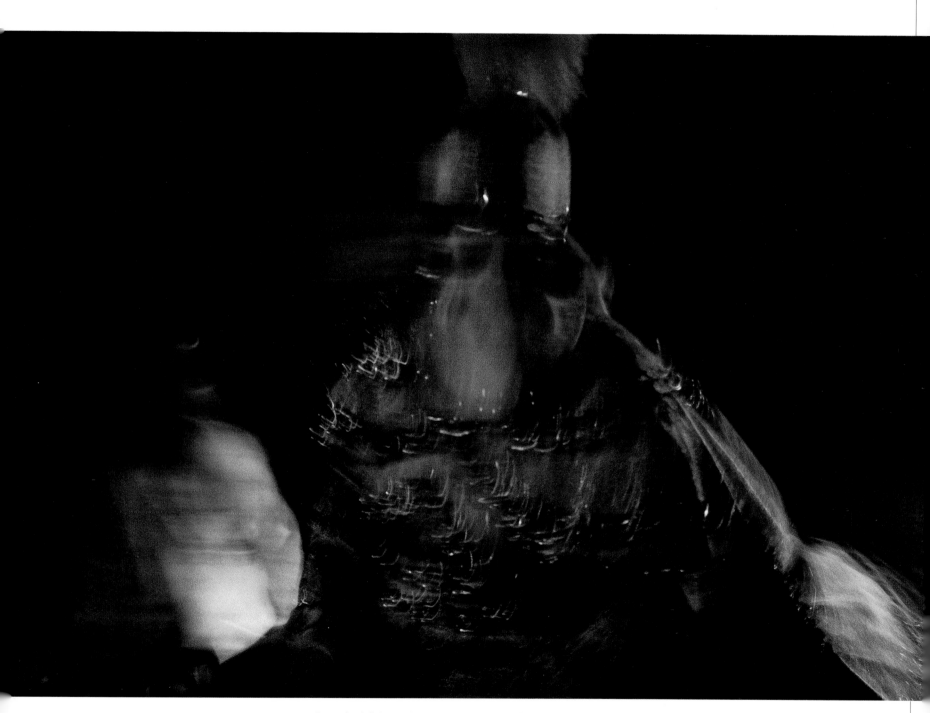

A masked duke on horseback looms out of the Mardi
Gras night, casting spurious riches to the throng.

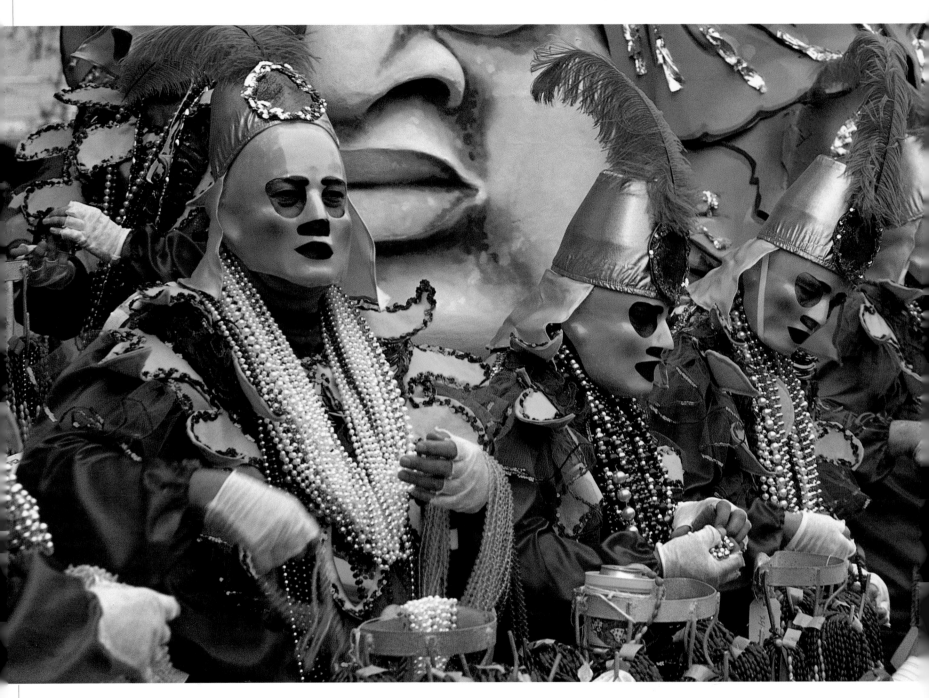

Color explodes from maskers riding a Rex float. Green, gold, and purple are the colors of Mardi Gras: green for faith, gold for power, and purple for justice.

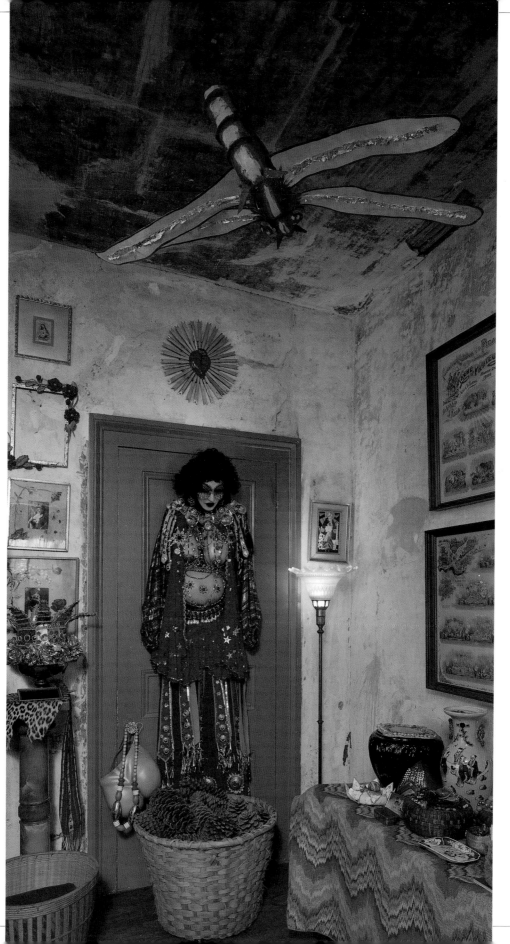

"She went out three years," says Paul Poché of his Whore of Babylon Carnival costume. He made it out of fantasy: fragments from his Aunt Florence's hats, old neckties, Christmas tree ornaments, a red chiffon cocktail dress, and a Bourbon Street hooker's outfit. Masking is an old tradition in New Orleans and has survived Spanish imperial proscription, wars, depressions, and even Protestantism. On one day of the year every man can be a king—or even a queen—and every woman too. On that day New Orleanians don't worry about their troubles because, for one day, they're someone else. Banker Morgan L. Whitney, Rex of the 1967 Carnival, commanded in his public proclamation that "melancholy be put to rout, and joy unconfined seize our subjects, young and old of all genders and degrees...that the spirit of make-believe descend upon the realm and banish from the land the dull and the humdrum and the commonplace of daily existence."

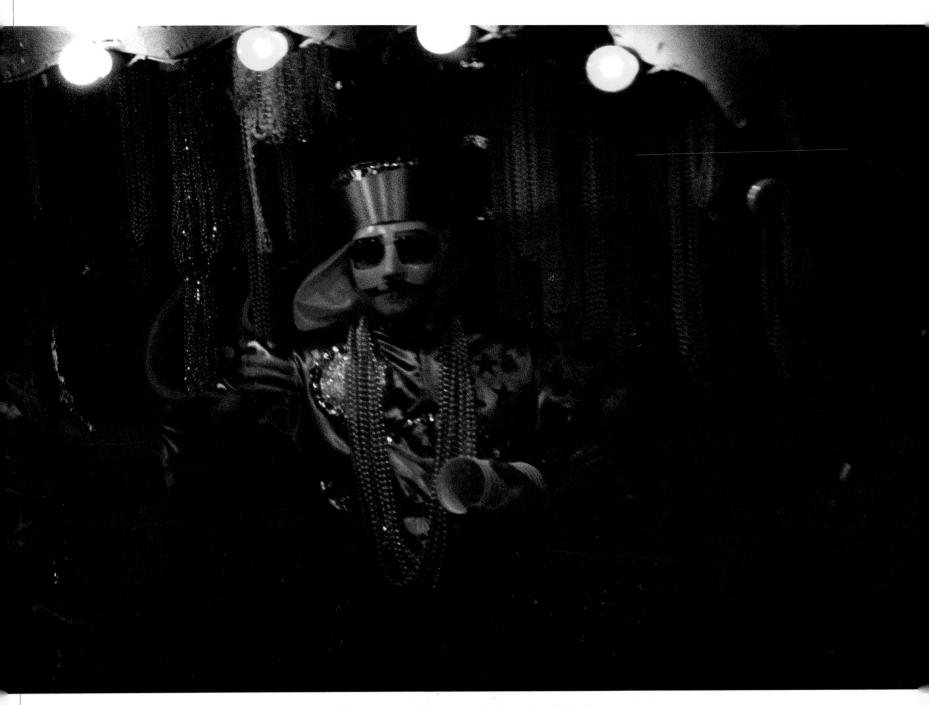

"Throw me something, mister!" A curtain of Mardi
Gras beads forms a theatrical backdrop for a masked
float rider tossing out souvenir cups.

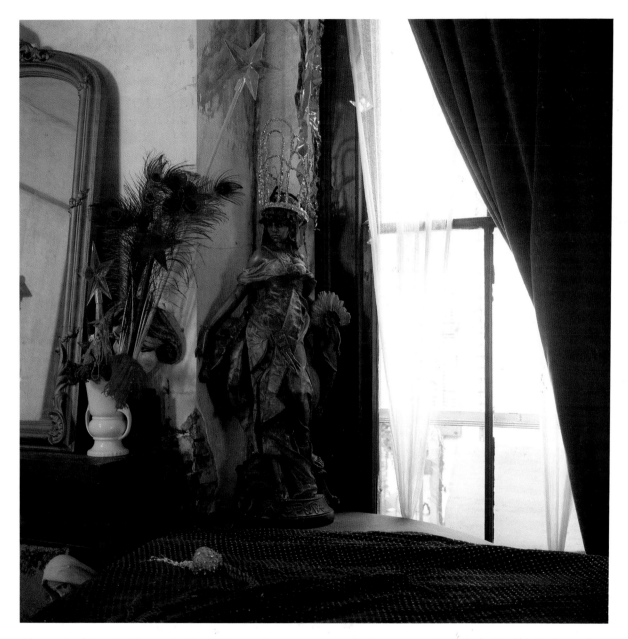

The spirit of Carnival lingers in New Orleans all year long. Plastic Mardi Gras beads show up in the unlikeliest of places. (Even the statue of staid Henry Clay in Lafayette Square wears some; loosen up, Henry!) Here a painted plaster statue of Cleopatra wears a Mardi Gras rhinestone crown. The dark cloth studded with paste jewels is an old Rex cloak. Peacock feathers and the tarnished, star-capped wand of a Twelfth Night reveler of the past stand in a white ceramic urn. The twelfth day after Christmas is the feast of the Epiphany, when the Three Wise Men paid homage to the Christ Child. That night opens the Carnival season that culminates on Mardi Gras, the day before Ash Wednesday and the beginning of the Lenten fast.

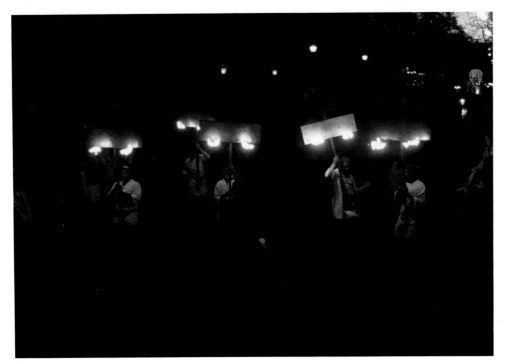

Perry Young wrote this description in 1931 of the first appearance of the Mistick Krewe of Comus in 1857: "At 9 o'clock, or thereabouts, the flare of torchlights shattered the darkness of Magazine and Julia Streets, bands burst into symphony, and the Mistick Krewe stood revealed—a company of demons, rich and realistic, moving in a procession that seemed to blaze from some secret chamber of the earth. They came! Led by the festive Comus, high on his royal seat, and Satan, high on a hill, far blazing as a mount, with pyramids and towers from diamond quarries hewn, and rocks of gold; the palace of great Lucifer. The demon actors in Milton's *Paradise Lost*. The first torchlight scenic procession in New Orleans, a revolution in street pageantry, a revelation in artistic effects." Here the *flambeaux* carriers precede the king of the Krewe of Babylon whose throne can be spied in the distance.

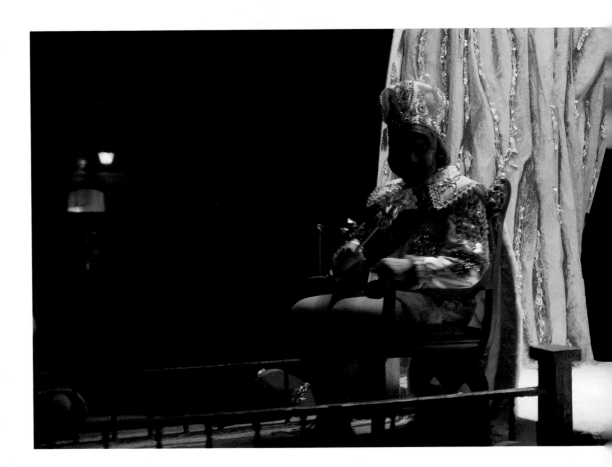

"Let joy be unconfined!" The king of the Krewe of Babylon regards his subjects from his rolling throne on elegant St. Charles Avenue.

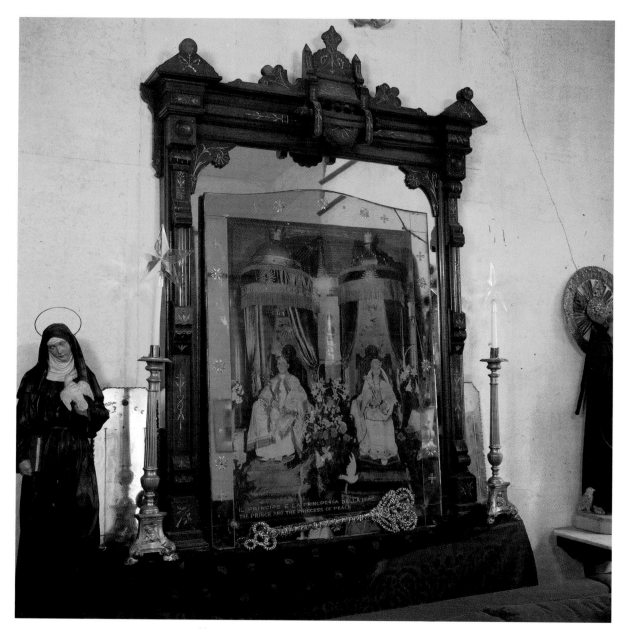

Rituals of transformation and days of celebration are essential to the living psyche of the Crescent City. The Christian calendar itself is strangely changed in New Orleans; the Carnival season that precedes Lent is more important in this city than the Holy Week that is its culmination. Tableaus in some New Orleans interiors play with this reversal. In this eclectic Bywater home, black-clad statues of Saint Scholastica (left) and Saint Benedict (right), brother and sister, flank an 1870s Eastlake-style mirror. Leaning against the glass is an old tinted photograph of the Prince and Princess of Peace from a long-ago Saint Joseph's Day tableau vivant. Saint Joseph's Day, also called *mi-careme* (mid-Lent), was a popular feast with the city's many Sicilians in the early twentieth-century French Quarter.

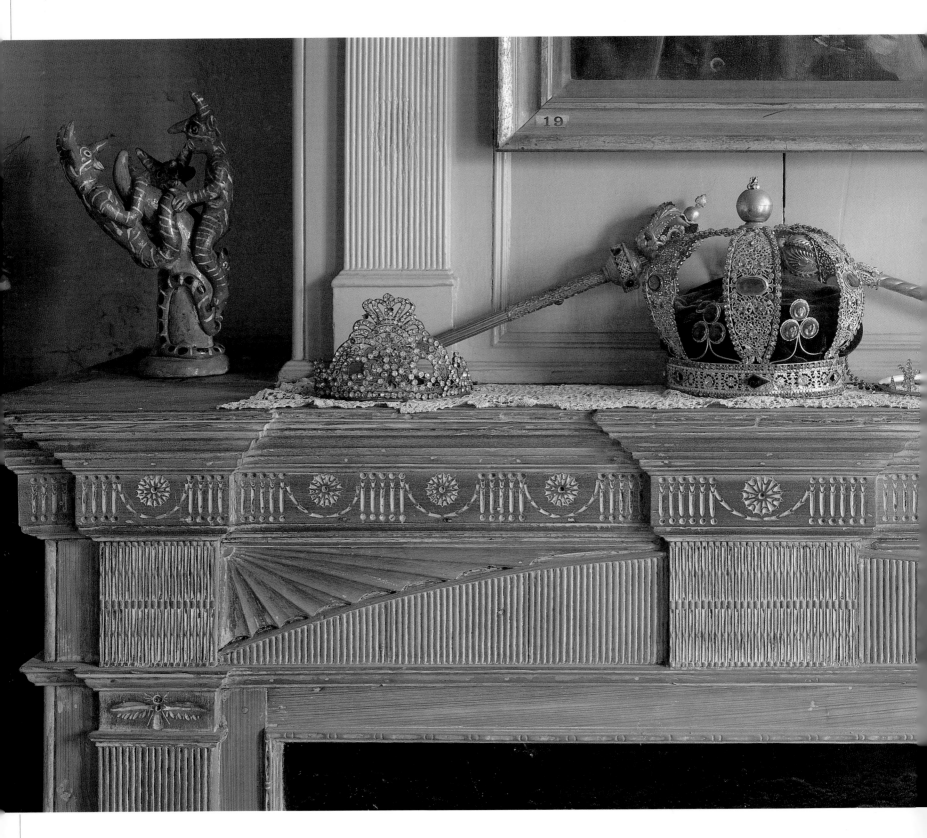

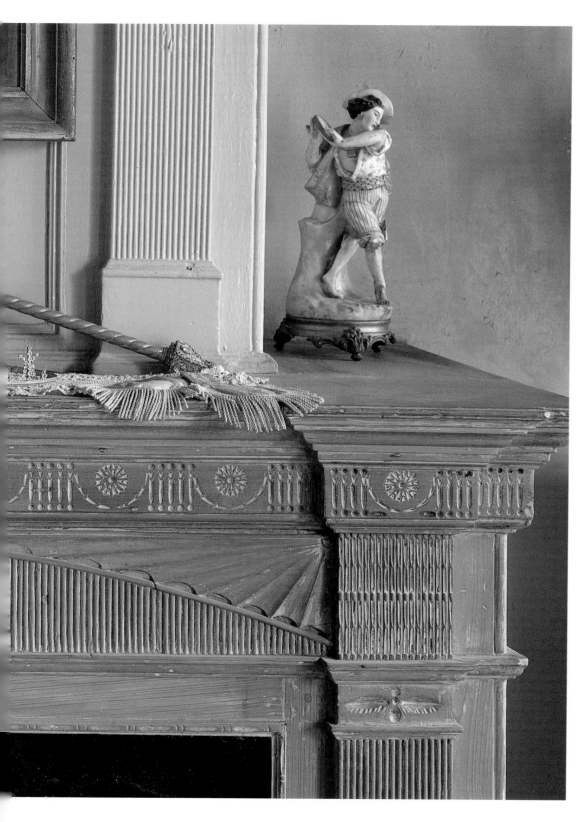

Each Carnival krewe selects one of its members to be king for a day, and the sovereign then chooses a young woman to be his queen. After a parade through the streets and the presentation of a tableau at a ballroom, the coronation of the queen takes place. Then all dance at a grand masquerade ball. "Once queen, queen forever" is an old Carnival motto.

Here an antique cypress mantel in a French Quarter parlor holds a paste-jewel crown and scepter, mementos of a long-ago night when Peterson Moon Yokum's mother was queen of a Carnival ball. She wore the tiara the year she made her debut. To the right a porcelain figurine beats a tambourine, to the left three devils cavort.

Ritual and grandeur, music and merriment, and persistent memories of a make-believe past pervade New Orleans still.

La Passé! La Passé! C'est là qu'est mon étoile.
C'est là qu'est mon trésor.

The past! The past! There is my star,
and there is my treasure.

—Armand Lanusse, 1836

AFTERWORD

Ten years ago, in the fall of 1993, *New Orleans: Elegance and Decadence* was first published. On the local scene, which is heavily reliant on the grapevine, there was little anticipation of the event. I had recently moved to New Orleans in the spring of 1991 and my collaborator Randolph Delehanty lived in San Francisco while the book was in production. Consequently, neither of us knew anyone in New Orleans and no one in New Orleans knew, or knew of, us. But during the course of this project, we met some truly extraordinary people. It was an exciting time that produced not only this book, but many of the friendships and acquaintances that have become the cornerstone of my life here.

My paramount concern was for *Elegance and Decadence* to be a romantic portrait of New Orleans. Even though it was a newly found place for me, I was hoping to become identified with New Orleans in the way that Eugene Atget is with Paris. I based the organization of my photo-essay on the landmark book edited by Arthur Trottenberg, *A Vision of Paris*, which juxtaposes Atget's photographs of Paris and its environs with excerpts from Marcel Proust's *Remembrance of Things Past*. I clearly had lofty ambitions that we managed to at least partially fulfill.

In retrospect, it has been a long decade since the release of *Elegance and Decadence,* in part because it has been a decade of profound personal change. But, through all the transitions, my devotion to and love of New Orleans as a place apart has grown and matured. Life is indeed large here, in every respect. When I look back at the places and events I photographed, I am struck by what has changed and what has stayed the same. Individuals whose homes and establishments I photographed only a little over a decade ago have, in quite a few instances, moved on. Fortunately for New Orleans, most of these transitions have produced equally intriguing abodes in other niches of the city. This project has become a life lesson for me in the relationship between the physical qualities that characterize place and the shifting bed of humanity that calls it home. New Orleanians are much like hermit crabs in the manner they constantly adapt and re-inhabit found shelter.

Elegance and Decadence began as a contemporary portrait of New Orleans and now serves as a portrait of New Orleans near the end of the last millennium. History has interceded, as it always does. The passage of time has, I feel, enhanced the meaning of the photographs, as the places and events they document slowly merge with New Orleans' ever–present past.

Richard Sexton
New Orleans, 2003

New Orleans is the only major city in the United States where the accepted pedestrian protocol is to offer a courteous "Mornin'" to passersby rather than avert one's eyes. Her hospitable people are what I treasure most, especially her vibrant artists. New Orleans made me feel very much at home, so much so that I moved there after writing this book. Though I am now back in San Francisco, I am old enough to divine the circular patterns in my life. Perhaps someday I will return to the mouth of the great river on whose banks I was born.

This book was conceived as a love letter to New Orleans, and this particular love affair has been amply requited. New Orleanians recognized something here that struck a chord with them. They—and those who do not know New Orleans but have heard of her allure—have embraced this book. *Elegance and Decadence* has become New Orleans' book as much as ours.

Now, a bit like the old wooden-wheeled floats that hide for a year in their dark dens before rolling out, renewed and resplendent once again, for Carnival, *New Orleans: Elegance and Decadence* reappears in this tenth-anniversary edition. Richard and I didn't seek to improve it. We have made only a few slight changes noticeable probably only to ourselves.

We want this book, like New Orleans itself, to be what it is. And we wanted to respect the moment and the personal circumstances of its creation. While some of what this book records has changed, the joyous spirit it sought to capture endures. We hope its reappearance brings as much pleasure in this new century as its initial appearance did at the end of the last one.

Randolph Delehanty, Ph.D.
New Orleans
Carnival, 2003

GLOSSARY

ABAT-VENT   French for "wind break." An almost flat extension of the roof supported by iron brackets that usually extends about three feet over the sidewalk.

BANQUETTE   French for "small bench," the local term for sidewalk. Originally referred to cypress planks laid alongside the drainage ditches that encircled French Quarter blocks.

BAY   A vertical division of the exterior or interior of a building marked not by walls but usually by windows or doors.

CABINET   A small room built paired in the rear corners of early Louisiana houses. One often enclosed a curving staircase to the attic; the other was used for sleeping or storage.

CARNIVAL   The Carnival season lasts from the feast of the Epiphany (the twelfth night after Christmas or the Feast of the Three Kings) to the midnight before Ash Wednesday, the first day of Lent, the annual penitential period in the Christian calendar. Mardi Gras, French for "fat Tuesday," is Shrove Tuesday, the last day of Carnival season. Carnival is a time of communal festivity and joy. *See also* krewe.

CAST IRON   Iron shaped by casting in molds. Especially popular in the 1840s and 1850s for railings, fences, and architectural ornament in often richly elaborate and naturalistic forms. Many pre-1840 houses later had cast-iron galleries attached to their facades. Distinct from wrought iron, which is shaped by beating heated rods and usually simpler in design. Wrought iron was popular in the eighteenth century, especially in the Spanish colonial period.

CENTER-HALL HOUSE   A Creole cottage to which Anglo-Americans introduced a center hall to separate the four rooms arranged symmetrically on the ground floor.

CREOLE   This word has a complex history which is explained in the introduction. Today it is usually taken to mean a person of French and/or Spanish descent; also Creoles of color, people of African and European lineage. Creole as applied to architecture refers to certain house types popular in the late eighteenth and early nineteenth centuries.

CREOLE COTTAGE   An early urban house form, square or rectangular in shape, of wood or brick with stucco, and built out to the sidewalk. Along the front were windows and French doors. The typical Creole plan consisted of four square rooms arranged symmetrically with no internal hallways. French doors connected the principal rooms, which were used for receiving guests, dining, and sleeping. In the two rear corners were *cabinets,* small rooms, one with a spiral staircase to the attic, and the other used for sleeping or storage. Between the cabinets was a loggia. Kitchens were often in separate outbuildings. Popular from about 1790 to 1850.

CREOLE TOWNHOUSE   Rectangular two- to four-story brick and stucco townhouses built principally in the French Quarter after the great fires of 1788 and 1794. They were detached, semidetached, or constructed in rows. Many had steeply pitched gable roofs with dormers. Usually only two rooms deep, with service wings attached to the rear and set at right angles to the main building. A long, narrow pedestrian passageway on one side led to an enclosed stair gallery placed between the main house and service wing. Double parlors, one behind the other, were often used as commercial space. On the second floor were two large rooms en suite. There were no internal hallways.

DEPENDENCY   An extension or wing of a house set at right angles to the main building and used as either slave quarters or as a kitchen, workrooms, or servants' or children's bedrooms.

DORMER WINDOW   A window placed vertically in a sloping roof with a roof of its own.

FAUBOURG   French for "suburb." Plantations subdivided into blocks and lots were sometimes named for the subdivider, such as Faubourg Marigny, the former Marigny plantation.

FAUX-BOIS; FAUX-MARBRE   Painted decorative surfaces imitating wood or marble; often applied to cypress wood.

FRENCH DOOR   A long window reaching to the floor and opening in two leaves, usually with glass in the upper sections. Individual leaves can be opened at angles to catch the breeze and direct it into the room. In New Orleans, many French doors are protected on the exterior by solid board-and-batten shutters, or louvered jalousies.

FRENCH QUARTER   Also known as the Vieux Carré. The original French section of the city begun by Adrien de Pauger in 1721; today a designated historic district bounded by Canal Street, Rampart Street, Esplanade Avenue, and the Mississippi River. Most of its buildings date from the later Spanish and American periods.

GABLE   The vertical triangular section of a wall formed by a pitched roof.

GALLERY   Exterior porches attached to a building and covered by an overhang or roof. Cast-iron galleries can be original to the building or later additions. Galleries shade the house, create spaces for socializing, and, when built over the sidewalk, protect pedestrians from sun and rain. Double gallery houses, popular during the antebellum period, are two-story buildings with galleries across their facade at both levels supported by pillars or columns.

GREEK KEY   A frame around a doorway or fireplace with a broad lintel and a slight flaring of the side mouldings from top to bottom. A motif in Greek Revival architecture popular in the 1850s.

GREEK REVIVAL   A style of architecture which drew its inspiration from ancient Greece as interpreted by American architects in the period from 1830 to the 1860s. In New Orleans, Greek Revival houses rarely produced the full temple form (as many plantation houses did), but rather employed Greek-inspired columns, door surrounds, entablatures, egg-and-dart mouldings, rosettes, and acanthus leaf motifs. Greek Revival buildings tended to simplicity, strength, and dignity. Cottages, middle-class houses, and mansions employed the style. White was the favorite color for both brick-and-stucco and frame Greek Revival houses.

KREWE   A Carnival organization that usually produces public parades and private masked balls. The first was the Mystick Krewe of Comus, a secret society established in 1857 and associated with the Pickwick Club. Today there are many different krewes active in the city and in its suburbs.

LEVEE   From the French for "raised up." An embankment, either natural or man-made, that prevents flooding.

MARDI GRAS   *See* Carnival.

NEUTRAL GROUND   An area between roadways equivalent to medians in other cities. Originally applied to the borders between faubourgs and to the median of wide Canal Street. Canal Street separates the old Creole city downriver from the new American city upriver. Many neutral grounds in the city's neighborhoods lie over covered drainage canals.

PAPIER-MÂCHÉ   French for "chewed paper." A light but strong material made from paper pulp mixed with glue, sizing, rosin, or other additives. Used to make traditional Carnival floats.

PORTE COCHERE   A covered entrance for vehicles. Usually seen only in costly houses, especially in the French Quarter.

RAISED HOUSE OR COTTAGE   Houses and cottages built off the ground on brick piers to offset frequent floods. The space under such houses, the *rez-de-chaussée,* was used for storage or a work space.

SHOTGUN COTTAGE   A long, narrow, one-story house with its rooms built one behind the other and with its doors aligned. Double shotguns are two-family houses built along the same plan with a shared wall. Popular working-class housing from the 1840s to the 1920s.

SHUTTER   A hinged movable cover for a window or door. Early French shutters were solid wood; later the Spanish introduced louvered shutters (jalousies) that provided both security and ventilation.

VIEUX CARRÉ   *See* French Quarter.

WROUGHT IRON   *See* cast-iron.

ABOUT THE AUTHORS

Richard Sexton was born in Atlanta in 1954 and raised in Colquitt, a small farming town in southwest Georgia. He is a graduate of Emory University, Atlanta, and later attended San Francisco Art Institute. Sexton is a noted photographer, writer, and speaker on the topics of architecture, design, and the built environment. He has produced features for publications such as *Abitare, Old House Interiors, Louisiana Cultural Vistas, Preservation in Print,* and *Southern Accents.* His photographs have appeared in *Archetype, Garden Design, Gulliver* (Periodici Rizzoli), *Harper's, Old House Journal, Preservation,* and *Smithsonian,* among others. Sexton is the author/photographer of *Vestiges of Grandeur: The Plantations of Louisiana's River Road,* the companion volume to this title, and is the photographer of *Gardens of New Orleans: Exquisite Excess,* both published by Chronicle Books. His earlier books from Chronicle include *The Cottage Book* (1989) and *Parallel Utopias: The Quest for Community* (1995). Sexton's multidisciplinary studio is based in New Orleans. He teaches photography at the New Orleans Academy of Fine Arts. His work is represented in New Orleans by A Gallery for Fine Photography. Contact: www.richardsextonstudio.com, rsphoto@bellsouth.net.

Randolph Delehanty, Ph.D., is a writer born in the Deep South, reared in the Northeast, long-time resident on the Pacific Coast, and very aware of all of America inside this frame. He was born in Memphis, Tennessee, in 1944 and raised in Englewood and Tenafly, New Jersey, in an English- and Spanish-speaking family. He holds degrees in history from Georgetown University, the University of Chicago, and Harvard University, where he was a Prize Fellow and where he earned his doctorate. In 1970, he moved to Berkeley, California, to study history independently at the Bancroft Library. Later he was the first historian for the Foundation for San Francisco's Architectural Heritage and then taught for many years in the Humanities Department at San Francisco State University. From 1995 to 1999, he was the first director of the University of New Orleans' Ogden Museum of Southern Art. He has written more than a dozen books, including *Randolph Delehanty's Ultimate Guide to New Orleans,* which explores the historical, architectural, literary, and musical dimensions of the Crescent City through twelve walking tours. Today Delehanty lives in San Francisco and is the historian for the Presidio Trust at the Golden Gate National Recreation Area. He is working on a book on the social changes reshaping all of California. Contact: randolph_delehanty@post.harvard.edu.

ACKNOWLEDGMENTS

Many hospitable New Orleanians helped us with this book, and it is a pleasure to thank them. For able assistance with the photography, we thank Craig Macaluso and Chris Snyder. For generously granting permission to reproduce the paintings in the introduction, we thank Roger Houston Ogden. We also wish to thank Kenneth W. Barnes, director of the Ogden Collection.

For allowing us to photograph their homes, shops, and gardens, and for helping us find evocative places to include in our book, we wish to thank:

Dorian Major Bennett
Pat and Thomas N. Bernard
Lisa Browning
Bethany E. Bultman
Roland Chiarra
Eugene D. Cizek, Ph.D., and
    Lloyd L. Sensat, Jr.
Marc and Mary Cooper
Louis and Mary Len Costa
Patrick Dunne
George Dureau
Joel Lockhart Dyer
R.J. Dykes III
Marcus Fraser
Christopher Friedrichs
Malcolm Heard, Jr., and
    Alicia Rogan Heard
Robert and Elizabeth Livingston
Jana Napoli
William C. and Betty Harris Norris
Peter W. Patout
Elmore Paul Poché
Ken Reynolds
Josephine Sacabo
Hubert and Nina Sandot
Stephen Scalia and Milton Melton
Henri Schindler

Shelby Sessums
Elizabeth Shannon
Mike Smith
Robert C. Tannen and Jeanne P. Nathan
Jon Tompkins
Mario Villa
Clifton G. and Jo G. Webb
Thomas and Mercedes Whitecloud
Peterson Moon Yokum

For historical guidance we wish to thank:

Pamela Arceneaux, The Historic New
    Orleans Collection
Arnold R. Hirsch, Ph.D., University of
    New Orleans
John Magill, The Historic New Orleans
    Collection
Preservation in Print, The Preservation
    Resource Center of New Orleans and
    the Louisiana State Historic
    Preservation Office
Sally K. Reeves, Notarial Archives,
    Civil District Court
Jessica Travis, The Historic New Orleans
Collection

INDEX